Lesbian Cinema after Queer Theory

Clara Bradbury-Rance

Subtext i all intertext

EDINBURGH
University Press

Edinburgh University Press is one of the leading university presses in the UK. We publish academic books and journals in our selected subject areas across the humanities and social sciences, combining cutting-edge scholarship with high editorial and production values to produce academic works of lasting importance. For more information visit our website: edinburghuniversitypress.com

Edinburgh University Press Ltd
The Tun – Holyrood Road
12 (2f) Jackson's Entry
Edinburgh EH8 8PJ

First published in hardback by Edinburgh University Press 2019

Typeset in Garamond MT Pro by
Servis Filmsetting Ltd, Stockport, Cheshire,

A CIP record for this book is available from the British Library

ISBN 978 1 4744 3536 9 (hardback)
ISBN 978 1 4744 3539 0 (paperback)
ISBN 978 1 4744 3537 6 (webready PDF)
ISBN 978 1 4744 3538 3 (epub)

Contents

Figures

Acknowledgements

This book began life in 2011 as a PhD at the University of Manchester, where I was supervised by Jackie Stacey. Discussing feminist film theory with the scholar whose work first beckoned me towards the field was, and continues to be, a privilege. Her attention to detail, painstaking annotations and clarifying reflections transformed my work. The pages of this book still reflect her patience, care and encouragement. Jackie, thank you. These pages – and in fact many of these acknowledgements – are also a product of the five years I spent working with Jackie on the Sexuality Summer School, which gave me not only an annual dose of theoretical invigoration, entertainment, art and conversation, but also deep and lasting friendships. For all these reasons, it is a project I feel immensely proud to have been a part of. I can only hope that this book has done justice to the feedback provided on the PhD by Patricia White and Kaye Mitchell, who were fun, inspiring and galvanising examiners. I received further wisdom from members of the Manchester English Department including David Alderson, Daniela Caselli and Laura Doan. For her rigorous reading and provocative questions, special thanks go to Monica Pearl.

At Manchester, I was funded by the School of Arts, Languages and Cultures and the Arts and Humanities Research Council. I also spent a snowy semester at the Five College Women's Studies Research Center in 2014, which provided a turning point in my thinking and ability to write again after a long interruption. For sound practical and conceptual advice at every stage in the preparation of the book manuscript, thank you to the editorial team at Edinburgh University Press, particularly Gillian Leslie and Richard Strachan, and to the anonymous reader of the manuscript for the generous and enthusiastic review that fuelled my final draft. I was invited to share chapters-in-progress at various points in the project's gestation at Critical Sexology, the Five College Women's Studies Research Center, Manchester Feminist Theory Network, University College London and the Universities of Gothenburg, Michigan, Stirling and Westminster. I also presented work at conferences at the Universities of Brighton, Cambridge, Cardiff and Glasgow. Thank you to my welcoming and generous hosts and interlocutors for providing me with the space to try out, relish and develop ideas.

I found my first full-time job at King's College London, where I ran the final lap to finish this book. All of my colleagues at King's have been welcoming, supportive, motivating and so often incredibly good fun. In particular, Rosa Andújar, Sophie Blackburn, Helen Brookman, Harriet Curtis, Zeena Feldman, Chris Holliday, Thea Jean, Simon Kaye, George Legg and Angel O'Donnell: thanks for the good cheer and the post-its. I have found the space here to commit to my teaching with as much rigour and feminism as my research, and to find in the classroom countless moments of inspiration.

I have been lucky enough to cultivate a group of mentors from far and wide whose interest and encouragement at different stages of the project and of my career has been motivating and humbling, whether they know it or not: thank you to Mary Capello, Lisa Downing, Richard Dyer, Mary Lynne Ellis, Rosalind Galt, Lisa Henderson, Noreen O'Connor, Jean Walton, Patricia White and Emma Wilson. Since the first semester of my undergraduate degree at the University of Exeter, Fiona Handyside's mentorship, as teacher then friend, has been profoundly influential. From BTP supervisions to cinema trips and spag-bol debriefs, I continue to cherish our conversations about the movies – and her writing about them.

My peers have been mentors in their own way and have guided me through the early stages of academic life. Thank you to my committed, attentive, patient and rigorous group of readers: Ronnie Barnsley, Jacob Breslow, Sam Colling, Rose Deller, Chris Holliday, Emma Spruce and Chris Vardy. I had invigorating conversations about academia and much else besides with Ilana Eloit, Laura Guy, Maurice Nagington, Meredith Nash, Ros Murray and Kathryn Oliver. Extra special thanks to Emma Spruce, for experience shared; to Chris Vardy, for distractions mundane and profound; and to Rose Deller, my comrade in work and play, for the breathtaking constancy of her support. I hope that Alice Barnaby knows everything she contributed to this project, intellectual, practical and emotional. I thank Helen Barron for so many years of being willing to talk it all through. Niklas Albin Svensson, Sophie Amili, El Evans, Tom Grant, Liz Hardman, Lydia Jones, Maia Kirby, Sarah Page, Mary Partington, Chris Richards, Shani Rousso and Clare Tyson also supported me through the emotional and physical interruptions that did their best to put a halt to this book's progress. My friendships with you all have made life excitable and sustainable.

For pep talks, humour and love, I thank my family: my sister Madeleine Bradbury Rance, my step-father Peter Speyer, my brother-in-law John Fosbrook, my nephews Owen and Bryn Fosbrook Rance, and my godmother Sue Davies and godsister Jess Drader. Thanks to the members of my mother's women's group, on-going since the 1970s, who during my childhood were a regular reminder that the personal is political. And, of course, overwhelming thanks to my mother, Sara Rance: I could not have written a word without your support. This book is dedicated to your feminism and your care.

Finally, to Preya Assi: thank you for making love, and life, an utter thrill.

Part of the analysis of *Nathalie* . . . and *Chloe* in Chapter Two was published as 'The Translation of Desire: Queering Visibility in *Nathalie* . . . and *Chloe*', in *Queer in Translation*, edited by B. J. Epstein and Robert Gillett (London: Routledge, 2017), pp. 144–55. Sections of the argument I make about *She Monkeys* in Chapter Four appear in 'Ambiguous Intimacy as Queer Potential: Touch, Desire and Adolescence in *She Monkeys*' in the journal *Feminist Theory* (2019). I am grateful to SAGE journals and Routledge for the permission to publish these earlier pieces in their present form. Publicity images for the film *Carol* (Haynes, 2015) are courtesy of Number 9 Films Ltd.

Preface

In 1998, the celebrated lesbian film scholar B. Ruby Rich wrote: 'I don't want to make the mistake of falling into that comfortable old victim box, complaining of absence in the midst of presence. We're not invisible anymore' (58). In 1999, Patricia White observed that lesbianism was by now 'an intelligible social identity, visible on the nation's television and movie screens' (6). And Julianne Pidduck signalled in 2003 the '"hypervisibility" of lesbian/gay/queer works' in North America (266). Two decades ago, then, it became possible to suggest that the lesbian had reached the realm of the visible.

Cultural visibility does not exist in isolation, of course, but rather arises out of the normalisation of anti-homophobia campaigns and the broadening of civil rights for LGB (more rarely TQ+) individuals, couples and families. Even in the era of Donald Trump's presidency – or perhaps as a response to it – diversity seems to have become the watchword of the cultural and other industries in the USA and beyond. Social media movements to end sexual harassment such as #metoo and #timesup have coincided with calls for further diversity across the sector.[1] In the twenty years since scholars started to speak of visibility as a possibility and probability, significant transformations have occurred in spheres from the military, to the Catholic Church, to marriage equality. Social visibility has been institutionalised, commodified and politically manoeuvred.

In autumn 2017, during the final stages of writing this book, I booked tickets for the London Film Festival and found that I was spoilt for choice. For romantic drama, the Billie Jean King biopic *Battle of the Sexes* (Jonathan Dayton and Valerie Faris, 2017); for social satire, Sally Potter's *The Party* (2017); and for the rumours of an unexpected genre twist, *Good Manners* (Marco Dutra and Juliana Rojas, 2017), whose blurb, as it turned out, withheld *another* twist, the centrality to the film's plot of lesbian desire. It may still be hard to imagine the lesbian version of the mainstream reality television show *Queer Eye* (David Collins, 2018–) coming into existence – a female journalist declares on Twitter that 'Queer Eye is fine but I would like a companion show with butch women helping straight women who want to feel comfortable being less performatively feminine' (Goldfield, 2018). It still seems unlikely that a lesbian film will match the reception of the gay romance *Call Me by Your Name* (Luca Guadagnino, 2017), which, unusually for an era of dizzying change and new release, played continually between October 2017 and March 2018 at the Curzon Soho cinema in central London (see Gant, 2018). However, the materialisation of at least three films with prominent lesbian narratives at the most important UK film event of the year speaks of unprecedented change. Lesbians on-screen in 2018–19 cross genres, tastes, moods, periods and audiences, including in *Disobedience* (Sebastián Lelio, 2017), *Vita and Virginia* (Chanya Button, 2018), *Colette* (Wash Westmoreland, 2018) and *The Miseducation of Cameron Post* (Desiree Akhavan, 2018). We begin to see popular culture mainstreaming lesbianism in a way that might not have been imaginable even at the turn of the century.

The same decades that have heralded remarkable transformations in the inclusion of lesbianism in mainstream political, social and cultural fields have also witnessed a revolution in the academic study of sexuality, which has veered away from the labels associated with the identity politics of 1970s and 1980s liberation movements. Critical discourses have increasingly replaced identity categories such as lesbian with the more fluid notions of queer sexuality. Situated against this context, *Lesbian Cinema after Queer Theory* takes as its starting point three interlinking observations: firstly, that lesbianism is more visible on-screen now than it has ever been; secondly, that even so, the discussion of the lesbian's screen presence is beset by comparisons to older models of representation; and, thirdly, that queer theory has forcefully ignited the discussion of sexuality over the past three decades but has concurrently diminished the perceived relevance of lesbianism as a term of engagement.

In this book, I read contemporary cinema through the history of the woman's screen image, arguing that historically compromising gaze structures and processes of visual mediation might, even now, surprise us by enabling us to comprehend desire's complexity. I root the discussion in the various registers through which feminist film theory has striven to capture these conditions of representability; in particular, I consider how psychoanalytic film theory has crafted the language for moving beyond the testimony of the physical, guiding us through the contradictory intelligibilities of social and corporeal relations and psychological internal worlds. Instead of rejecting it on the grounds of its alleged sentencing of lesbianism to the non-place of sexuality, the book puts psychoanalysis into dialogue with films that explore precisely such anxieties. Because of sexist, homophobic and racist processes at work in mainstream cinema more broadly – even amidst the changes recounted above – the lesbian has historically been given visual form only in male (and often white, straight, cisgendered) fantasy. Lesbian self-representation has been alienated. Through an attendance to the ways in which these socio-historical contexts have become formal cinematic languages on-screen, what has emerged is a further challenge to the easy categorisation of lesbianism. Indeed, central to the book is the discursive and photographic legacy of those very systems of representation.

Instead of being chosen solely on the basis of their contribution to the visibility effect (for instance, breadth of distribution or garnering of mainstream awards), the films discussed in this book bring to the fore the paradoxical nature of this so-called visibility. I include male directors in the corpus, undoubtedly urging (and not without my own ambivalence) new mechanisms of subversive identification. Throughout, I identify and theorise the kinds of cinematic language through which the figure of the lesbian has continued to be made legible on the screen. In doing so, I argue that, rather than providing another identity category, queer is the charge or potential through which lesbianism is enabled to expand its borders. To take up queer theory's terminological challenge with a sense of productive provocation rather than alienation is to ask important questions. How do we maintain critical and political attachments whilst acknowledging their production of ambivalence? When should we mobilise the universal or the particular? How do we account for lesbian studies' discursive exclusions and, in particular, its whiteness?[2] This book will be observed as occupying a particular habitus that is indebted primarily to the narrative structures of classical Hollywood and its legacy. However, its corpus includes several co-productions, gesturing towards a new regime of the image that cites transhistorically and spreads transnationally. Such films help to construct conceptual configurations of lesbianism's visual possibilities, even as I indicate the frequent Americanisation of transnational sexual imaginaries. *Lesbian Cinema after Queer Theory* builds a conceptual foundation from unexpected parallels, convergences and citations.

Developing from the context provided by the Introduction, Chapter 1 establishes a framework for thinking about the history of lesbianism in cinema through debates within feminist film theory. The chapter analyses *Mulholland Drive*, a film that intertwines the conventions of lesbian representation with cinema's own conditions of production. By virtue of its Hollywood setting, conventional thriller tropes and Technicolor aesthetic, the film looks back to the censorship practices of the mid-twentieth century's Motion Picture Production Code, a context the chapter explores through work on the parameters set for lesbian representation by classical Hollywood cinema and the (non-)place of the lesbian in the visual field. *Mulholland Drive* articulates a widespread cultural paradox: the juxtaposition of the lesbian's absence and her threatening over-presence. If the thriller relies on the doubling of the woman for its structuring anxieties and motivations, the lesbian amplifies this existing threat. Throughout this book, I explore the paradoxical demands for the lesbian to be read both as pathologically singular and as threateningly doubled. Acknowledging the perhaps uncomfortable parallels between contemporary cinema and classical Hollywood, this chapter stages the key feminist debates that underpin many of the book's ongoing theoretical interlocutions.

Chapter 2 argues that absence and presence are forced onto the same page in a reading of *Nathalie . . .* (Anne Fontaine, 2003) alongside its remake *Chloe* (Atom Egoyan, 2009). *Nathalie . . .* is a film about a woman's suspicion, and then re-staging, of her husband's affair. Structures of homoerotic looking complicate the plot's ostensible focus on heterosexual desire. The film creates a series of spaces in which two women's shared experience of sexual interaction with the same man creates a derivative voyeurism. A vicarious lesbian eroticism depends on what is *not* shown rather than what *is*. In contrast, the explicit consummation of desire that marks *Chloe*'s (arguably) radical adaptation is necessarily paired with explicit violence. Through the increased visibility of sex in the remake, it becomes in the original a structuring absence. Through a reading of this juxtaposition, and in dialogue with feminist work on visibility and representation, the chapter challenges the conception that increased visibility equals inevitable progress.

The momentum of the book thus shifts gears here from the sharpened lines of the lesbian figure in *Mulholland Drive* towards the generically indeterminate and ambiguously erotic desires of the subsequent films of the corpus.

Chapter 3 explores the impulse to equate sexual identity with liberation. In *Circumstance* (Maryam Keshavarz, 2011), spaces of cinema, fantasy and surveillance become sites of projected selfhood in the face of identity's seeming impossibility. The chapter argues that the spatialisation of cultural idealisation is intensely evoked by the film's narrative of adolescence in a non-Western, Islamic state that nevertheless is premised upon a familiarity with or desire for global queer and youth cultures. Queer functions spatially to trouble a fetish of identity through which it is itself constructed and desired. Against a compromised narrative of cultural oppression, the private domestic sphere in *Circumstance* becomes a threatening locus of sexual potential and then sinister surveillance. The woman's image is both the source of patriarchal anxiety and its solution, while representable homosexuality is aestheticised through whiteness. In this context, the chapter argues that *Circumstance* generates a smoothly exoticised idealisation of a Western elsewhere through which a fantasy of out lesbian sexuality is made visually possible.

Chapter 4 analyses the ambiguous intimacies generated by the competition that permeates desire in *Water Lilies* (Céline Sciamma, 2007) and *She Monkeys* (Lisa Aschan, 2011). The chapter argues that the films' adolescent sporting cultures produce a lesbian potential that is generated, but then immediately contained, by negotiations of control. The queerness of lesbian desire is evoked here as a series of affects outside of figurative norms. We are always left just out of reach of the consummation of desire that we cling to as narrative convention is resisted. While the internal process of coming *into* desire transpires through sensory abundance, mutual eroticism is marked and suspended by *not quite touching*. The chapter advances a reading of an affective mode of filmmaking that is saturated with desire but not defined by desire's labelling. While Chapters 2 and 3 unsettle the visibility imperative of discourses surrounding lesbian cinema, Chapter 4 disturbs the positivity of lesbian legibility by positing a queer affect that resides, contrary to expectation, in the spaces between bodily exhibitions of desire.

The analysis at the heart of Chapter 5 interrogates the status of the sex scene as the only available register through which to read lesbian cinema in popular discourse. A confusing clash of ideological standpoints frames the debate around *Blue Is the Warmest Colour* (Abdellatif Kechiche, 2013), which has been the subject of extensive media scrutiny ever since its Palme d'Or triumph at the Cannes Film Festival in 2013. It has been lauded as a universal love story, hailed as a significant political milestone and derided as a misogynistic appropriation of the female body by a male director. The film's infamously explicit sex scenes are asked by critics not only to be satisfactory images of the act itself, but also of lesbian identity more broadly: of the film's legibility as lesbian. The chapter explores instead how desire functions beyond the remit of visual evidence, considering how sex in *Blue Is the Warmest Colour*, unmediated by music or the dominance of close-ups that populate the rest of the film, creates a disjuncture between what is seen and how it is perceived. As this chapter argues, the film's disorganised diegesis throws us into a time and space out of sync with the linguistic logic through which its discursive sphere has registered.

Even in a changing context of social and cultural representation, still we see visual citations of earlier models and forms that complicate the lesbian's contemporary screen figuration. Gesturing back to and developing the context provided by Chapter 1, my reading of *Carol* (Todd Haynes, 2015) in Chapter 6 reveals the circularity of lesbianism's visual regimes. The protagonist commands the film's compass through an expansive gaze. Rather than directed exclusively at its object, desire is diffused across a sweeping affective repertory: misty windows, sheets of rain and saturations of city light; lingering musical themes; the revival of celluloid grain. *Carol*'s visual repertoire draws on twentieth-century visual conditions of marginality that continue to be provocative and seductive; alongside this cinematic heritage, however, it can also be read as a queer melodrama whose erotic register recalls the exhilarating ruptures of the New Queer Cinema. The chapter argues that lesbian potential is indebted to the suspended terms of mid-twentieth-century cinematic homoeroticism, breaching the logic of visibility's progression.

While *Lesbian Cinema after Queer Theory* provides a close focus on the cinema, it also proceeds to do so in a context of television's dominance in the race towards lesbian visibility. The contemporary field of visual cultural studies has been shaped not only by television's accessibility but also by its scope. That medium's long-running narratives have transformed the visibility of the lesbian in the basic terms of minutes on-screen. While records of cinematic visibility can of course follow this criterion, the films analysed in this book are chosen for what I consider to be specifically cinematic features. New media platforms have made theatrical film viewing an increasingly rare experience. However, the context of digital technology in fact necessitates more than ever an attention to cinema's specificities. Temporally, films present a very particular relationship between part and whole, between ephemeral moment and overall scope. This is a condition of the feature film's capacity (and the relative scarcity of the moments that make it up) as well as a symptom of the theatrical context of viewing. Watching a film from start to finish with no planned interruption draws our attention to sequence and pace: the currency of time has a heightened value. Spatially, the cinema as a location intensifies the act of viewing, concentrating the screen's affective pleasures.

Rather than advancing a conventional history of the recent past of lesbian representation or an overview of the films that have made the lesbian visible, in *Lesbian Cinema after Queer Theory* I analyse a series of films released in the past two decades alongside the invigorating theories of sexuality that problematise their legibility *as lesbian*. These films are united by an emphasis on the diegetic role of spectatorship and voyeurism in the construction of desire. They all include scenes of what I think of as intensified spectatorship, revealing the ways in which the cinematic apparatus links desire to the image. Central to this book's aim is the reconsideration, through queer theory, of theoretical arguments about the tensions between identification and desire. These lie at the very heart of debates over what constitutes lesbianism in the visual field. This book negotiates these theoretical tensions in order to mark out the ways in which we might simultaneously trouble and sustain lesbian cinema in the era of the visible.

Introduction: Looking after Lesbian Cinema

The unprecedented increase in lesbian representation in political, social and cultural spheres over the past two decades has coincided with a shift in theoretical consciousness. In a paradoxical feat of what could be called unhappy timing, the lesbian's delayed and uneasy path towards visibility has coincided with queer theory's dominance in the academic study of sexuality. The result has been a comparable *invisibility* in the very intellectual field that might have accounted for these representational transformations. *Lesbian Cinema after Queer Theory* takes this up as a structuring problem. Queer theory has generated a new field of figurations, pushing at the limits of lesbian legibility. It has also generated the potential for nuanced and sensitive renderings of debates about sexuality on the screen. While timely, politically significant and intellectually exhilarating, such changes provide a provocation to the lesbian whose identification is often dismissed and disavowed as an anachronistic term of attachment. As one such lesbian, claiming my identity category even as I am invigorated by its disruption, I ask: what does it mean to write about lesbian cinema after queer theory?

As this project began to unfold, circa 2011, I found myself looking for a corpus that would chronicle the new visibility of lesbian cinema. What I did not anticipate was the question: 'but Clara, what *is* lesbian cinema?' Two women are aligned across time and space by a coloured filter reflecting and obscuring their image. A gaze is shared between two girls across discrete shots, spatially disconnected but aligned by framing. A woman reclines face-on in the background behind her lover who lies in profile in the foreground, their two sets of lips fused on the two-dimensional screen. Another tells explicit sexual stories to a companion who watches as intently as she listens. A young woman's fantasy of a stranger is signified through flashes of colour. A teenage girl's gaze isolates its object but is left unnoticed and unreturned. Another kisses the trace of lipstick left by a playful kiss on a window pane. Here is a series of cinematic moments that read, to me, as lesbian. But the word lesbian no longer seems to allow for their full description. It does not fully account for their complexity, excitement, anticipation, ambivalence and intractability. Twenty-first-century lesbian cinema emerges after the advent of queer theory; lesbian cinema chases after queer theory's theoretical provocations. Just as I want to celebrate lesbian visibility, I am instructed to trouble it, to find trouble in it, to see how it causes trouble. I am moved to consider the relationship between cultural visibility and theoretical legibility. Just as the lesbian is made progressively visible in one domain, in the other she becomes fixed as a figure of the past to get over, to be moved beyond. This trouble becomes both a launching site and the site of a defence, a paradox that eventually proves to be central to this book's rationale.

TROUBLING VISIBILITY

Lesbian Cinema after Queer Theory explores how the figure of the lesbian in contemporary cinema is marked by a paradoxical burden of visibility and invisibility produced at the convergence of queer and feminist discourses. There are relatively few scholarly monographs in film studies written under what Valerie Traub calls the 'sign of the lesbian' (2015: 7). Existing contributions to the field indicate a prior invisibility, historically interrupted only by invocations of pathologisation, isolation and tragedy. They chronicle both the pains and pleasures of fantasy identifications; persistent tropes, codes and conventions; sideways glances and peripheral characterisations. We hear of the lesbian's marginal presence in classical Hollywood and early cinema (Corber, 2011; Horak, 2016; White, 1999), the pathological figurations to which she is insistently reduced (Hart, 1994; Coffman, 2006; Cairns, 2006; Weiss, 1992), and her inception as the product of a spectator's fantasy and of the cinema itself (Kabir, 1998; Whatling, 1997). Recurring scholarly interventions figure the lesbian either as 'overwritten by cliché' (Love, 2004: 121), or as condemned to fall entirely 'outside sexuality's visual field' (Jagose, 2002: 2). She is lost in the slippage between, on the one hand, the inherent negativity of the female as absence to male presence and, on the other, the difficulty of homosexual difference.

The figure of the lesbian I speak of here is not a precursor to, but rather created by, her cinematic image. She functions through repetition, through tropes, through stereotypes. And yet to issue a corrective to invisible pasts in the form of the promise of visible futures is, paradoxically, to issue a new set of threats. As Zeena Feldman writes of the 'politics of visibility', 'being seen can gesture misrecognition' (2017: 2). We might not recognise what others are now allowed to see of us, or what we now see of ourselves. As Peggy Phelan warns, the route to visibility must be acknowledged as a process of naming and fixing, even if it is to be politically championed (1993: 1). Annamarie Jagose contests therefore the 'efficacy of assuming visibility as the standard measure for sexual legitimacy' (2002: 231), while Amy Villarejo argues that 'the demand to make lesbians visible, whether as ammunition for anti-homophobic campaigns or as figures for identification, renders lesbian static, makes lesbian into (an) image, and forestalls any examination of lesbian within context' (2003: 6–7). Even as we recognise the undoubtable 'cultural interventions that visibility politics have made' (Beirne, 2008: 26), we catch sight of the trouble with visibility: it fixes just as it names; it dismisses some as it champions others; it distracts; it normalises; it fossilises. Palatability can sacrifice politics. To make visible is to refine the spectrum of who and what is shown.

The long-awaited *making visible* of the lesbian on the cinema screen has followed a course of monumental representational change. Now more than ever, everything is marked by the ways in which it can be turned into an image. New photographic technologies have transformed the availability, immediacy and regularity of video production and distribution. Digital – and increasingly mobile – platforms have widened the remit and spectrum of what is made and seen. Mainstream conventions in film and television, as well as in other visual media such as video games and web series, have shifted towards an increase in the sexually (and violently) explicit. In 2000, Judith Mayne conceded a simultaneous desire to 'affirm visibility and [to] question it' (xxi). Since 2000, this process of affirming and questioning visibility has become even more charged. The paradoxical positioning of the lesbian in film has always meant reading between the lines, against the grain. Such metaphors serve us well. Now, subversive erotic identifications are met by the possibility of looking for lesbians on-screen – and finding them. The process of what Mayne calls 'finding the lesbians' might now confront, surprise or alarm us in ways we hadn't previously imagined (Ibid.: xviii). Especially in this context of visual and social change, we might disavow the pleasurable evidence of the sex scene in favour of an otherwise frustrating ambiguity. We might champion the refusal of identity's naming even as we long for out role models. We might be committed to films that forsake their commitments to us. We might discover identifications in heteronormative spaces. We might be overwhelmed by affect before we engage with politics. We might discover that our intellectual pleasures counteract our aesthetic pleasures. We might find anticipation sexy. We might divert calls for seriousness. We might be excited by the need to look, and to look again. We might want to find a new way to describe any or all of these 'mights'. We might want to call them queer.

An edited collection on 'queer film and video' published in 1991 by the collective reading group Bad Object Choices, containing essays by Mayne, Cindy Patton, Stuart Marshall, Richard Fung, Kobena Mercer and Teresa de Lauretis, asked: *How Do I Look?* This question – and its implicit extensions (how do I look *in* film / how do I look *at* film) still define processes of viewing, enforcements of type and recognition, structures of visibility and invisibility, and mechanisms of identification. As film and video become queerer and queerer, however, we return to another question, the 'where' that accompanies the 'how'. In 1999, Patricia White introduced her book *Uninvited: Classical Hollywood Cinema and Lesbian Representability* by asking: 'when representation is forbidden, *where* do we look?' (16, emphasis added). Perhaps what is radical, twenty years on, is to repeat the question: when representation is granted, *where do we look*?

A BRIEF HISTORY OF COMPLICATED ERASURES

The lesbian's era of visibility has coincided with more general transformations in production and distribution across screen media, including rising numbers of international co-productions and new digital platforms for transnational dissemination. However, even in this context of change and opportunity, the conversation continues to be shaped by the requirements of conceptual and historical ground clearing. Invisibility is entrenched in the existing discursive field surrounding the history of lesbian representation. Rather than the recipient of a clean break between a historical invisibility and a contemporary visibility, the lesbian is marked by a discourse that foregrounds the relationship between the two. As Traub writes of the 'knowledge problem' that defines the lesbian as term and category, 'it is crucial to insist [. . .] *not* that "the lesbian" actually *has been* invisible, impossible, inconsequential, or apparitional, but that this figure's representational status has hinged on a dialectic between visibility and invisibility, possibility and impossibility, signification and insignificance' (2015: 286). In other words, the lesbian stands in for an anxiety rather than for herself.

What is most evident in many early figurations, spanning genres from the romance to the thriller, is the persistent framing of lesbianism in the singular, whether as pathetically doomed to loneliness (*The Children's Hour*, William Wyler, 1961) or as sinisterly and even parodically seductive (*The Killing of Sister George*, Robert Aldrich, 1966). In some of the most enduring figurations of lesbianism in twentieth-century cinema, the seductive protagonist is coded as embodying a stable or essential lesbian sexuality while her heterosexual counterpart is primed to undergo a process of transformation. In the mid-1980s, *Desert Hearts* (Donna Deitch, 1985) signalled a new optimism. Ten years later, however, Jackie Stacey expressed surprise that Deitch's film did *not* make way for 'a long line of popular lesbian romance films with "happy endings"' (1995: 92).

The 1990s is prominent as a significant turning point – a decade of change by the end of which we were to understand that lesbianism *had been made visible* both on the cinema screen and in the academy – Andrea Weiss's *Vampires and Violets: Lesbians in the Cinema*, the first full-length monograph solely dedicated to lesbian cinema, was published in 1992. Even by this point, however, as the lesbian in the social and political realm had been increasingly normalised and her difference reduced, earlier tropes continued to mark contemporary cultural productions. In a survey of films doing the festival circuit in 1995, Rhona Berenstein noted that 'lesbians are not born, they're seduced' (1996: 125). At least that's the impression Berenstein got from the majority of the lesbian films on offer in which women 'need to be coaxed into their lesbian-ism' by a more experienced 'dyke' character (Ibid.). In cult films such as *Claire of the Moon* (Nicole Conn, 1992) and *When Night Is Falling* (Patricia Rozema, 1995), the ostensibly straight female lead is seduced into her lesbian desire by a more experienced and already-out lesbian figure. In a similar vein but under the guise of another genre, the later years of the decade set in motion the production – though far more rarely theatrical distribution – of coming-of-age narratives such as *Show Me Love* (Lukas Moodysson, 1998); *The Incredibly True Adventure of Two Girls in Love* (Maria Maggenti, 1995), repeated by Maria Maggenti with a twist a decade later in *Puccini for Beginners* (2006); and, in a genius parody, *But I'm a Cheerleader* (Jamie Babbit, 1999).[1]

Rather than manifesting a decisive break with the twentieth century's systems of (non-)representation, the twenty-first century's increased turn to visibility has been the result of a staggered series of smaller steps. Television heralded change for the 2000s, where the medium's long-form narrative format might (unlike Berenstein's line-up) screen lesbian relationships 'well out of the closet' (Berenstein, 1996: 125). *The L Word* (Ilene Chaiken, 2004–9) unequivocally marketed itself on a newly enabled 'commodification of les-bianism as a category of identity' (Wiegman, 1994: 3). The show instituted a new era of visibility, taking on a *Sex and the City* (Darren Star, 1998–2004) remit and commodifying the middle-class Los Angeles 'lipstick lesbian' ('Same Sex, Different City' was its tag line). The show also provided, in its almost exclusively female directorial and writing team, credits for directors whose films have otherwise struggled to receive international distribution.[2] Even so, Eve Kosofksy Sedgwick spoke the mind of many of the show's viewers after its second season: 'I will be relieved', Sedgwick wrote, 'when the writers decide they have sufficiently interpolated straight viewers and can leave behind the lachrymose plot of Jenny's Choice' (2006: xxiv). 'Jenny's Choice' – the ingénue's discovery of a lesbian desire that turns her world upside down – characterised several outputs of the early 2000s, including *Kissing Jessica Stein* (Charles Herman-Wurmfeld, 2001), *Imagine Me and You* (Ol Parker, 2005), *Room in Rome* (Julio Medem, 2010) and *Kiss Me* (Alexandra-Therese Keining, 2011). The ready-established lesbian couple did however increasingly appear in films such as *Producing Adults* (Aleksi Salmenperä, 2004) and *Break My Fall* (Kanchi Wichmann, 2011), while a renewal (or maturing) of Clea DuVall and Natasha Lyonne's formative *But I'm a Cheerleader* partnership took a reassuringly undramatic form in DuVall's directorial debut *The Intervention* (2016). The lesbian couple reached something of a disgruntled apotheosis in 2010, when the 'family values movie' *The Kids Are All Right* (Lisa Cholodenko) was in the top ten films released in its opening weekend in the UK box office (see Colleen Benn, et al., 2010, British Film Institute, 2018).[3] Lisa Cholodenko's film exemplifies the move towards what I have argued elsewhere is a postfeminist lesbian cinema (see Bradbury-Rance, 2013).[4]

In the aftermath of a wave of equality laws privileging the couple form for homosexuals as well as heterosexuals, the lesbian's cultural visibility seems to engender the fixing of her theoretical legibility. The lesbian is increasingly equated with 'the normal, the legitimate, the dominant' – namely, everything queer is not, according to David Halperin's definition (1997: 62).[5] The paragraphs above reveal just one version of lesbian screen visibility. A parallel trajectory, also beginning in the early 1990s, indicates the possibility of an alternative. The New Queer Cinema was a moniker charted and coined by B. Ruby Rich to capture a series of films that were 'fresh, edgy, low-budget, inventive, unapologetic, sexy, and stylistically daring' (2013: xxiv). While the movement most notably made the names of male directors like Todd Haynes, Isaac Julien and Gregg Araki (see Pramaggiore, 1997; Pick, 2004), it also opened up marginal spaces for lesbian films such as Cheryl Dunye's *The Watermelon Woman* (1996), Rose Troche's *Go Fish* (1994) and Cholodenko's *High Art* (1998). These simultaneously resisted both the overinvestment in the happy ending and the disappointment of the failed lesbian romance. José Esteban Muñoz argues that 'being ordinary and being married' are 'desires that automatically rein themselves in, never daring to see or imagine the not-yet-conscious' (2009: 21). The New Queer Cinema radically refused to rein itself in.

If there is a certain lag in the field of the theatrically distributed feature film, it has been overemphasised by contrast with the small (and smaller) screen (see Griffin, 2016; Beirne, 2014; Monaghan, 2016). What Stuart Richards has called a 'New Queer Cinema Renaissance' (2016) can be observed in films such as *Weekend* (Andrew Haigh, 2011), *Stranger by the Lake* (Alain Guiraudie, 2013) and the wide oeuvre of Xavier Dolan, including *Laurence Anyways* (2012) and *Tom at the Farm* (2013). Of the (few) lesbian films on Richards's list, Desiree Akhavan's *Appropriate Behaviour* (2014) was pre-empted by its director's self-publicised web series *The Slope* (2010–12) and Dee Rees's *Pariah* (2011) was followed up first by a film premiered on HBO (*Bessie*, 2015) and then the Netflix-distributed *Mudbound* (2017). Meanwhile,

Jill Soloway followed up her indie film *Afternoon Delight* (2001) with the series *Transparent* (2014–) which piloted on Amazon Prime rather than on broadcast television, and publicity provided by sites such as YouTube helped to pave the way for, or even fund, works such as Campbell X's *Stud Life* (2012) (see Mayer, 2016: 176). Arguably, the primary site of potential for queer productions that resist the mainstream commodification of lesbianism has stepped in the twenty-first century into the digital realm. The move towards the era of the visible has been neither linear nor consistent.

LESBIAN INVISIBILITY IN QUEER TIMES

We can see that two trajectories, running in parallel, constitute the 'progress' narrative that has attached to the lesbian's journey from invisibility to visibility over the past few decades. One has seen the overwhelming visibility of lesbianism as an identity category and the emergence of distribution spaces (albeit often virtual ones) for self-identifying lesbian filmmakers. The other has seen the increasing prevalence of *queer* recognition at film festivals that, in correspondence with the academic context, serves to institute a new kind of invisibility in which the lesbian is subsumed under broader queer representational categories. When *Blue Is the Warmest Colour* (Abdellatif Kechiche, 2013) won the prestigious Palme d'Or at the Cannes Film Festival in 2013, it made history. The award had never before been won by a film with a lesbian narrative. Nor had the Queer Palm, instituted in 2010 at the same festival, until it was awarded in 2015 to *Carol* (Todd Haynes, 2015). Yet, both of these triumphs also expose the precarious nature of such success. Unlike the Academy Awards, which predominantly celebrate mainstream Anglo-American films made within the studio system, with a single category devoted to 'foreign language' films, Cannes sets the tone for the reception of an international corpus of films that become recognised as high art (see Perriam and Waldron, 2016).[6] Whilst the Queer Palm is independently sponsored and does not appear in the Cannes official list of awards, its selection from amongst the best (broadly understood) 'queer' films in the festival's official programme provides a simple demonstration of lesbian visibility in one of the most significant institutions of prestige in the international art house film circuit. Between 2011 and 2018, ninety-two films were candidates for the award. Of those, across seven years, just twenty-four were directed by women.[7] And of those, none has won the award, while a tiny minority of the nominated films (whether directed by men or by women) have lesbian narratives.[8]

The parallel histories of queer and lesbian cinema have converged and diverged. A web search for scholarly articles on 'lesbian film' and 'queer film' reveals an equivalent rise in the usage of both terms between the years of 1990 and 2000. However, from the year 2000 onwards, searches in five-year periods indicate a steady drop in results for 'lesbian film' and a striking rise in results for 'queer film'.[9] When she coined the term 'Queer Theory' as the title of a conference in 1991, de Lauretis proffered a possible solution to the 'politically correct phrase "lesbian and gay"' in which 'differences are implied but then simply taken for granted or even covered over by the word "and"' (1991: v–vi). 'Queer Theory' was thus 'arrived at in the effort to avoid all of these fine distinctions in our discursive protocols, not to adhere to any one of the given terms, not to assume their ideological liabilities, but instead to both transgress and transcend them – or at the very least problematize them' (Ibid.). However, the taking-for-granted-ness of the word 'and' seems to have migrated along with the terminological shift. What we can now observe is a trajectory whereby lesbianism has been theorised, problematised and then dissolved in queer theory's new intellectual paradigm. Nick Rees-Roberts employs the word 'queer' in the title of his book *French Queer Cinema* with the understanding that it will be read as 'convenient shorthand for lesbian, gay, bisexual and transgender identities' (2008: 3–4). He states in the same introduction, however, that his corpus will 'focus primarily on gay male sexuality (due to the lack of "out" lesbian filmmakers and of lesbian self-representation)' (2008: 3–4). Edited collections on queer cinema often follow a similar kind of flattening out of gender difference, or otherwise assign lesbian films to one distinct chapter whose naming as such marks it as other from the rest of queer's apparently simpler significations (see for instance Griffiths, 2006; Dawson, 2017; Peele, 2007). The majority of collections on 'queer' or 'gay' cinema exclude lesbians both as contributors and as objects of study, rendering insecure the equation of political progress with screen visibility. A presumed incompatibility between lesbianism and queerness sees lesbianism either marginalised within, veiled by or distinguished as other from queerness (for rare exceptions, see Benshoff and Griffin, 2006; Stacey and Street, 2007; Perriam, 2013). Rather than necessarily a direct exclusion on the part of these authors and editors, this tendency demonstrates the overwhelming use of queer as an umbrella term that in fact serves a series of paradoxically conflicting options: to make lesbianism redundant, to designate her otherness, or to disguise her absence. To explore representational visibility on-screen alongside discursive visibility in scholarship is thus to observe a longstanding anxiety about the processes of conflation through which 'the very name "lesbian" disappear[s] under the rubric "queer"' (Garber, 2009: 67). Even this linguistically equalising term is revealed to subsume the lesbian into a discursive field that excludes her.

And yet. For Sedgwick, queer refers to 'the open mesh of possibilities, gaps, overlaps, dissonances and resonances, lapses and excesses of meaning when the constituent elements of anyone's gender, of anyone's sexuality aren't made (or *can't* be made) to signify monolithically' (1993: 8). For Sara Ahmed it describes those 'specific sexual practices' that, for her, intrinsically involve 'a personal and social commitment to living in an oblique world, or in a world that has an oblique angle in relation to that which is given' (2006: 161). These spatial metaphors are not only exceptionally exciting but also theoretically productive for the paradoxical process of locating lesbian legibility on the contemporary screen. Gaps and overlaps, oblique angles: these are the spaces of lesbian cinema in the twenty-first century.

Long before the blooming of queer theory in the academy, lesbian was a term subjected to the onus of clarifying self-definition. Tamsin Wilton, for example, exposes the need to preface 'any exploration of lesbian issues with [. . .] the catechism of undecidability: the formula of question and response which problematizes the definition of "lesbian"' (1995: 3–4). Traub begins an article on lesbian film with that very formula, asking, 'What is a lesbian?' (1995: 115). Crucially, she immediately refuses to answer, arguing that to do so would '*fix* that which is fundamentally unstable' (Ibid., see also Tasker, 1994). This anti-definition could itself now be described as queer. And yet, lesbianism is more often than not positioned as queer's outdated precursor. The 'feminist-as-lesbian' is a figure named by Victoria Hesford as she who is legible 'as a *shorthand notation* for women's liberation' (2013: 16–17, see also Jagose, 1994). A possible reversal of Hesford's construction – the lesbian-as-feminist – might also function to accommodate lesbianism's burden of signification, for the term 'lesbian' is asked not only to indicate the figure of the lesbian woman but also the progressive politics signalled by that figure (see also Villarejo, 2003: 6–7).[10] In the early second-wave feminist movement, lesbianism was, in Hesford's words, 'something closer to what we now call *queer* – a practice of subverting existing social identities and of anticipating future forms of social and sexual life' (2013: 239, original emphasis). Such equations are rendered increasingly unstable. The figure of the lesbian has come to signify not only the liberatory politics of the feminist movement but also its exclusions. The two terms together – lesbian + feminist – hold within them a quality that, in Elizabeth Freeman's words, 'seems to somehow inexorably hearken back to essentialized bodies, normative visions of women's sexuality, and single-issue identity politics that exclude people of color, the working class, and the transgendered' (2010: 62). When women's liberation itself increasingly becomes a shorthand for trans-exclusionary platforms, lesbianism is moved further away from the conceptually queer potential of its past.

What we see is that, in short, lesbianism becomes 'unrecognizable across domains' (Wiegman, 2012: 130). The struggle is to find a way to accommodate, in Susan Stryker's terms, the 'diverse particularities of our embodied lives' (2007: 67). Rosalind Galt and Karl Schoonover state that 'queer film theory is always a feminist project for us' (2016: 11). Here, queer always = feminism (see also Marinucci, 2016 [2010]). In the bid for inclusion and intersectionality, the single-issue presumption that haunts lesbianism's claim is systematically pitted against queer theory's less troubled intersectional advances. Nevertheless, Robyn Wiegman suggests that the reduction of lesbianism to an identity category disavowed by queer theory, and the consequent resistances to it by those who claim queer instead as their term of attachment, rely on 'making the lesbian solid enough to perform their own self-fashioning reclamations – indeed it is their proximity to and intimacy with her that makes their divergence from her possible' (2012: 130–1). The combined histories of queer and lesbian as terms of attachment and political motivation have run not only in parallel but through mutual constitution.

WHEN WE SEE IT

Queer has been defined theoretically as '*whatever* is at odds with the normal, the legitimate, the dominant' (Halperin, 1997: 62); as that which is 'not yet conscious' (Muñoz, 2009: 21); as the very status of 'unthinkability' (Butler, 2002: 18). These definitions provide a methodological challenge for the *finding* of queerness in visual representation. As I have outlined above, lesbianism's history of radical political utopianism suggests that the lesbian is no more straightforwardly legible. In lesbian feminist writing on the subject, cinema must variously bear the burden of 'social responsibility' (de Lauretis, 1994: 114); must be 'passionately linked to the lesbian community, both in the sense of political struggle and in the banalities of daily life' (Becker, et al., 1995: 42); must remove itself from 'the discourse of the gendered subject [assumed] within a heterosexist authority system' (Hammer, 1993: 71). Villarejo locates the 'lesbian people, lesbian places, lesbian things' (2003: 22) of her book *Lesbian Rule: Cultural Criticism and the Value of Desire* in a documentary film corpus, in which 'lesbian is right there, staring at you, haranguing you, imploring you, or telling you stories' (Ibid.: 15). Documentary is Villarejo's chosen site of lesbian potential, construction and rhetoric in a project that, she writes, stands 'as an elegy to' the term lesbian, if that term is (but, she says, probably isn't) 'in its final hours, slowly to be overtaken by the term *queer*' (Ibid.: 7). For Lee Wallace, who focuses on the relationship between sexual identities and cinematic form while leaving behind the psychoanalytic bases of earlier monographs on lesbian film, lesbianism 'disclose[s] itself within the visual field' (2009: 81). Instead of sexuality being implanted *into* film, it is constituted in Wallace's theorisation *by* film, in which the *mise en scène* is more than just 'the suturing medium of the diegesis' (Ibid.: 55). Cinema's visual codes and how they are directed, shot, edited and interpreted are paramount to the creation of meaning. Mayne reflects in the introduction to *Framed: Lesbians, Feminists, and Media Culture* that someone analysing the state of interest in lesbian cinema in a couple of decades may well 'wonder at the choices, perhaps finding quaint the continuing preoccupation with Hollywood, or the fascination with Garbo and Dietrich, or the desire to make such lists in the first place' (2000: xxi). Still, a corpus must be found. In their book *Queer Cinema in the World* (2016: 15), Galt and Schoonover insist on a 'radical openness' to finding queerness in cinema where they might not expect it. *Lesbian Cinema after Queer Theory* maintains a similar approach to lesbianism in the cinema.

To exemplify the opportunities and dangers of this critical task, I want to pause here on a particular example. At the end of 2016, I watch Park Chan-Wook's *The Handmaiden* at the London Film Festival. It is 11 a.m. on a Saturday morning, and the enormous festival screen on London's Embankment holds a full house. Laughter and heady sighs resound audibly in the hall. Park's film was premiered earlier in the same year in competition at Cannes Film Festival: at the beginning of the next, it will be screened again in London at BFI Flare: London LGBT Film Festival (which by 2018 has become London *LGBTQ+* Film Festival, having begun life as London Lesbian and Gay Film Festival). The film appears in the popular press in several critics' top-twenty lists for the year 2017 (see *The Guardian*, 2017; *Time Out*, 2017; *The Independent*, 2017; *Wired*, 2017). *The Handmaiden* is an adaptation of the widely acclaimed and loved neo-Gothic novel *Fingersmith* (2002) by the lesbian writer Sarah Waters, who publicly endorses the film. In cinematic form it becomes a spectacle of erotic looking. It is a literary adaptation that is visually ravishing; a Cannes prize goes to the production designer Seong-hie Ryu for her exquisite set pieces. The film easily becomes a recognisable element in its director's oeuvre: it is a vengeance film to accompany *Sympathy for Mr. Vengeance* (2002), *Old Boy* (2003) and *Lady Vengeance* (2005), as befits Park's auteurist motives. It owes an obvious debt to classical Hollywood cinema's systems of the image, and is compared with classics such as *Rebecca* (Alfred Hitchcock, 1940), *The Spiral Staircase* (Robert Siodmak, 1946), *Les Diaboliques* (Henri-Georges Clouzot, 1955) and *The Haunting* (Robert Wise, 1963). It has a male director, though the sex scene that is rapturously described in review after review is reportedly shot only by a female cameraperson, a female soundperson and the two actresses. Presumably to absolve him from accusations of voyeurism, Park is absent from the scene's filming. In the UK, the film receives an 18 rating, for 'strong sex' (2013); it is also exceptionally violent.

I love *The Handmaiden*. I find it sexy, stylish and compulsively watchable. What the film has in common with the principal case studies of this book is a gesturing to the precariousness of the image in a visual field that insistently cites the past. Its contemporary production context enables the mainstreaming of its explicit sex scenes. Yet, its complex narrative unsettles our attachments. We fail to know what the visible image has really offered to us. Its chronology threatens to make lesbianism impossible: a misremembering, a figment of the imagination or a misrecognition. *Lesbian Cinema after Queer Theory* highlights the reworking of several genres – from the thriller to the domestic melodrama – to consider how they mediate, and produce, lesbianism. It observes how the cinematic apparatus itself masquerades, performs, conceals and, even then, highlights desire. If the possibility of visibility yields a burden of evidence, then looking backwards can yield vicarious and divergent eroticisms.

SEX, DESIRE, EROTICISM, AFFECT

This book is indebted to a conceptual debate between two theories of desire that remain outside the trajectory of queer theory's dominance in the study of sexuality: de Lauretis's Freudian reading of the specificity of lesbian desire (1994) and Stacey's reading of homoerotic identification and the multiplicity of women's spectatorship practices (1994). While they both position themselves in opposition to past manifestations of psychoanalytic feminist film theory that failed to account for lesbian desire, a tension arises in the contrasting distinctions these scholars make between sexuality and eroticism. Taking from Freudian psychoanalysis the desiring potential of sexed subjects, de Lauretis's work on lesbian desire is known for its focus on lesbian specificity and for its theorisation of what Freud himself 'could not imagine but others can – a lesbian subjectivity' (1994: xiv). In contrast to Laura Mulvey's early refusal of lesbian desire outside of the female spectator's masculine identification, de Lauretis posits a lesbian cinema 'constituted in relation to a *sexual* difference from socially dominant, institutionalized, heterosexual forms' (Ibid.: xii, original emphasis). It is this emphasis on the *sexed* and *desiring* nature of subjectivity that underpins de Lauretis's project. Her primary reservation is the risk of conflating desire and identification and thereby de-sexualising lesbianism.

Stacey, on the other hand, looks at processes of desire that move away from the specificities of 'lesbian subjectivity'. Nevertheless, her intervention focuses not on 'de-eroticising desire, but rather eroticising identification' (1994: 29). Her work urges us to consider those multiple processes of identification that are yielded by sometimes-fixed identities. The choice of the word 'homoerotic' (Ibid.: 28) – a psychic category rather than a social one – allows her to recuperate desire within cinematic identification not only for lesbian women but for all women, where homoeroticism is an aspect (one of many, she argues) of the pleasures that cinema can afford female spectators, multiplied beyond those restricted to masculine versus feminine positions. Brought into popularity in the years after the 1994 publication of both Stacey's *Star Gazing* and de Lauretis's *The Practice of Love*, the term queer has since been mobilised to cut through the dichotomies that threaten to cloud their debate. My use of queer throughout this book is informed, if not by her use of the word itself, then by Stacey's analysis of those ambiguous modulations of eroticism and desire. Moreover, my reading of both of these theoretical texts in dialogue with queer theory provokes the impetus for this book's intervention, in which homoeroticism is reconfigured as the queer potentiality of lesbianism.

The debate between de Lauretis and Stacey that I have briefly charted here evokes a central concern of the book with how to understand sexuality's representability without sex. As Mandy Merck writes, it is 'the love scene' that, of all possible visual options, holds a 'particularly symbolic function: the ability to represent "lesbian experience"' (1993: 167). Michel Foucault famously announced that the nineteenth century was the period in which the delineation of behaviours made way for the categorisation of identities, so that 'the homosexual was now a species' (1998 [1984]: 43). Yet in contemporary cinema, it seems, the lesbian must still be evidenced by the behaviours that were her identity's precursor. Sexual specificity determines lesbian legibility; sex becomes the visual evidence through which sexuality registers. As Ann Cvetkovich argues, however: sometimes, in some contexts, 'what counts as (homo)sexuality is unpredictable and requires new vocabularies; affect may be present when overt forms of sexuality are not' (2007: 463). In *Lesbian Cinema after Queer Theory*, whilst attending to the 'vital re-centring of the body' that has been characteristic of feminist theory's turn to affect (Pedwell and Whitehead, 2012: 116), I use queer as an elaboration (rather than replacement) of lesbianism that captures what is not only before speech but also before (sexual) touch (see also Koivunen, 2010). In the face of contemporary visibility's paradoxical imperatives, I gesture to an embodied dynamic not defined by a directional relationship between subject and object (or between the lesbian and the one whom she will seduce), but a mood of sexual potential. Desire is not limited to the familiar 'genres' of encounter (Berlant, 2008: 4) that unfold in dialogue, character, or the satisfaction of a shot/countershot sequence. Affects spread across a film's timeframe. Repetitive visual motifs leave traces of desire on the screen.

In the introduction to a special issue of *Women's Studies Quarterly* on 'queer method', Heather Love champions queer scholarship for the ways in which it has 'dealt with untidy issues like desire, sexual practice, affect, sensation, and the body' (2016: 346). To employ such a 'knowledge project' (Ibid.) as a method for reading lesbian cinema in queer times calls for us to dwell on unruliness and untidiness: not merely to resist identity and identification but to find them in uncomfortable places. Acknowledging or observing cinematic strategy can, as Caroline Bainbridge writes of Susan Streitfeld's *Female Perversions* (1996), 'disrup[t] and challeng[e] the spectator's desire for identification, repeatedly seeking to alienate us from the potential for pleasure' (2008: 55). Conversely, our seeking and finding of pleasure in unlikely places can be precisely what alienates us from ourselves. Just as the New Queer Cinema reinscribed pleasure through resistance to domestic normativity and the mainstreaming of homosexual desire, so reading lesbian cinema as queer might entail an alienation from the very pleasures that we have fought to see represented.

I argue in *Lesbian Cinema after Queer Theory* that lesbianism is a term to which 'it remains politically necessary to lay claim', precisely because it lays its 'claim on us prior to our full knowing' (Butler, 1993: 20). 'Lesbian' and 'queer': these terms do not fulfil their imaginatively political potential equally, nor do they perform the same theoretical function. To write definitively about lesbian film under the banner of queer theory reduces queer's potential to move beyond the norms of difference; yet to write instead about queer film, without specifying lesbian difference, loses sight of the ways in which social and cultural structures of normativity and marginality have structured the terms of lesbian representation. The lesbianism I claim is highbrow and lowbrow; it is friendship and fun; it marks emotional and sexual intimacies. It is sometimes attached to my feminism (though not always). The lesbianism I claim is politics and pleasure. To claim an identity category is different from exploring the historical trajectory of that category and its affiliations; even if I do both, the former supports the motivation for this book while the latter defines its content.

Given new understandings of the limits of the sexual encounter on the cinema screen, what is the relationship between the explicitly seen and the marginally sensed? How do cinematic spatial and temporal disorientations map on to the claiming of a defined visibility? How does contemporary lesbian cinema hinge on an interplay between the singular and coupled figuration of the lesbian, and how does it both generate and anticipate anxiety in response to the blurring of the two? In order to answer these questions, *Lesbian Cinema after Queer Theory* brings together a set of films that all negotiate the ubiquitously linear path that is presumed to consummate the story of lesbian sexuality. The films analysed in this book produce complex, insistent and ambivalent links and networks of sex, desire and eroticism. They emerge sometimes as symptoms of generic citation and sometimes of generic indeterminacy. No matter the age of the protagonist, all of the films analysed present not desire's confirmation but its precariousness. Through the lesbian's historical cultural invisibility and the law's refusal to mark her as it has the gay man, figurations of lesbianism in terms of 'immaturity' or 'incompleteness' are used to pathologise her through the discourse of the passing phase (Roof, 1991: 5). Yet these same terms might, in another context, be read queerly, as in Jack Halberstam's suggestion that the reclamation of a queer adolescence 'challenges the conventional binary formulation of a life narrative divided by a clear break between youth and adulthood' (2005: 153). Here, the very same words we use to describe queer's refusal to fix sexuality become those we use to contemplate the lesbian's historical relation to absence. Even as they promise to emancipate us, shifting terminologies have the potential to reinscribe problematic mechanisms. I am reluctant to call this a book about the *queering of lesbian cinema*. Instead, I argue, the productive relationship between queer theory and lesbian film is based on the queerly paradoxical structure of lesbianism itself: a latent potentiality for queerness based on the history of the compromised image.

Just as Judith Butler famously observes that feminist debates over gender evoke a 'sense of trouble, as if the indeterminacy of gender might eventually culminate in the failure of feminism', I have countered a similar response to the indeterminacy of sexuality (1999 [1990]: xxix). Following Butler, the stimulus of *Lesbian Cinema after Queer Theory* is the notion that, if such trouble occurs in the queering of lesbianism, 'trouble need not carry such a negative valence' (Ibid.), but rather set out a mode of relation between the two that is mutual rather than either synonymous or substitutive. The danger, in a context of progress ushered in by visibility, is that, in asking the lesbian to do the performative work of queer, we retreat into a heterosexist ideology of lesbianism as a 'phase'. Taking this 'phasing' as its provocative risk, this book asks a series of questions about the conditions of lesbian legibility in a corpus of films that, rather than exemplifying the period's newfound visibility, trouble the visible itself.

CHAPTER 1

The Woman (Doubled): Mulholland Drive *and the Figure of the Lesbian*

The grinning face of a young woman forms a translucent screen against the city lights of Los Angeles in the final shot of David Lynch's *Mulholland Drive* (2001) before the film fades to black (see Figure 1.1). Platinum blonde hair blends with washed-out skin and a broad smile. Pale pink lips are barely distinguishable from teeth, cheeks, hair or eyes. Colourful architectural flashes highlight the omission of detail in an unadorned face. The woman gazes over the top of the buildings against which she is super-imposed; the focus of her gaze remains for us an abstraction. But we have seen this face before. The smile recollects her character's arrival in Hollywood at the beginning of the film. She bears the lightness of the aspiring actress's potential but has by now found only heartbreak and revenge. Her figuration here is a depleted facsimile of the narrative's optimistic beginning. Translucent, half-figured, the precarious vagueness of her visible image is doomed to repetition.

This sequence aligns the lesbian with invisibility. It conjures the historical characterisation of the lesbian's cultural presence as only ever 'an impalpability, a misting over, an evaporation, or "whiting out" of possibility' (Castle, 1993: 28). The character behind the face in Figure 1.1 desires, wants, loves, hurts, fucks and kills. Over the course of the whole film, we see her body, her breasts, her sweat, her tears, her snot. But in this particular visual moment, her corporeal presence is flattened, reduced to a vacant smile. She is aesthetically 'whited out' to make way for the opaque city of dreams to which she is in thrall and which she both haunts and is haunted by. Whiteness already enables an invisible process of de-racialisation: it is presumed to be unnoticeable in a representational system in which white skin passes as universal (see Dyer, 1997a). The extreme whiting of the image in Figure 1.1 accentuates the conditions of (white) lesbian representability in classical Hollywood cinema. Her blonde hair is characteristic of mid-century Hollywood glamour; it recalls Marilyn Monroe, the enduringly irresistible pin-up. It is also metaphorically imperative as a device of invisibility. Blonde-haired, not possessing but rather lacking colour, she succeeds at femininity but not at corporeality; muted by gender, she is not quite the subject of her own image.

In the title of Patricia White's field-defining book on lesbian cinema,

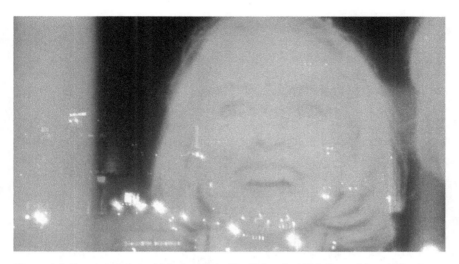

Figure 1.1. Frame grab from *Mulholland Drive* (David Lynch, 2001). Betty (Naomi Watts) as a vision of Hollywood.

Classical Hollywood Cinema and *Lesbian Representability* find themselves levelled by equivalence in the semantics of the title's first word, *Uninvited*, which suggests the lurking 'presence of the absence' that is part of Hollywood's own system of representation (1999: 24). Yet, White's account of 'Classical Hollywood Cinema' demonstrates that 'Lesbian Representability' is not entirely forestalled by this uninvitedness, but rather distorted, veiled or delayed. *Mulholland Drive*, and my reading of it in this chapter, remembers this history. The film encapsulates the paradox of representation for the lesbian: a figure defined by a long history of stereotypes, but also historically associated with invisibility. This ideological unconscious of cinema's visual form has become so familiar as to be common knowledge. As we are led to understand by the few authors of books on twentieth-century lesbian cinema, the lesbian image on the cinema screen has classically been made metaphorically translucent. An 'apparitional trope' is evidenced in, but extends beyond, ghost films 'with eerie lesbian overtones' such as *Curse of the Cat People* (Gunther von Fritsch and Robert Wise, 1944), *The Uninvited* (Lewis Allen, 1944), *The Innocents* (Jack Clayton, 1961) and others (see White, 1999: 61). The lesbian, we are presumed to know already, is nothing but a spectre.

Just as *Twin Peaks* (Mark Frost and David Lynch, 1990–1) drops the history of Hollywood cinema into its character names (Dale *Cooper*, *Audrey* Horne, *James* Hurley and *Norma* Jennings) and indeed its casting of stars (Russ Tamblyn, Richard Beymer), *Mulholland Drive* relishes the citational practices that pay tribute to its Hollywood setting, even as it is produced in a changing context.[1] In an era of digital record and projection, the indexicality of image to corporeal presence is itself flattened. The woman's eerie translucence in Figure 1.1 now indexes the conditions of Hollywood production with even greater effect. If, as Laura Mulvey writes, the relationship between the cinema's 'material base and its poetics' is dissolved into digitally abstract form, we are left pondering the relationship to the real of film when we no longer depend on 'the physical link between an object caught by a lens and the image left by rays of light on film' (2006: 18). For a director like Lynch, the resultant loss of quality of digital provides 'more room to dream' (American Film Institute, 2010). In this new digital age, debates on film within the academy and beyond have also responded to and attempted to regulate a trend that blurs the boundaries between cinema and television (with increasing evidence of the aesthetic quality of the latter still frequently denied or dismissed). A theatrical screening of a Netflix Original was booed at Cannes, while the inclusion of *Twin Peaks: The Return* (Mark Frost and David Lynch, 2017) among the international film magazine *Sight and Sound*'s best films of 2017 confused and infuriated readers (the decision was studiously defended by editor Nick James [2018]). Originally pitched as a television pilot but turned down by potential broadcaster ABC and re-conceived as a feature film, *Mulholland Drive* doubles down on its visionary cinematic stakes while embodying the potential of the digital age. In a mocking nod to its compromised scope and mode of consumption, the film's DVD release eschews the ubiquitous chapter markers that allow a film to be divided up for serial viewing; even its distortion of diegetic chronology must be experienced immersively from start to finish. This distorted temporality is epitomised by the shot in Figure 1.1: it closes the film, which has reached a bleak conclusion, but its depiction of lightness and pleasure belongs to an earlier diegetic moment. Dreamlike in incoherence, the woman at its centre is created by the cinema itself – by a tribute to Marilyn's hair, by Los Angeles's lights, by the digital effects that modify her image towards an oxymoronic overexposed obscurity. As a film that embraces such retrograde figurations, *Mulholland Drive* symptomises cinema's self-referential response to a changing field of representation. If there is a cultural imaginary that insistently aligns the figure of the lesbian with invisibility, *Mulholland Drive* is launched from within that discursive site.

Drawing on feminist film theory's conceptualisations of the woman's image and of the woman *as* image, this chapter deciphers two sides of cinema's figuration of the lesbian: her frequently theorised absence (as woman who lacks and as historically invisible figure) and her threatening over-presence (doubled by partner or by mirror). Instead of leaving behind the pathologisation of lesbianism that Heather Love (2004) argues is rendered through the chronically tragic figuration of the lesbian, *Mulholland Drive* can be read as a film *about* that history. Love argues that *Mulholland Drive* is all about the clichés that burden the figure of the lesbian. As I argue, these are specifically *cinematic* clichés. The lesbian takes on a specific threat and specific anxiety when she is rendered in cinematic form: whited out, flattened out, singularised, specularised. Drawing on parallels with classical thrillers such as *Rebecca* (Alfred Hitchcock, 1940) and *Vertigo* (Alfred Hitchcock, 1958), and contemporary counterparts such as *Basic Instinct* (Paul Verhoeven, 1992) and *Black Swan* (Darren Aronofsky, 2010), this chapter charts the different cinematic models of femininity, from paranoid woman to *femme fatale*, in order to contemplate a contemporary response to classic images (and non-images). Constructed through citation to a classical age of cinema and to its director's own auteurism, *Mulholland Drive* tells a story about Hollywood in order to trace the paradox of lesbian figuration in that very system of production. While lesbianism is made narratively impossible by the film's reworking of conventional generic demands, this chapter argues that the image signifies the possibility for lesbianism through the identification with, and idealisation of, the film star. My readings of all of the films in this book dismantle the primacy of the couple for conceptualising contemporary lesbian cinema. This chapter inaugurates that project by addressing the ways in which the tension between the figure and her double can be seen as central to cinema's relationship with lesbianism.

IN THE REALM OF THE ALREADY SAID

The dominant statute of the Motion Picture Production Code (1934–68) effectively forbade explicit homosexual representation on-screen for much of the twentieth century. Commonly known as the Hays Code after its first president, William H. Hays, the Code was adopted by the Motion Picture Producers and Distributors of America (now the Motion Picture Association of America), a trade association originally founded in 1922 to protect the film industry against federal intervention and to manage the morality of its films and stars (see Kuhn, 1988). What it induced was strident censorship of what were perceived to be immoral images on-screen. Even under its jurisdiction, however, filmmakers became adept at emitting signs in their films through visual codes rather than through explicit narrative details (see Wallace, 2009). Brett Farmer writes that 'although Hollywood's role as an institution of heteronormativity is indisputable and its representational strategies of homophobic abuse glaringly evident, this in no way exhausts the vast range of cinema's signifying effects' (2000: 5). Farmer's focus on fantasy as a mode of engagement allows for modes of subversive interpretation, even of Hollywood's 'indisputable' heterosexuality. Ellis Hanson, furthermore, writes in the introduction to a collection on queer theory and film that 'Hollywood, despite its history of censorship and its pretence to heterocentrism, is one of the queerest institutions ever invented' (1999: 7). These counter-readings of Hollywood as an institution form part of the gay male theorisation of the body's relationship to the visual field. Lesbianism meanwhile has a specific relationship to censorship and invisibility, or rather to a recurring *lack* of outright censorship that renders the lesbian more presently absent throughout twentieth-century cinema than her male counterpart. Indeed, Annamarie Jagose begins her history of lesbian invisibility in her book *Inconsequence* with precisely these differences: 'even more than male homosexuality – that love that famously dared not speak its name', she writes, 'female homosexuality has been ambivalently constituted in relation to the logics of vision: it is less the subject of prohibition than of an incredulousness that would deny the space of its possibility' (2002: 3). Analysing a series of literary case studies, each of which manifests the persistent sequentialisation of desire that normalises heterosexuality, Jagose argues that sexual identity always follows belatedly from the apparent symptoms of its existence. Jagose's book is significant for its decentring of the paradigm of visibility for the study of lesbianism. Whilst the Motion Picture Production Code inevitably paired homosexuality with prohibition, Jagose argues that invisibility is an inevitable condition of lesbianism in the visual field to begin with, rather than a symptom of stalled progress to be redressed.

This conditioning takes a particular form in the generic precedents of the thriller. If, as Jagose writes, lesbian invisibility is 'not a failure but a strategy of representation', then *Mulholland Drive*'s play with the lesbian image reveals that 'strategy' to be a structuring condition of the thriller itself (Ibid.). The lesbian has become attached to a series of cultural clichés – the seductress, the murderer, the victim – that are manifestly adopted via the thriller's generic conventions. *Mulholland Drive*'s figurations hinge not only on a geographical location in Hollywood, but on a location in this very history of the genre, exemplifying a complicated circulation of representational constitutions and recuperations. At the film's narrative turning point, an ensemble of characters is abruptly replaced by doppelgängers played by the same cast but differently characterised. In this switch, the central actresses must 'work against the lesbian romance they have previously assisted to visual consummation' (Wallace, 2009: 100). What Lee Wallace sees as the undoing of lesbian romance, however, might instead be read as signifying *Mulholland Drive*'s staging of an illusory romance that reveals the conditions of production of the cinematic lesbian.

The film begins with a façade of a conventional linear narrative. Betty (Naomi Watts) is a young actress new to Hollywood. Upon arriving as a guest at her Aunt Ruth's apartment, she is surprised to discover Rita (Laura Harring), a woman who has lost her memory after a mysterious accident on Mulholland Drive. Together, they try to unearth the identity of Rita, who can remember nothing about her past but the name 'Diane Selwyn'. This name belongs to a woman who, after tracking her down, they find dead in an apartment. Fearing for her safety, the brunette Rita disguises herself in a blonde wig with Betty's help. Betty and Rita progress from amateur detectives to lovers. Their sex scene – prompted by Rita's transformation – initiates an unexplained expedition to the sinister Club Silencio, which in turn instigates the film's crucial twist. Established over the course of two hours as the protagonists of the incumbent narrative, Betty and Rita disappear altogether and are replaced by two new characters, Diane and Camilla, played by the same actresses. We now follow Diane (Watts) down a nightmare journey of unrequited love for Camilla (Harring), who, in the film's second sex scene, cruelly ends their relationship. Diane eventually engineers Camilla's murder before desperately resorting to her own suicide. Meanwhile, the film is punctuated by forays into the narrative of Adam (Justin Theroux), consistently characterised throughout the film's two parts (what I will from now on call Act One and Act Two) as a director dealing with the Mafia's attempt to control the casting of his new film. Adam's subplot becomes imbricated in the major story when it is established, in a final scene, that the reason for Diane's heartbreak is his engagement to Camilla.

Like the original *Twin Peaks* or its reboot, *Mulholland Drive* engages our attention not through the forward motion of a narrative that can easily be synopsised, but through the feeling that a different kind of knowledge is produced by the disruption of any such motion. A sexual climax abruptly results in the termination of narrative coherence; lesbian desire is never allowed to find its momentum. The lesbian's sequential figuration in *Mulholland Drive* functions through the recycling of generic cliché. The difficulty of summarising the film's synopsis comes from the fabrication of its own dream language. Multiple layers of dream-casting abound: the characters, the film set, the wider context of production. Angelo Badalamenti's score choreographs our attachment to the film's generic devices; his work on other Lynch projects, including *Twin Peaks* as well as *Blue Velvet* (1986), *Wild at Heart* (1990), *Lost Highway* (1997) and *The Straight Story* (1999), prepares *Mulholland Drive*'s viewers for the mysterious goings-on that unfailingly characterise those other texts. While the narrative suffers from indecipherability, the film reliably offers regular appearances from a stock of generic characters – hitmen, police, the dead body – who act as continual reminders that meaning is being constituted as generic induction, through sound and image if not through narrative conclusion. However, if we read *Mulholland Drive* not only as a film that obeys

Figure 1.2. Frame grab from *Mulholland Drive*. Dancing couples are joined by black silhouettes in front of a 'purple screen'.

Figure 1.3. Frame grab from *Mulholland Drive*. Betty greets her imaginary fans.

the generic plotting of the thriller but one that *pastiches* it, we can understand why its adherence to what White calls the 'overdetermined images' of inter-textuality might operate beyond the level of narrative structure (1999: 17). In Richard Dyer's words, pastiche 'accepts and indicates what is really the case in all cultural production, that it exists by virtue of the forms and frameworks of meaning and affect available to it'; pastiche thereby 'acknowledges itself as being in the realm of the already said' (1997b: 179). Even as the synopsis eludes us, the knowledge of a few simple defining features – an inexplicable crash, an investigation, a romance – places *Mulholland Drive* wordlessly 'in the realm of the already said'.

On the soundtrack of the film's first scene, slow atonal strings with no orienting beat attend a black screen with bold white credits. Just as we begin to anticipate the motivation for this forebodingly sombre soundscape, it is interrupted by the rhythmic drums of upbeat swing music. Several couples jitterbug in front of a purple screen that reveals the mechanics of semi-digital filmmaking: the dancing figures in the foreground seem two-dimensional, even more so as they are accompanied by projected black silhouettes of additional dancing couples (see Figure 1.2).[2] By announcing its artificiality and half-finished form, this 'purple screen' draws our attention towards the absence of whatever contrived backdrop might have been (but, crucially, wasn't) added in postproduction. Eventually, the two soundtracks (the sombre and the swing) start to merge, as the translucent image of a brilliantly lit and smiling woman – the character we later meet in her fully opaque form as Betty – is layered over the dancing jitterbugs (see Figure 1.3). The cheers and applause that greet Betty's overexposed profile are then hushed by the heavy sighs of a figure in a bed, shot in close-up. We will later discover that here lies the decomposing body of Diane Selwyn – whose name is Rita's only memory in Act One and who is Betty's reincarnation in Act Two. At this point, we do not see the body that we later discover lurks beneath these red sheets; on this occasion, it is the musical, rather than visual, clue that does the generic work of alerting us to the thriller's fatal linchpin. The superficiality of cinematic signifiers such as the purple screen meet the exhilaration of movement in the jitterbug sequence; the glare and glow of celebrity meet the threat of failure. *Mulholland Drive* announces the thriller genre as that which frames lesbian desire only as an impossibility. The narrative thread concludes with the singular figure of the abject lesbian, for the happy, shiny Betty as idealised image is just that: an image, a spectre. As Diane, she is the dead body beneath the red sheets; as Betty, she is the translucent profile. Crucially, she must be both at once.[3]

SEEING DOUBLE

The lesbian imaginary set up by cinema and the discursive field that surrounds it brings together invisibility and the single–double paradox under the umbrella of anxiety. Judith Roof argues that 'configurations of lesbian sexuality' in the parallel discourses of 'psychoanalysis, cinema, literature and literary criticism' hinge not on 'lesbian sexuality per se, but the anxieties it produces' (1991: 5). In other words, the terms through which lesbianism is finally figured simultaneously figure an incumbent anxiety. *Mulholland Drive*'s generic affiliation is premised on an absence that forms the inherently contained opposition to the film's most present image: that of the lesbian as the woman in excess. I linger again on our translucent image of the figure of Betty that begins *Mulholland Drive* (see again Figure 1.1). As we negotiate a wobbly pan back and forth across the horizontal axis of the image, another figure hovers just out of the frame, donning a matching blonde wig and bright smile (see Figure 1.4). These women are lovers, friends, rivals and doppelgängers; whatever the configuration, the image of just one will do, standing in for both. The partner hovers around the single lesbian figure while the spectre of singularity marks even the romantic couple. As Andrea Weiss writes in the opening pages of *Vampires and Violets*, the first full-length monograph on lesbian cinema, the lesbian image is routinely reduced to singular figures such as '*the* lesbian vampire' or '*the* sadistic or neurotic repressed woman' (1992: 1, emphases added). Rarely granted romantic occupation of the couple form, she is marked out as other from the heterosexual woman who is assumed to be her passive victim. This sexuality is frequently compounded not only with predatory self-assurance but also with violence. Reaching its peak in the early 1990s, the erotic thriller constructs the lesbian either as threatening obstacle or as laughable insignificance or, as in *Basic Instinct* and *Single White Female* (Barbet Schroeder, 1992), as both at once. The figure of the lesbian as somehow suspect or degenerate reinforces these films' reassuring displays of

Figure 1.4. Frame grab from *Mulholland Drive*. Betty is joined by the spectre of a partner, Rita (Laura Harring).

heteronormativity. The murderous seductress is a stereotype standing in for the lesbian's more broadly suspected perversion 'within a patriarchal framework' (Rueschmann, 2000: 102).

However, as a paradoxical counterpoint (or rather counterpart) to the singular female figure, it is the doubling of the woman that has structured narrative drives from *Metropolis* (Fritz Lang, 1927) to *Sisters* (Brian de Palma, 1973), *That Obscure Object of Desire* (Luis Buñuel, 1977) and *The Double Life of Veronique* (Krzysztof Kieślowski, 1991).[4] The woman represents a threat to the coherence of the male ego, the source of both his pleasure and his potential undoing (see for instance Mulvey, 1975). This male ambivalence about woman's duplicity is brought into visual form by mirrors, doppelgängers, portraits and disguises. In *The Life and Death of Colonel Blimp* (Michael Powell and Emeric Pressburger, 1943), the woman's doubled image is created through the use of the same actress (Deborah Kerr) for different parts, onto which the man might project and reconcile his ambivalent desires. In the 1990s and 2000s, this trope accommodates heightened anxieties not only about female sexuality *tout court* but about lesbian sexuality specifically. Lesbian killer couples became a renewed arthouse trope of sexual daring and empowered deviance in the 1990s, and four were released within a single year of one another, evidencing the desire for what Michele Aaron reads as 'risky or *risqué* delights' (1999: 72): *Heavenly Creatures* (Peter Jackson, 1994), *Fun* (Rafal Zielinski, 1994), *Sister My Sister* (Nancy Meckler, 1994) and *Butterfly Kiss* (Michael Winterbottom, 1995). This very trope has been most recently resurrected in the Chloë Sevigny vehicle *Lizzie* (Craig William Macneill, 2018) and parodied by Ingrid Jungermann in the comedy horror *Women Who Kill* (2016). This is a motif not only of characterisation but of vision: the transposition of the lesbian couple into a nightmareish double form serves to lay bare existing anxieties about the woman's sexual excess (see Kuhn, 1982: 35). In *Basic Instinct*, it is in renée hoogland's words 'precisely in her role of "double" that the haunting figure of the lesbian underlines her function' (1997: 40; see also de Lauretis, 2010: 32). *Black Swan* explicitly uses the visual double to characterise excessive female competitiveness, violence and the threat of lesbian sexuality. The film uses technology to intensify a recognisable historical trope. The female characters in Aronofsky's film are always mediated in some way, whether simply through the multiple reflections of the dressing room juxtaposed with the duplicitous chatter of gossiping dancers, or the CGI that turns mirrors into uncanny projections of macabre alternate realities. As *Black Swan* shows by relishing a turn to cliché cloaked (and read) as arthouse creativity, the lesbian is doubly dangerous to conventional systems of representation because she not only multiplies the existing threat of women's sexual desire, but also redirects it.

Mulholland Drive turns all of the female figures into one woman in order to vanquish the double threat of the lesbian couple. In an essay on lesbian sexuality and violence, Lynda Hart concerns herself with the murder(s) central to the controversial *Basic Instinct*.[5] Hart invokes a disruption at the heart of the detective genre, the tropes of which inform the foundations of her argument.[6] What makes *Basic Instinct* noteworthy, Hart argues, is its inability, or its refusal, to deliver what its genre promises: an unambiguous answer to the inevitable generic question: whodunnit? Hart's argument suggests that what produces this generic failure is precisely what enables the genre's ubiquitous thrill: the female threat to the male protagonist. *Mulholland Drive* self-consciously embraces the conditions and consequences of *Basic Instinct*'s narrative model, by playing with intertextuality, pastiche and the Hollywood setting itself in order to harness its commitment to a figuration of the Woman as always multiple but embodied within a single figure. *Basic Instinct* offers a succession of female characters, each of whom has a murderous potential and, crucially, embodies a clichéd figure of womanhood, from the lover and the mistress to the colleague and the suspect. *Mulholland Drive* adheres to the very same paradoxical structure: a dead body, a host of women as potential suspects. Hart states that 'one woman will not do the trick. Men need one who does it and one who doesn't do it' (1994: 133). In Hart's reading, it does not matter which of the women committed the murder, only that it was *one of them* (and not one of the men).

The duplication, merging and distortion of these roles are thus enabled and heightened by cinema's form, accentuated in *Mulholland Drive* as fantasy is put at the heart of the narrative drive. Fantasy has been understood as pivotal in the construction of sexuality by Freudian scholars such as Jean Laplanche and Jean-Bertrand Pontalis, who read it as the very 'setting' of desire (1986 [1964]: 26). Elizabeth Cowie famously converts this to the specifically cinematic '*mise en scène* of desire' in her essay 'Fantasia' (1997 [1984]: 133). Teresa de Lauretis is also indebted to Laplanche and Pontalis's theorisation of desire and fantasy in order to argue, in *The Practice of Love: Lesbian Sexuality and Perverse Desire*, that 'it takes two women, not one, to make a lesbian' (1994: 92). This is not a simple argument for the primacy of the lesbian couple. Rather, we are compelled to understand that it is not only individualised fantasy, but rather *shared* fantasy, that forms the site of lesbian subjectivity. De Lauretis's case study of lesbian representation, *She Must Be Seeing Things* (Sheila McLaughlin, 1987), portrays 'two women who share a common fantasy' (de Lauretis, 1994: 92). Sheila McLaughlin's film is about two women, one a filmmaker: 'one makes movies, the other doesn't. But doesn't she? In a sense, they both do. Both make movies in their minds' (Ibid.: 86). Fantasy as the setting of desire is a visible motif in a film about filmmaking. However, like *Mulholland Drive*, McLaughlin's film additionally distorts, and even unravels, any strict rules about the distinction between what is fantasy and what is reality; what is seen and by whom; when seeing double is *being* double. The sameness and difference of two female bodies in proximity – seeing, being seen, or both at once – create a series of illusions. For de Lauretis, 'the' lesbian subject is a figure split and doubled by the fantasy of the screen. Again, this is not simply to say that the lesbian is constituted through her inclusion in a couple. Her constitution is an intensely cinematic one, the condition of her legibility visual rather than strictly social. The 'specularization' of her own image produces 'the subject as both subject and object, autoerotically doubled and yet split from itself and invested in the fantasmatic pursuit of the other (and in this sense, as well, it takes two women, not one, to make a lesbian)' (Ibid.: 96). Rather than 'lesbians' or 'a lesbian couple', in de Lauretis's precise and precisely repeated wording, a duo ('two women') is condensed into a singular figuration ('a lesbian') that contains the partner, as double, within it. This chapter now asks how cinema, as a site of fantasy, can both produce such double figurations and also account and compensate for the anxiety they produce. We might agree that she is 'two women not one'; we might not. Regardless, the tension surrounding the lesbian figure is generated by the threat of her doubled composition.

Most readings of *Mulholland Drive* reduce the lesbian storyline, in Wallace's words, 'to the status of a wish-fulfilment fantasy anchored in the kind of sexual psychosis Hollywood frequently makes cognate with lesbianism'

(2009: 100).[7] The film's lesbian representation hinges on precisely the tendency that Wallace critiques, betraying the illusion of normality attributed to this familiar trope of 'sexual psychosis' and reflecting it back to its viewers as fantasy. And yet, for Love, Lynch 'scrambles' the two plots usually available to lesbian characters: the abject, heartbroken, lonely woman and the innocent schoolgirl. Love writes that Lynch refuses 'to respect the distance between the comic and the tragic versions of female same-sex desire', instead showing 'schoolgirl capers and abject lesbian longing to be two aspects of a single fantasy' (2004: 123–4). Just as the film switches between vantage points that show first the glistening illuminations of LA and then its murky horrors, the role of the actress is passed around among characters and, with each exchange, switches from an embodiment of optimism to one of pessimism and back again: Betty, glowing and aspirational (Watts, Act One); Rita, a mere appropriation of a bygone star (Harring, Act One); Diane, unemployed and dejected (Watts, Act Two); and finally Camilla, the radiant star of Adam's film, whose glory must come at someone else's expense (Harring, Act Two).[8] The character of the actress narrativises the visual doubling at the heart of the anxious mythology of lesbian sexuality. Impersonation is systematically linked to lesbian desire. What Love calls the 'single fantasy' in *Mulholland Drive* is that which is brought about through the actress, appropriated and re-appropriated as an image whose meaning transfers between Betty, Rita, Diane and Camilla. The multiple characterisations of the actress simultaneously proliferate erotic narratives. They also provoke the pathologisation of those narratives through, on the one hand, the confirmation of anxieties about sexual excess, and, on the other, the suspicion that lesbian desire is not just *sometimes* but rather *only ever* a performance.

OF HOLLYWOOD, IN HOLLYWOOD

Consummating the film's multiple and divergent figurations of desire and threat is the titular highway that winds through the hills of Los Angeles: Mulholland Drive. In an early sequence that follows the jitterbug contest, the anterior view of a black car dissolving into the dark scene around it initiates a pan that captures LA's shimmering landscape. In the car as it winds its way up the highway is the woman who will become, via the crash we are about to witness, the amnesiac Rita. She is marked both by the glamour of the pearls around her neck and by the contempt of the Mafiosi in the front seat in whose hands her fate resides. In a series of close-ups and long shots, her image alternates with the landscape of the city through which she moves. Defined by juxtaposition, she is a figure *of* Hollywood *in* Hollywood. As both impotent amnesiac woman (Rita) *and* potential *femme fatale* (Camilla), Rita fails to know

Figure 1.5. Frame grab from *Mulholland Drive*. Rita chooses her name.

and fails to *be known*. Rita might be curious about what she has forgotten, and keen to recover her memory, but, like the 'Paranoid Woman' as described by Mary Ann Doane, she is unbearably 'revealed as impotent in terms of the actual ability to uncover the secret or attain the knowledge which she desires' (1987: 135). The insert included in *Mulholland Drive*'s original DVD release lists '10 clues to unlocking this thriller'. What becomes clear, as you follow for example the instruction to 'pay attention to the red lampshade', is that such 'clues' are arbitrary: 'unlocking' is not the name of the game here. This is a thriller that refuses to make its mystery solvable or even really knowable.

If lesbianism is made narratively impossible by generic demands (if Act Two undoes the lesbian romance of Act One, as Wallace claims of *Mulholland Drive*), its possibility is enabled through erotic identification. When Betty first discovers the stranger Rita in her aunt's empty apartment and demands to know her name, the construction of the shot that follows places the amnesiac woman to the side of a mirror that occupies half of the frame. In the mirror is reflected a poster of *Gilda* (Charles Vidor, 1946), in which a *femme fatale* dominates the shot spatially and symbolically. In her signature role as the eponymous Gilda, Rita Hayworth is often cited as the classic *femme fatale* (see Dyer, 1998 [1978]): she is suspiciously, then maddeningly, then destructively seductive. Commonly stereotyped in the *film noir* through a chiaroscuro lighting regime and a *mise en scène* populated with reflective surfaces that highlight her fundamental duplicity, the *femme fatale* is central to the narrative but must also be the victim of its fatal conclusion. If she can be read not only through her demise but rather her 'exciting sexuality' (Place, 1998 [1978]: 48), as in

Figure 1.6. Frame grab from *Mulholland Drive*. Rita is caught trespassing.

Gilda, *Kiss Me Deadly* (Robert Aldrich, 1955) and *Woman in the Window* (Fritz Lang, 1944), nevertheless at the root of all of these characterisations is the paradoxical demand that she be both (though this theorisation has been open to interrogation, see Farrimond, 2018). When Betty asks to know her name, the stranger panics and sources a name from the poster: Rita (see Figure 1.5). Rita embodies Hayworth not only through naming but also through the appropriation of the actress's significance in this role.

Just as Jackie Stacey theorises the eroticisation of identification in classical Hollywood cinema, so *Mulholland Drive* characterises its actresses through identification with those same Hollywood figures. In Stacey's words, 'identification involves the *production* of identities, rather than simply the confirmation of existing ones' (1994: 172, emphasis added). Rita's naming most explicitly confirms this identity production. Rita embodies not Hayworth herself, but an erotic identification *with* Hayworth. In other words, Rita takes on the image of Hayworth *as an image*. It is in this way that desire is folded into the image. Her adopted subjectivity is constructed through the image in simultaneity with her desirability. Rita's adoption of Hayworth's name yields a further convoluted series of identifications. Rita is duplicated by reflection not only in the mirror images that populate Act One of *Mulholland Drive*, but by Betty, who functions as Rita's foil. In their first meeting, they are unified by the camera frame but separated by the translucent screen of the shower that distorts the image and creates a diffracted frame within the frame (see Figure 1.6). This 'ambivalent' screen – to use the central tenet of Judith Mayne's (1990: 41) reading of *The Big Sleep* (Howard Hawks, 1946) – makes Rita both victim and threat. Thus the *femme fatale* meets her paradoxical demand. This is a demand met vicariously by Betty too: Rita's body, soon to evoke the ideal woman, is now made translucent behind the glass just as Betty's was by overexposure in the opening sequence (see again Figure 1.1).

Rita's character, like her name, is premised on the adoption and embodiment of an image. Indeed, it is as an image that the woman's place has been characterised in the history of cinema. Yet, this is more complicated than her mere objectification. In Alfred Hitchcock's *Rebecca*, the portrait of the family ancestor whose costume the heroine (Joan Fontaine) appropriates (just as Rebecca de Winter has done in the past) comes to represent Rebecca's own image.[9] The portrait on the wall is not of Rebecca, but of an image that Rebecca herself has assumed. This is an image that has been read within feminist film theory as standing in for the maternal signifier (see de Lauretis, 1984; Doane, 1987; Modleski, 1988). As White (1999: 64) discusses in her account of these scholars' responses to Hitchcock's film, the erotic potential of the mutual identification by which the heroine and Rebecca are linked (the fact that they have both dressed up as the ancestor in the portrait) has become a source of discord and even ambivalence for feminist theorists.[10] *Mulholland Drive*, through its navigation of a complicated plot and rejection of linearity, promises to repeat this erotic identification. De Lauretis (1984: 152) attributes to *Rebecca*'s heroine a 'double figural identification', in which her desire is manifest in a tension between the 'narrative image' (Rebecca de Winter, unseen as character but dominant as portrait and force) and the 'narrative movement' (led by the heroine, whom we see in the flesh but who remains nameless). This tension produces a homoeroticism that hauntingly pervades the film. The heroine must enable both of these directions of desire; she must function 'not as a mirror, a flat specular surface, but as a prism' (Ibid.). The woman as prism is literalised in *Mulholland Drive* in the diffraction of the image of one woman as the repeated identification of all women in the film. The shower screen and its prismatic distortion of Rita's body is the first visual clue to mark out this trajectory. In *Rebecca*, only one woman is seen (the nameless protagonist) but she must occupy the position of desire for/of both women. In *Mulholland Drive*, both women are seen but they must be narratively merged into one. What de Lauretis calls the woman's static 'narrative image' guides the many characterisations in *Mulholland Drive*.[11] Fantasy is a scene of desire, wherein identification is eroticised (where erotic identities are indeed constituted through identification) and desire is maintained through a network of looks that do not only presuppose sex as an act.

Becoming friends after their first meeting and happily sharing the borrowed apartment together, the two women embark on an expedition to discover the story of Rita's lost identity. Costume initially marks out a visual

Figure 1.7. Frame grab from *Mulholland Drive*. Rita and Betty come to a realisation of Rita's identity.

Figure 1.8. Frame grab from *Mulholland Drive*. Rita dons a wig in disguise.

division between Betty and Rita, prolonging the film's preoccupation with women as opposites on the one hand and doppelgängers on the other. But this visual principle is disrupted in the characters' visit to the apartment of the mysterious Diane Selwyn, whose name is Rita's only recollection in her amnesiac state. Betty and Rita's discovery of the decomposing body, which we must imagine belongs to Diane herself, is a perverse twist in which the half-image of the translucent Betty/Diane in the opening sequence is fleshed out but through decay. She is a figure now evoked not just aesthetically 'in negative space', as Martha Nochimson writes of the film, but in the narratively negative space of mortality (2004: 167). As Betty and Rita run out of the building, frame appears to be layered on frame to create a visual distortion (see Figure 1.7). This technological decomposition results in metaphorical merging. Responding to Rita's flustered attempt to cut off her hair in the wake of the shocking discovery of the death of Diane Selwyn (Rita's would-be namesake), Betty insists: 'let me do it'. 'It' seems to be a diminishing of the two women's visually defined difference. The camera pans along the wall to reveal Rita in a wig to match Betty's blonde coiffeur, their pairing delivered to us in a reflection (see Figure 1.8). If Rita's titular prototype Hayworth was first reflected to her in a mirror, Betty, her new visual prototype, is reflected to her now. The transformation is swiftly juxtaposed with a move to the bedroom and a reference to their doubled image confused with something akin to sexual farce, as the instruction 'you don't have to wear that in the house' is misread by Rita and she removes, instead of her blonde wig, the towel that covers her naked body. The tentative movement of the camera as they begin to kiss is exploratory, drifting from eyes to mouth and down to breasts, and mirrors the curiosity of their rather hackneyed dialogue: 'Have you ever done this before?' Their desire is presented both as exciting (the lighting produces a sweaty sheen, while the soundtrack allows for their audible sighs) and almost inevitable (the path from Rita's entry into the bed,

Figure 1.9. Frame grab from *Mulholland Drive*. Betty and Rita are beckoned to Club Silencio. NB: For the sake of clarity, the brightness of this image has been increased from the original.

to a maternal goodnight kiss, to a passionate embrace, is seamless, and the camera's movement remains slow and fluid). A simple crossfade (an extension of Figure 1.8) compresses the image of Betty alone with that of her and Rita in the mirror. The predictable cinematic tropes of lesbian desire – the tension between single and double, the merging of two women in a single sexual act – are here worked through in a single scene.

Identification and merging pre-empt sexual activity, which then uncannily pre-empts another unexpected narrative turn. A sweep of orchestral strings follows the camera's pan up Rita's body to reach a still shot of her face in profile against Betty face-on in the background (see Figure 1.9). Rita's lips move as if dissociated from the rest of her face, ventriloquising for the silent Betty behind her: 'Silencio'. Fused on a two-dimensional screen, the lips speaking silently ('Silencio') make possible the very image that speech cannot replicate. This is one such image that defies the narrative movement towards lesbian impossibility. It is also implicated in mystery and narrative frustration. Their departure from the bedroom comes abruptly as they rush into a taxi and then to a nightclub, the seams of transition between these disjunctive urban spaces removed. The sexual 'arrival' that the scene has led us to expect is withheld; instead, the film thrusts its figures into another kind of arrival, at the enigmatic Club Silencio. The tonality of the post-coital romantic strings gives way to a surreptitious atonality that introduces us to the location, an old theatre that intensifies the scene's intra- and extra-diegetic play with the anxieties and absurdities of performance. Mysterious aural and oral tricks link Club Silencio to the bedroom, both of them spaces in which we start to doubt what it is that we see and hear. The whole room glows with a blue haze that consolidates the fantastical theatrical setting with Lynch's oneiric tone of choice.[12] As the singer Rebekah del Rio performs, lighting brings her face into the foreground and detaches her from the pitch-black stage. The same lighting device similarly disconnects Rita, and then Betty, from the scene that they share. 'It's all recorded,' announces the MC on stage, as del Rio's body falls to the floor even as her voice continues to sing Roy Orbison's 'Crying' with the same level of intensity.[13] The pieces of the narrative we have become accustomed to begin to unravel.

This series of scenes seemingly presents the only available sequence for the lesbian within the confines of the genre, and institutes the 'switch', in which the same set of actors is induced to perform as a new cohort of characters. The film provides sex as a climactic feature of narrative transformation emphasised through literal character transformation. *Black Swan* is another film featuring the illusory duplicity of the performer's narcissistic desire: Nina (Natalie Portman) and her doppelgänger, Lily (Mila Kunis), have sex in a scene in which their bodies look to be on the verge of mutation, an illusion exacerbated by a manipulative edit (see Lindner, 2017a). Nina's discovery that the encounter never happened in 'reality' both unsettles and sanctions the film's figuration of lesbianism. The psychological horror genre continues to figure female sexual predatoriness in this way, *The Neon Demon* (Nicolas Winding Refn, 2016) another example of lesbianism's deployment as a tool of generic climax. And in *Thelma* (Joachim Trier, 2017), science fiction meets adolescent drama, the most absurd and captivating scene one in which the protagonist dreams of a snake that takes over her body in a moment of sexual ecstasy. The idealised image of lesbian desire in *Mulholland Drive*'s sex scene is revealed by Love to be a 'ghostly effect produced by the social impossibility of lesbianism' (2004: 124). The transformational cliché of lesbian sex as a mere vehicle confirms it as both reality and dream, both artifice and spectacle. It is really nothing but a plot device.[14]

De Lauretis's reading of the Hitchcockian model of narrative (itself a citation of a mythological model, as she argues) articulates the way in which such 'divided or doubled desire[s]' are punished in classical Hollywood cinema (1984: 155).[15] We might read de Lauretis's analysis of *Vertigo* as a step-by-step account of the structuring dynamics necessitated by *Mulholland Drive*'s generic adherence. It is precisely through duplication that the woman as lesbian becomes a threat. When a film enlists 'the terms of a divided or double desire', de Lauretis writes, it must follow a set of rules (Ibid.). In *Vertigo*, that divided or doubled desire is operated by 'the person Judy-Madeleine who desires both Scottie and the Mother', for 'Madeleine' (Kim Novac) in that film loves both protagonist Scottie (James Stewart) and also the image of the Mother as Carlotta Valdes, whose portrait we see but who remains a detached figure (see also Tania Modleski's reading of de Lauretis's analysis, 1988: 101).[16] In *Mulholland Drive*, the doubled desire (of the lesbian) must, it seems, be divided, here by the attention of the heterosexual man. De Lauretis argues that:

> when a film accidentally or unwisely puts in play the terms of a divided or double desire (that of the person Judy-Madeleine who desires both Scottie and the Mother), it must display that desire as impossible or duplicitous (Madeleine's and Judy's, respectively, in *Vertigo*), finally contradictory (Judy-Madeleine is split into Judy/Madeleine *for* Scottie); and then proceed to resolve the contradiction much in the same way as myths and mythologists do: by either the massive destruction or the territorialization of women. (1984: 155)

In a startlingly clear resurrection of the terms that de Lauretis sets out for *Vertigo*, *Mulholland Drive* displays desire as 'impossible' *and then* 'duplicitous': Betty and Rita's desire is dissolved into the nullity of a narrative black hole (impossible) before being rendered as just another love triangle that ends with lesbian heartbreak (duplicitous). That same desire is 'finally contradictory': in *Vertigo* 'Judy-Madeleine is split into Judy/Madeleine', while in *Mulholland Drive* Betty/Rita becomes Betty-Rita but then also Diane/Camilla. If this contradiction must ultimately resolve with 'either the massive destruction or territorialization of women', *Mulholland Drive* offers both. Territorialised by the Hollywood scene itself, by its very logic, the film's women are ultimately destroyed: the self-violence and suicide of *one* effectively kills *all* women.

ALL THE NARRATIVE NEEDS

After the extraordinary identificatory mobility of Act One, in Act Two, *Mulholland Drive*'s narrative is re-ordered into the model its genre commands us to expect: we must remember that the 'already said' – as Dyer categorises the pastiche (1997b: 179) – was, indeed, said all along. The generic framework of the first act sets up the 'behaviours and affects' that Jagose argues becomes the basis of a retrospective assembly of sexual identity (2002: x). These behaviours and affects are always 'imitative and belated' (Ibid.), always conjured through reference to the acts that are presumed to be their precursor. In one of the first encounters of Act Two, Diane and Camilla (the newly incarnated Watts and Harring) share a sex/break up scene infused with what calls to be read as an intentional superficiality. They play their roles according to the instructions of the thriller; generic mechanisms are made parodically patent, as they are across Lynch's oeuvre. Here they take on the reproduced and echoed performance of the Club Silencio scene that initiates their switch. Familiarity is unsettled by unexpected reversals. Diane (Betty), suddenly topless, leans into Camilla (Rita) in a perversion of the maternal leaning that initiated the first storyline's sex scene. What proceeds is a characterisation of lesbian desire and heartbreak that cinema history has taught us to hope for. This is then highlighted as a cinematic figuration of lesbian impossibility as the scene is abruptly succeeded by a visual cut to the panels of a film set. Diane, dressed in period costume, walks into a static scene, and fragments of the story come together as Camilla, the star of this film-within-the-film, is kissed by director Adam while Diane is agonisingly induced to stay and watch. The sequence jumps to a shot of the close-up face of a teary-eyed and snotty-nosed Diane, whose point of view comes in and out of focus with the fast heartbeat-like zoom of the camera as she masturbates. What will happen in the aftermath of this scene of misery is, we must surmise through the labyrinthine reveal of the plot's chronology, Diane's perpetration of homicide and then of suicide, both acts of desperation. The signalling of fantasy through masturbation brings into stark relief the limits of any sexual encounter, insomuch as it troubles (both interrupts and questions) the evidencing of desire in the requital of a mutual physical act. These juxtapositions couldn't more clearly lay out the terms by which desire, always regulated through the fantasies of its consummation, shifts the lesbian from lonely single to part of a couple and back again.

Through a narrative that explores the conditions of cinematic production in Hollywood, *Mulholland Drive* illustrates the conditions of figuration for the cinematic lesbian. The film paints its images as if in twentieth-century Technicolor, revelling in the surface affects of just these kinds of clichés. But in a film in which every fiction is open for unravelling, a narrative path cannot possibly be pinned down, and the only workaround is to refuse the conventional model of narrative analysis that relies on the linearisation of a synopsis for the basis of understanding. Without employing the term 'lesbian' or self-identifying as a 'lesbian film', *Mulholland Drive* articulates, through its pastiche of the thriller genre and its Hollywood setting, the tensions of lesbian configuration in cinema, which hinge on an anxiety about 'the lesbian' as two women and hence as the threat of the woman, doubled. The lesbian is a threat because her sexuality indicates that she is inherently two (de Lauretis's statement that 'it takes two women, not one, to make a lesbian' [1994: 92] conveys to me not a self-evident meaning but an indication of the source of cultural anxiety). Several films have demonstrated the enduring potential for lesbian doubling and desire to provide a film's principal 'twist', as in *Bound* (Lana and Andy Wachowski, 1996), *Black Swan* and *Side Effects* (Steven Soderbergh, 2013). *Mulholland Drive* shows how cinema manages this threat through a fantasy of the second lesbian as a mere spectre, double, doppelgänger of the first. Lesbianism is forced into a singular figuration that contains the absent partner (as double) within it.

Mulholland Drive espouses an aesthetic of the 'already said'. It is a pastiche of all that the thriller needs in order to provide the spectator with what she expects and demands. *Mulholland Drive*'s generic appeal functions through the thrill of suspense. Yet what resides most firmly in the 'realm of the already said' is that which necessarily remains conversationally unsaid, the figuration of lesbian desire. Cinema constructs the lesbian as a double of the already threatening woman and simultaneously responds to her excessive threat by punishing her with systematic obscurity. Two women occupy positions in a triangulation; one must be eliminated in order to achieve the necessary heterosexual union. One woman is all the narrative needs to succeed. Where in Hart's reading of *Basic Instinct*, the detective story requires one woman who did it and one who did not, the love triangle only needs one woman who is rejected and one whose femininity is sanctified through heterosexual arrival. *Mulholland Drive* represents this bind through the archetype that sees Camilla reject Diane for Adam. Yet, if lesbianism is made narratively impossible by generic demands, the possibility exists for lesbianism to be signified through erotic identification: in mirror images, in the idealisation of the film star and in the refusal of linearity that enables these erotic fascinations to cross multiple relations and gazes, erotically and auto-erotically. If the film sets up two sides of a fantasy – and we do not ever know which is wish and which is fulfilment – then it presents desire as always fantasy. Fantasy here is the site of desire's recognition – our engagement with cinematic citations of earlier images of desire – rather than the site of desire's consummation. The girl does not always get the girl. Ultimately, sex in *Mulholland Drive* is both initiated by, and results in, the fragmentation of the couple and the disintegration of our perception of them as separate beings. Continuing this analysis of the contradictory relationship between visibility and invisibility in cinema's production of lesbianism, Chapter 2 considers the necessary troubling of the ease with which sex can be read as the visual evidence of sexuality. Attending to spaces of fantasy through which the female protagonist figures her own desire for and through the other, the chapter argues that the triangulation of desire does not necessarily subordinate lesbian subtext, but rather complicates it by unsettling its singularity.

Merely Queer: Translating Desire in Nathalie . . . and Chloe

Troubling the requisites of both mainstream publicity and lesbian subcultural recognition, Anne Fontaine's *Nathalie* . . . (2003) is part of an oeuvre in which heterosexual activity is counterbalanced by looks between women. Fontaine's *Dry Cleaning* (1997) uses the motif of the love triangle to exhibit how a 'guilty, middle-class couple "clean up" the evidence of their transgressive, sexual desires' (Tarr and Rollet, 2001: 218). *The Innocents* (2016) takes place in a female homosocial setting interrupted by men – a Polish convent in the aftermath of the Second World War. In *Adore* (2013), the parallel desires of two female best friends for each other's sons creates a complicated triangulation, or rather multiplication, in which homoeroticism is created by each woman's desire for the other's resemblance. This preoccupation with the intrafeminine gaze resonates with a wider corpus: in François Ozon's *Swimming Pool* (2003), a charge of eroticism is exhibited in tandem with jealousy and competition. Sofia Coppola's *The Beguiled* (2017) rarely strays from conversations about the (beguiling) man who provides its central motif, yet the film's aesthetic is driven by the looks among the group of women who plot against him, akin to those shared by many of Coppola's other female protagonists (see Handyside, 2017); the desire he introduces into their homosocial haven produces an erotic complicity. Even if these films fail – and indeed challenge the terms of – the renowned 'Bechdel test' of gender equality, which measures a film's merits based on its inclusion of 'at least two women' who 'talk to each other' about 'something besides a man' (Bechdel, 1986: 22), their structures of homoerotic looking complicate their ostensible foci on heterosexual desire in action or in conversation.

The eponymous protagonist of *Nathalie* . . . is introduced to us in a point-of-view shot that roves around the bar in which she works, panning across the faces of other women before pausing and zooming in on Nathalie (Emmanuelle Béart) in isolation.[1] As the shot becomes a close-up, Nathalie turns towards the camera (see Figure 2.1). The gaze she returns is that of Catherine (Fanny Ardant), a middle-class, middle-aged woman whose incongruous presence in the bar is matched by her unusual motivation. Discovering early in the film that her husband Bernard (Gérard Depardieu) has been

Figure 2.1. Frame grab from *Nathalie* . . . (Anne Fontaine, 2003). Nathalie (Emmanuelle Béart) is introduced.

Figure 2.2. Frame grab from *Nathalie* . . . Nathalie and Catherine (Fanny Ardant) meet for the first time.

cheating on her, she decides to hire a sex worker who will seduce Bernard and recount tales of their affair. This transaction introduces the potential for a derivative voyeurism. In Nathalie's episodic retellings of these sexual encounters, we are given no visual clues, no graphic exposition of events. Rather, we witness the telling of a story by one woman to another, who, as a consequence, is enabled to participate retrospectively. The first shot of the two women together is one in which their coupling is tentative, Nathalie brought into the frame through the mirror behind Catherine's seat (see Figure 2.2). There is a resonance here with Édouard Manet's *A Bar at the Folies-Bergère* (1882), in which we see a woman – sullen or pensive? – standing with a mirror behind her giving us our only, reflected, access to the multiple bodies taking up space in the bar in which she works. The optical tricks that play on our perception leave us precariously unsure of our spectatorial positioning. Just as in that famous painting, in Figure 2.2 we mistake our own gaze for that of the mirrored Nathalie. The visual doublings in *Nathalie* . . .'s mirror shot, like those explored in Chapter 1, alert us to a broader tension between duplicity and trust foregrounded in the film's complicated plot. While the mirror multiplies them and moderates our access to Nathalie, whom we see only through reflection, the women *look* directly at one another without mediation. This intense shared gaze connects them before any words are spoken, establishing the mood of a film in which it is what remains unsaid that eroticises a relationship otherwise unconsummated through sexual action.

In his reading of *Nathalie* . . ., Slavoj Žižek rejects any claim to the relationship between Catherine and Nathalie as lesbian: 'the trap to avoid', he writes, 'is to read this intense relationship between the two women as (implicitly) lesbian: it is crucial that the narrative they share is heterosexual, and it is no less crucial that all they share is a narrative' (2006: 190). For Žižek, the (verbal) narrativisation of heterosexual desire is what determines the film's erotic register, justifying the injunction *not* to call it lesbian. Countering Žižek, I argue in this chapter that the dynamic in *Nathalie* . . . is defined by the eroticism of the gaze. What Nathalie and Catherine share is not just a narrative, not just a *hetero*erotic recollection of a heterosexual act, but rather a potential-ised *homo*erotic intimacy that is reinscribed through fantasy. Referring to the shared narrative as the 'lesbian subtext', Žižek writes that it 'distracts us' from the pre-eminence of the women's desires as they are rendered through words, not acts (Ibid.: 189). Žižek links his reading of *Nathalie* . . . to a famous scene in *Persona* (Ingmar Bergman, 1966) in which Alma (Bibi Andersson) recalls an orgy in conversation with Elisabet (Liv Ullman). In Alma's recollection, 'we see no flashback pictures; nonetheless the scene is one of the most erotic in the entire history of cinema – the excitement is in how she tells it, [the story] resides in speech itself' (Žižek, 2006: 189). Žižek makes an important distinc-tion here, observing that eroticism in both *Persona* and *Nathalie* . . . arises from the recollection of that which is not visualised. He asserts that it is the recol-lection of sex – that which for him remains a 'heterosexual' narrative – that provides the film's erotic potential.

The eroticism of *Nathalie* . . . is based on a series of translations: deriva-tions, reflections and impersonations. Desire is produced through stories rather than encounters; the gaze is often reflected; the object of desire impersonates its subject. Queer theory has actively disturbed 'the labels that have been used to define, limit and indeed naturalize the distinction between heterosexuality and homosexuality' (Bristow, 1997: 194). This chapter thus re-reads Žižek's recommendation to divorce lesbian possibility from hetero-sexual visibility, understanding instead that a surface heterosexuality might hold within it a queer undercurrent. I argue that Nathalie and Catherine's relationship can be read as a queering of heterosexuality through the eroticis-ing of the homosociality that triangulates it. The narrowly defined and singu-lar figuration of lesbianism is de-centred, the eroticism in their relationship neither text nor subtext. Recounted through a series of homosocial spaces, moreover, the women's shared experience of sexual interaction with the same man creates a third relation of queer recollective eroticism that first depends on, but then sidelines, the heterosexual narrative.

This proposed reading is complicated by a remake, *Chloe* (Atom Egoyan, 2009), which orchestrates a far less ambiguous delineation of the erotic triangle. Emma Wilson suggests that Atom Egoyan's films 'have always dis-solved divisions between queer and straight, showing characters discovering unexpected possibilities in erotic situations' (2010: 29).[2] Yet these divisions are arguably solidified again in *Chloe* by the dissolution of eroticism's ambigu-ity. *Chloe* barely changes the original film's structure, borrowing lines (such as Nathalie's seductive opening gambit, 'Do you want to buy me a drink?'); visual motifs (the preponderance of glass and mirrors); and characterisa-tions (Catherine in both films is a gynaecologist, whose job necessitates a mechanical intimacy with women's bodies, while she insists that Nathalie/

Chloe pretend to be an interpreter). This last metaphor initiates a sequence of interpretations, or translations, from actions to words and, as I will explore, onwards from words to images. In the original film, the genesis of the plot occurs when Catherine hears a romantic voicemail from another woman on Bernard's phone. In *Chloe*, Catherine (Julianne Moore) sees a romantic photo of her husband David (Liam Neeson) and his student via a text message on his iPhone, just the first instance of many in which the remake makes graphic – as in visual, but also as in explicit or indisputable – what is only implied or obscured in the original. There are two crucial differences between the two films related to this 'making graphic'. Firstly, in *Nathalie . . .*, the tales that Nathalie brings back to Catherine remain at the level of language, while in *Chloe* they are not only verbally described in detail by Chloe (Amanda Seyfried) but also visually re-enacted. Secondly, in *Chloe*, the first stage of narrative climax is provided by the 'lesbian' sex scene between Catherine and Chloe that is absent from the first film. This predominance of visually coded sex in the remake has a retrospective effect on our reading of its absence in the original.

Nathalie . . . is generically dubious. It is not just thriller, neither merely romance nor family melodrama – though it hints at the tropes and climaxes that characterise all of those genres. *Chloe*, on the other hand, is a consummate example of an erotic thriller. This marketable generic adherence, its bigger budget and its superior box-office figures coincide with a move towards an unprecedented visibility in the twenty-first century.[3] This version of visibility has had broader consequences for feminist discourse. In *Elle* (Paul Verhoeven, 2016), the B-movie thriller reigns as a generic motif in an explicitly sexual and violent rape revenge story. The use of video game design as a narrative backdrop confirms the paralleling of technology and visibility. *Elle* and the conflicted responses to it, as to other contemporary films like *Nocturnal Animals* (Tom Ford, 2016), has engendered questions about explicitness in relation to sexual violence, empowerment and sensationalism, as exemplified in an illuminating written debate between Erika Balsom ('For') and Ginette Vincendeau ('Against') in *Sight and Sound* magazine (2017). Of course, their direction by men, like *Chloe*'s, heightens the potential affront to feminist readings of these films as purveyors of an empowering visible erotics, more than, say, Virginie Despentes and Coralie Trinh Thi's famously controversial *Fuck Me* (2000; see Beugnet, 2007). *Chloe*'s utilisation of the possibility of explicit lesbianism to convey narrative features otherwise confined to the merely erotic is thus part of the more general adoption of graphic displays of sexuality and violence.

In Chapter 1, I discussed the overt clichéing of lesbianism, the 'already said' status of lesbianism's pathological dismissal in classical Hollywood

Figure 2.3. Frame grab from *Nathalie . . .* Nathalie recalls her sexual encounter with Catherine's husband.

cinema (Dyer, 1997b: 179). Drawing on dialogues within feminist film theory, I gave an account of the pessimistic imaginary of lesbian representability. I proposed that it is through the fantasised duplicity of the lesbian – her status as the woman in excess – that she becomes a threat. I argued that *Mulholland Drive* exhibits the symptoms of a broader cultural anxiety that takes the form of a paradox: the lesbian's perpetual absence in representation coexists with the threat of *too much presence* (there is never only one of her). In this chapter, I take up queer theory's intervention into the discussion of desire and visibility. Drawing on the wider context of *Chloe*'s generic affirmation, I interrogate how the tension between absence and presence characterises the desire for visibility in contemporary mainstream genre cinema. The chapter asks what is lost in a move to make sex the visible object of sexuality's representation. It considers how what Žižek calls 'lesbian subtext' might be read through what I argue is a queer spatialisation of desire. The chapter reads the two films – *Nathalie . . .* and *Chloe* – together in order to 'open [. . .] them up', in Fiona Handyside's words, 'to new relations beyond themselves' (2012: 56). By addressing the relationship between *Nathalie . . .* and its remake, I complicate the terms through which the *burden of the visible* asks the newly available image to stand in for all prior facets of its invisible form.

MERELY EROTIC

In *Nathalie . . .*, Catherine's sexuality is voiced by Nathalie, who speaks the words that Catherine is unable to. Nathalie describes explicitly the sexual acts that Catherine might want to experience with Bernard but has not, must not or cannot. The film manifests this voicing not by explicitly representing the actions that Nathalie's words describe, but through the settings in which these verbal narrativisations take place. Sexuality here is articulated through the relationship between Nathalie and Catherine's verbal and spatial reloca-tion of desire and subjectivity. In the dressing room at the back of the bar – a women-only space to which Catherine gradually gains more legitimate access – Catherine and Nathalie are constantly framed and re-framed by their doubles in the mirrors situated around the room (see Figure 2.3). As the women actively inhabit the space, Nathalie tells, in graphic detail, the story of her first sexual encounter with Bernard. Not only do the women's spatial positions change, but their reflections also confuse and distort their singular-ity. Instead of replacing or sublimating the heterosexual gaze as in scenes between Catherine and Bernard, these movements exacerbate or accentuate the intensity of the homoerotic gaze. Nathalie's recreations of her (fictional) sexual encounters with Bernard create an erotic of recollection in spite of a distancing from sexual activity.

As Fontaine recalls, her actresses, Ardant and Béart, refused to make explicit any of *Nathalie . . .*'s subtextual lesbian content. In an interview, the director recollects what she sees as a lack of 'erotic rapport between the two actresses' (DP/30: The Oral History of Hollywood, 2009). Fontaine's regretful recollection accompanies the 2009 release of Egoyan's film rather than her own. A reading of *Nathalie . . .* and *Chloe* in conjunction allows for the staging of a debate about how this term – the erotic – finds room next to, or against, the sexual. In 'Desperately Seeking Difference' (1987) and *Star Gazing* (1994), Jackie Stacey puts forward a now-seminal understanding of the erotic pleasures of identification. Her concern across this work is not with 'de-eroticising desire, but rather eroticising identification' (1994: 29), achieved by paying attention to the erotic looks in films such as *Desperately Seeking Susan* (Susan Seidelman, 1985) and *All About Eve* (Joseph Mankiewicz, 1950). Teresa de Lauretis (1994: 120), in her response to Stacey, demands that we ask what it is about these looks that makes them more than either merely homosocial or merely imitative of familial structures of intimacy such as in the 'relatively continuous' feminine bonds established by Eve Kosofksy Sedgwick in *Between Men* (1985: 5). If lesbian desire must be (homo)sexual in order to avoid falling into what de Lauretis designates 'a representation of lesbianism that is heterosexually conceived' (1994: 120), then what is the rela-tionship between homosexuality and the sex that is presumed to be sexuality's proper rendering? Across this debate, we are to understand that, first, lesbian desire is threatened with desexualisation if conflated with nonsexual forms of homoerotic intimacy; and, second, a representational imperative exists in which lesbianism must be defined by sex, rather than by desire. De Lauretis's work highlights a fear that desire and sexuality might become conflated in a way that obscures the 'sex' of sexuality. Repetitive models of conflation and obscuration disguise not only sexuality as *mere* desire, but also sexuality as *mere* sex. This sets up a presumption of what constitutes the 'erotic rapport' that Fontaine perceives to be missing in her film.

I repeat the use of 'mere' in order to borrow explicitly from de Lauretis, who uses the word throughout her book *The Practice of Love* in order to account for those characteristics that seem beside the point, inferior or irrelevant (Ibid.: see pages xiii, 17, 90, 111, 130 and 244).[4] In what is for me the most interesting example, de Lauretis writes that

> this emphasis on the *sexual* is by no means intended (there should be no need to say it) to reduce lesbian subjectivity to a mere matter of sexual behavior or sexual acts, as if these could be isolated from all other aspects, qualities, affects, social determinations, and achievements that make up each human being as a complex individual and a unique contributor to her or his culture. (Ibid.: xii–iii)

Over the course of de Lauretis's book (see Note 4 for further examples), 'mere' is applied to the body; to sexual behaviour, as in intercourse; and to sexual behaviour, as in, more broadly, *acts*. These examples provoke us to ask: how might sexuality exceed the confines of *mere* sex whilst remaining – as is key for de Lauretis – sexual? What work does the 'merely' play here? Merely subtext, merely erotic, merely queer? As de Lauretis writes in an analysis of David Cronenberg's *Crash* (1996): in 'sexual encounter after sexual encounter, the body is invaded by the sexual as a drive with no reachable aim or object choice, beyond gender and beyond desire [. . .] *Crash* is about more than sex' (2011: 247–8). Sexuality is, precisely, excess, that which exceeds all of these *mere* encounters, bodies, acts and behaviours.[5] What de Lauretis means to suggest in this later work seems to be that the queerness of sexuality extends beyond gender or 'orientation': that sexuality *itself* is queer, insomuch as it is pure drive, uninhibited by the regimes of normativity both beyond and within LGBTQ+ cultures and communities (see also 2010). The fascinating paralleling of these intellectual paths – instituting the use of 'queer' as theory in the academy (1991) whilst maintaining the call for lesbian specificity (1994) and radically defining queer's relation to sex (2010, 2011) – make de Lauretis a theoretical figure to announce the paradoxes inherent in the discussion of lesbian cinema after (and in) queer theory.

QUEERING IDENTIFICATION

In both *Nathalie . . .* and *Chloe*, the climax of the narrative occurs when we discover that the alleged sexual encounters between Nathalie/Chloe and Bernard/David have never actually taken place. The characters are, and remain, strangers to one another. Each film discloses this fiction very differently. *Chloe*'s general advance of visibility exposes the romantic wish-fulfilment of the eponymous character, who insists that her romance with Catherine is 'so, so real'. In *Nathalie* . . ., however, there are clues that disrupt any such bid for authenticity: 'I fake it – it's my job', Nathalie says to Catherine.[6] The notion of faking applies to both her roles here: giving the illusion of orgasm and enabling Catherine's fantasy; both require a necessary duplicity. In *Mulholland Drive*, fantasy is seen to be the basis for desire as all characters are revealed to be actors, all declarations revealed to be performance. As the MC at the sinister Club Silencio announces: 'it's all recorded'. In that scene, the performer's overwhelmingly convincing display of emotional distress is revealed to be uncannily artificial through the revelation of the lip sync. If sexual climax is something that can be faked through professional repetition, then sexual fantasy can be, too. To avow this is to see repetition as part of an erotics of cinematic lesbian representability rather than its obstacle.

In *Nathalie* . . ., 'Faking it' is part of Nathalie's adoption not of another person's *identity* but of her *identification*. Lesbianism might be, as Patricia White announced in 1999, an 'intelligible social identity' (6), but queer identification – even as it is attached to the specificity of lesbian same-sex desire – might still refuse intelligibility. In this way it is potentially more aligned to queerness, which, for Glen Elder, Lawrence Knopp, and Heidi Nast, should be read as 'a term of political engagement and not necessarily an identity' (2006: 203). Identification in this context describes an encounter with desire rather than a self-definition based upon that desire. In *Nathalie* . . ., through this doubly layered identification, the two women are merged in their shared ownership of desire for one man. Catherine's desire for Bernard, and her growing desire for Nathalie, are acted out in fantasy. And, because Nathalie and Bernard's encounters are not shown on-screen, the focus must be on the space of the telling. As the two women circle the dressing room, Catherine is reincarnated as a reflection in the mirror and as the fantasised object of Nathalie's recollected sexual encounters. If the 'boundary between self and ideal [. . .] produces an endless source of fascination', as in Stacey's formulation (1994: 173), *Nathalie* . . . simultaneously fictionalises and articulates a desire that holds that boundary within it. The reflections exposing the cyclical imitations that the women take on by and for one another also expose the inherently imitative structure of the image itself.

In cinema, the spectator is caught up in what Jean Laplanche and Jean Bertrand Pontalis call fantasy as a 'sequence of images' designed to lead her through a network of ambiguous positions of desire and identification (1986 [1964]: 26). The subject does not find the place of the object in fantasy, but rather finds herself in it. However, she 'cannot be assigned any fixed place in it' and may, despite being always part of the fantasy and present in it in some form or other, take a somewhat 'desubjectivized form' (Ibid.). For this reason, lesbian specificity is particularly difficult to decipher in its fantasy form – which is, as de Lauretis argues, with Laplanche and Pontalis, the only form in which desire takes shape. In *Nathalie . . .*, these identifications are given shape by Nathalie's erotic recollections. As we are reminded by Žižek's emphasis, 'it is no *less* crucial that all they share is a narrative' (2006: 190, original emphasis). And yet, it is precisely the narrative-within-the-narrative that makes the queerness of sexuality the register of its visualisation.[7]

What is of particular interest in de Lauretis's reading of *She Must Be Seeing Things* (Sheila McLaughlin, 1987), which began my discussion of lesbian singularity and doubling in Chapter 1, is her observation of how, as the 'filmmaker within the film', the figure of the lesbian 'constructs a *vision* of things – events, emotions, relationships and possibilities' (1994: 87). In *She Must Be Seeing Things*, Jo (Lois Weaver), a filmmaker, watches a film that she has made alongside her girlfriend Agatha (Sheila Dabney). In de Lauretis's reading of the film, filmmaking itself is a method for the dominant female protagonist to articulate her desire for another: the 'words and images she has put together' become '*a figure of desire for Agatha*' (Ibid.: 89, original emphasis). Crucially for de Lauretis's analysis, Jo and Agatha watch the film *together*. It is the act of simultaneous viewing that allows the viewed sequence to function as an 'enacted' lesbian fantasy (Ibid.: 90). Diegetic spectatorial positioning informs our meta-spectatorial intrigue or pleasure. The frame and *mise en scène*, not only of the film within the film but also of the women's viewing of it, 'mediate and complicate our own, purposefully distanced, spectatorial relation' to the scene (Ibid.). What is important here is the simultaneity of the viewing of desire's visual incarnation. This occurs similarly in *The Clouds of Sils Maria* (Olivier Assayas, 2014), in which an actress (Juliette Binoche) is asked to play the role of the older of two women engaged in a destructive lesbian affair. She thus takes part in the revival of the very same play in which, as a young actress, she had made her name as the younger of the two characters. The film gestures to the angst of Margot Channing (Bette Davis) in *All About Eve*, and what produces its potent homoeroticism is not the lesbian action of the play, which we never witness, but the rehearsals of it in which Binoche's character Maria reads her lines with her assistant Valentine (Kristen Stewart). Here it is their impersonations of roles played on and off the stage that build up the erotic tension. Whether on a film set as in *Mulholland Drive*, or in the theatre as in *Black Swan* (Darren Aronofsky, 2010), the production of a fantastical show re-situates the female protagonist in an alternative scene that allows her to watch (a version of) herself. It is in this other scene that she discovers the figure of the lesbian as an Other who both is and is not herself.

Catherine's scheming arrangement with Nathalie is ostensibly designed in order to reignite her relationship with Bernard. Yet, he remains visually sidelined. Nathalie's recollection itself is pivotal; even more so is the fact that these events are only recollected in dialogue with Catherine. The encounters are necessitated by Catherine, without whom they would have no reason to occur. Even Nathalie's name, her characterisation and her fabricated occupation are all constituted by Catherine's wilful imagination. Fontaine describes this genesis as a 'creation of the character' of Nathalie (DP/30: The Oral History of Hollywood, 2009). The French word that Fontaine uses is 'personage', which can be translated not only as person or character, but also *figure*. We are asked to consider, when watching Bergman's *Persona*, whether Alma's persona is created prior to or by virtue of her engagements with Elisabet. We are asked something similar in *Nathalie . . .* The multiple translations of Fontaine's 'personage' pinpoint the way in which Catherine effectively creates someone who can figure, or bring into representation, her own desire.

Later work by Stacey picks up this trope in what we might call a more overtly queer vein. Exploring the negotiations of impersonation in the film *Gattaca* (Andrew Niccol, 1997), Stacey suggests that 'impersonation requires the repetition of duplicity', and asks whether *Gattaca* makes 'visible the internal contradictions of identity that will lead to its ultimate failure?' (2010: 128).[8] These 'internal contradictions' also generate the potential for the queer inhabitation of multiple sites of identification. The eponymous protagonist of *Nathalie . . .* represents both the impersonation of someone else's fantasy and a fantasy of impersonation itself: she is what Catherine would like to be (the desired object for Bernard), just as Bernard is what Catherine would like to be (the sexual agent, even the adulterer). Because the impersonation is not visually rendered in this original film, we are allowed to imagine that Catherine might in fact play both roles. The film functions not just through a single reversal of sexual roles, but rather a series of reversals. As a science-fiction film, *Gattaca* might be a generically curious intersecting text for *Nathalie . . .* However, Stacey's reading of it illuminates the relationship between film history and desire's queer trajectories, revealing its preoccupation with the function of the cinematic image and the apparatus of delusion. *Gattaca*'s 'genetic impersonations figure', Stacey writes, 'multiple chains of vicariation that disrupt the singularity of gender and sexuality and the authenticity of its embodied form' (Ibid.: 133).[9] In *Gattaca*, we are presented with what we might see as a conventional love triangle. In fact, Irene (Uma Thurman) is the woman who triangulates the homoeroticism between the film's main protagonists, Vincent (Ethan Hawke) and Jerome (Jude Law).[10] Although Irene 'might be understood as a heterosexual object of desire', her 'role is inextricable from the intimacy between Vincent and Jerome – an intimacy that is itself founded on a desire to become the other' (Ibid.). What is important here is, firstly, that heterosexuality is not the automatic obstacle to homoerotic desire but potentially its unexpected conduit, and, secondly, that the disentanglement of heterosexual presumption from hetero-social interrelations 'figures', to use Stacey's term again, a divergent eroticism. It is the equivalent substitutions emerging from Catherine and Nathalie's non-literalised erotic explorations that in *Nathalie . . .* queer the 'singularity, intentionality and directionality' of desire (Ibid.: 134). *Chloe*'s direct depiction of lesbian sex reinforces, on the other hand, the very intentionality that the original film disavows.

BURDENING RECOGNITION

Processes of conflation and obscuration occur when sexuality is *made visible* through sex. Peggy Phelan's book *Unmarked: The Politics of Performance* analyses the oft-assumed relationship between the feminist Left and visibility politics through readings of performance texts, addressing 'the implicit assumptions about the connections between representational visibility and political power' (1993: 1). Contrary to the liberating march of progress that a politics of visibility often assumes, the move to represent what Phelan calls the 'hitherto under-represented other' actually serves to 'name, and thus to arrest and fix, the image of that other' (Ibid.: 2). In this way, the lesbian becomes a figure who must stand in for a series of cultural ideas and anxieties. By virtue of being made visible, the lesbian becomes an object of what I want to call 'burdened recognition'.

The anticipated 'sex scene' that is withheld in *Nathalie . . .* is enacted in *Chloe* as befits the climax of an erotic thriller. Following a build-up of attraction over the course of the film and provoked by David's overfriendly greeting of a female student, Catherine hastily makes her way in a taxi to a hotel and solicits Chloe's company. As they sit together on the bed in the warm glow of the hotel room light, Catherine stares into the cracked and tarnished mirror in an all-too-easy metaphor for fractured sense of self and murky morals (see Figure 2.4). This is yet another familiar story: lesbian desire routinely performs a disintegration of a protagonist's principles in films such as *Wild Things* (John McNaughton, 1998), *Cruel Intentions* (Roger Kumble, 1999), *Pretty Persuasion* (Marcos Siega, 2005) and *Jennifer's Body* (Karyn Kusama, 2009). Two of these films also perform this desire as a triangulation or displacement of heterosexuality. *Chloe*'s hotel room sex scene emphasises Catherine's ambivalence regarding Chloe's demonstrative desire – persistently displayed to us through narrative details as pathological rather than endearing. The scene shows not a radical embrace of lesbianism unfounded in the earlier

Figure 2.4. Frame grab from *Chloe* (Atom Egoyan, 2009). Catherine (Julianne Moore) addresses her ambivalent desire for Chloe (Amanda Seyfried).

film, but rather a now-clichéd move to use lesbianism in order to propel the otherwise straight female character forwards in her journey of self-discovery. In contrast to *Nathalie . . .*, whose storyline keeps its potential thrills at bay, *Chloe* embraces the demands of the thriller, forcing the potential of lesbian desire to its ultimate conclusion. The explicit consummation of sexual desire between Chloe and Catherine is necessarily paired with the explicit violence that is invoked through citation as a generic inevitability.

Citation and pastiche run throughout this book's chapters, highlighting the dream language of desire that White reads as key to subtextual lesbian representation in the classical Hollywood tradition (1999: 17). *Chloe* cites not only the original film from which it is adapted, but also key generic tropes in order to pair sexual desire and violence. *Chloe*'s register of heightened sexual visibility is tied up in the film's adherence to the dramatic principles of the thriller. We know that the thriller works on the basis not only of a particular set of narrative events, but also of the pace and mood of disclosure (see Neale, 1980; Bordwell, 1989; Derry, 1988). *Chloe* directly replicates the series of events written into *Nathalie . . .*'s script while altering its generic mood by replacing subtlety with suspense. Worked out *through* suspense, sexual visibility is a generic necessity for the sake of the narrative twist. What this in effect displays is the prevalent presumption of the spectator's inability to contemplate, in advance, the possibility of lesbian desire between two female protagonists like Emily (Rooney Mara) and Victoria (Catherine Zeta-Jones) in *Side Effects* (Steven Soderbergh, 2013). *Atomic Blonde* (David Leitch, 2017)

Figure 2.5. Frame grab from *Chloe*.
Catherine dons the symbolic hairslide of her
dead lover.

Figure 2.6. Frame grab from *Vertigo* (Alfred
Hitchcock, 1958). Judy (Kim Novac) as
Madeleine/Carlotta.

likewise pivots a key generic climax on its protagonist's strategic bisexuality.
The pairing of Corky (Geena Gershon) and Violet (Jennifer Tilly) in *Bound*
(Lana and Andy Wachowski, 1996) is the ultimate example of this trope,
drawing similarly on the *film noir* as central aesthetic and narrative motif.
Moreover, while the absence of sex in *Nathalie . . .* may recall the historical
invisibility of the lesbian in cinema, *Chloe*'s sexual presence is reminiscent of
the threat of the woman immortalised in the figure of the murderous *femme
fatale*. This characterisation yields her simultaneous confirmation and viola-
tion of the heterosexual matrix.

We already know the most basic synopsis of Chloe's plot: Catherine has
negotiated for Chloe to seduce Catherine's husband David and report back
what has happened. This almost exactly replicates the transaction at the
heart of *Nathalie . . .* But while in the original film Catherine initiates their
first interaction, in the remake it is Chloe. In a bathroom of a restaurant she
drops a hair slide on purpose and then, pretending that it is not hers, suggests that Catherine take it. The rest of the narrative proceeds with Chloe
as the initiator. Such an apparently subtle difference forces Chloe into the
role of the obsessive disruptor of family life, setting in motion a series of
disturbing engagements with Catherine and her family, which include seduc-
ing Catherine's son Michael (Max Thieriot).[11] If, as Sedgwick has argued,
women are routinely reduced to their use by men as items of exchange, Chloe
is effectively punished for destabilising these terms of transaction (1985:
25).[12] In a final act of desperation, Chloe threatens Catherine, pressing the
sharp end of the now-symbolic hair slide to her throat before kissing her.
It is when Catherine realises that her son is watching this climax of sex and
violence that she pushes against Chloe, letting her fall backwards to her death
through one of the dramatic glass walls of the architecturally ostentatious
house. The hair slide, the accessory with which this train of events is begun,
provides a visual motif at the very end of the film that makes explicit a reference to the ambivalently erotic doublings of Alfred Hitchcock's heroines. In

Chloe's finale, family stability is resumed: the penultimate three shots are of mother, father and son sharing affectionate looks across a crowded room. This resolution is visually infiltrated, however, by Chloe's hair slide, which creates in Catherine's hair a coil reminiscent of the imitative gesture of Judy/ Madeleine/Carlotta in *Vertigo* (Alfred Hitchcock, 1958) (see Figures 2.5 and 2.6). In Tania Modleski's description of Hitchcock's film, Scottie recreates Judy as Madeleine as 'a living doll' (1988: 91). If Catherine has similarly reinvented Chloe in fantasy, if she has reincarnated her 'according to [her] ideal image' (Ibid.), this image becomes one with which, subsequently, to self-identify. Catherine still morbidly manifests identificatory desire through the image even beyond the death of the object of her identification.

Replicating and championing key tropes in pathological lesbian film history, *Chloe*'s characterisation thus intertwines lesbian sexuality, lesbian impotence, lesbian menace and lesbian punishment.[13] Obsession and excessive desire have become quintessential characteristics of the psychological thriller's generic appeal, most notably with the appearance of Alex Forrest (Glen Close), the 'bunny boiler' (see Leonard, 2009; Jermyn, 1996) of *Fatal Attraction* (Adrian Lyne, 1987). Variations on this same theme can be found in *Misery* (Rob Reiner, 1990) and in *Black Widow* (Bob Rafelson, 1987), whilst the contrastingly indifferent reception of the male antagonist of *Pacific Heights* (John Schlesinger, 1990) demonstrates a gendered double standard. Sex becomes shorthand for the thriller's mandatory figuration of female sexuality. In the erotic thrillers that borrow from mid-twentieth-century *film noir*, the *femme fatale* remains the genre's main object of desire and fear, as Julianne Pidduck (1995: 65) writes in a discussion of 'neo-*noir*' films such as *The Hand that Rocks the Cradle* (Curtis Hanson, 1992) and *Body of Evidence* (Uli Edel, 1993). She might share 'her predecessor's smart mouth and sexual savvy', but must up 'the ante of earlier, more muted cinematic codes of sexuality and graphic violence' (Ibid.).

Sex in this story of lesbian sexuality must signify three conflicting registers of failure: excess, disappointment and violence. *Chloe*'s generic adherence gestures to the protagonists of films like *Fatal Attraction* who are drawn by the desperation of their own domestic situations to allow themselves to be seduced by the inevitably murderous woman whose sexuality presents her ultimate threat. Domestic disturbance is a theme that has commonly generated anxiety in genres from the thriller to the melodrama. Often associated with this trope, Moore's screen presence in films such as *Safe* (Todd Haynes, 1995), *Far from Heaven* (Todd Haynes, 2002), *The Hours* (Stephen Daldry, 2002), *The Private Lives of Pippa Lee* (Rebecca Miller, 2009) and *The Kids Are All Right* (Lisa Cholodenko, 2010) has evoked a domestic maternal promise that fails to provide what we want from it and from her: reassuring (familial) familiarity. *Far from Heaven* looks back to a mid-twentieth-century melodramatic aesthetic in which the home has a heavy presence; indeed, key to the family melodrama, according to Thomas Elsaesser, is the 'function of the décor and the symbolisation of objects', whose excessive dominance in the *mise en scène* takes on the significance of domestic oppression (1987: 61). In *The Kids Are All Right*, we see how a trajectory towards the domestication of lesbianism via fertility and adoption rights, equal marriage and the wider acceptance of 'new' forms of family brings lesbianism into the home, but never unproblematically (see Bradbury-Rance, 2013). In Stacey Passon's *Concussion* (2013) (and in a different vein, Jill Soloway's *Afternoon Delight* [2001]), we observe the potential aftermath of this domestic acceptance: what happens when domesticated desire is taken out of the home again. As if to capture these anxieties, in *Chloe* the home itself literally precipitates Chloe's death, as she falls through a window of the house following a final embrace with Catherine. Rather than the de-eroticisation of the lesbian relationship that Lee Wallace (2009: 131) argues is the home's modus operandi, what we observe here is the forcing of lesbianism into conformity because the primary lesbian subject (Chloe, the initiator) is killed off by the home itself. Here the film again reveals a Hitchcockian subtext. John Fletcher writes about the way in which the exhibition of 'the female gothic' in *Rebecca* (Alfred Hitchcock, 1940) hinges on a structuring 'intrusion into a space which has been the scene of a desiring and/or murderous action in the past' (1995: 344). *The Duke of Burgundy* (Peter Strickland, 2014) epitomises the neo-gothic house whose monumental and suffocating presence is taken on by the sexual dynamic between the two women inside its walls. The home in *Chloe* takes on a Gothic sensibility not only through Chloe's climactic death but also through that death's continual foreshadowing – for instance, the abundance of scenes shot through the glass that will ultimately kill her. It is this suspenseful effect that also generates the exquisite thrill of the genre, what Catherine Spooner argues is the Gothic's intrinsic concern: 'the production of pleasurable fear' (2006: 30).

Chloe's juxtaposition of two spaces, home and hotel, accentuate this pathological demand for restitution of lesbianism's diverting energy away from the home. The sex scene described above takes place in the hotel in which Catherine's meetings with Chloe began, and the entrance of which we have watched her look down on from her affluent office. Class and professional differences in both films accentuate the instabilities in the power relations between Catherine and Chloe/Nathalie, overdetermined in the older/ younger couplings that have become a curiously unremarkable art cinema trope (*American Beauty* [Sam Mendes, 1999]; *Lost in Translation* [Sofia Coppola, 2004]; *A Single Man* [Tom Ford, 2009]). This is highlighted in the pairing of

Love Crime (Alan Corneau, 2010) with its prompt remake *Passion* (Brian de Palma, 2012): the competitive, potentially erotic and ultimately murderous relationship between a younger woman and her female boss is heightened in the latter film by sexual manipulation. Unlike in the move from *Nathalie . . .* to *Chloe*, the replacement in the remake of Kristen Scott Thomas's significantly older woman by the younger Rachel McAdams (who is almost the same age as her counterpart Noomi Rapace) undermines the erotic potential of the age difference between Scott Thomas and Ludivine Sagnier in the original. In *Chloe*, Catherine embodies the maternal role. Her literal status, high up in a private doctor's office from which she surveils Chloe at work between hotel and taxi, only exacerbates a fact that is exposed and troubled in *Nathalie . . .* but not in *Chloe*: while this transaction is for Catherine one of potential desire, it must for Chloe be also financial. If the physical touches between Catherine and Nathalie in *Nathalie . . .* sometimes replicate those between mother and child, they are shared in both directions; both women play mother, both child, in a radical demurral of hierarchies of status, class and age. It is in *Chloe*, by contrast, that the one-sided maternal analogy provides a lesbian character whose sexuality must then be dismissed as childlike. Chloe disturbs what Kathleen Stewart identifies as the middle class's 'womb of safety and stasis' (2005: 326). She is at once *femme fatale* and *femme* (or rather *fille*) *impotent*. It is her induction into the domestic setting that highlights her class, age and power difference, and the domestic setting that must signal her inevitable demise. As in *Marnie* (Alfred Hitchcock, 1964), which, according to Robert Corber, 'interrogated the construction of female subjectivity in relation to patriarchal social and economic arrangements' while nevertheless 'reinstall[ing] marriage and motherhood as the "happy ending" of female sexual development' (2011: 19), Chloe is the scapegoat for the failure of this requisite narrative endpoint.

The sex worker's presumed role is to be reliably ready to shift sexual and spatial zones: as the character announces in her voice-over at the beginning of the film, 'I can become your living, breathing, unflinching dream, and then I can actually disappear'. This statement foreshadows Chloe's dramatic death at the end of the film in yet another re-write of the trope of lesbian invisibility. Discussing *Chloe* with an emphasis on its representation of prostitution, Handyside argues that the film's regressive trajectory emerges in the killing off of Chloe, the doubly other lesbian-prostitute who must be punished for her transgression of the patriarchal order (2017: 259). Lesbian desire is generically conflated with obsession and then (usually fatal) punishment. Handyside's reading of *Chloe* argues that the film reworks the prostitute's 'visible invisibility' (Ibid.). This paired term captures the predictability of invisibility: her presence is defined solely through her absence. Just such generic predictability is what sustains our interest in the film's narrativisation of desire.

PARAMETERS OF VISUAL FORM

Aligning the inevitability of sex (bringing fantasy to reality as 'a living dream') with the inevitability of death, Chloe's visibility is reworked by a genre that traps her in a double bind: the visibility of sex fixes the figure of the pathological lesbian along the lines of her generic heritage. The weight of meaning generated by her image obscures sexuality's complexity behind sex as an act made visible. Thus, through what we might otherwise call the 'hypervisibility' (Pidduck, 2011) of sex in *Chloe*, it retrospectively becomes in *Nathalie . . .* a structuring absence.[14] When we read *Nathalie . . .* through the language made available by its remake, we fix the image of desire in the language of sex. However, as Jacqueline Rose writes, 'sexual representation' must 'take in the parameters of visual form (not just what we see but how we see – visual space as more than just the domain of simple recognition)' (2005 [1986]: 231). Any discussion of representation risks the overstatement of an original, coherent, transportable *thing* (however abstract) that is simply reflected in image, or *re*-presented. Representation always provokes, produces and *means* more. Michel Foucault's proposition that 'nothing has any meaning outside of discourse' (1972, in Hall, 2003: 45) may have become a theoretical axiom but remains politically uncomfortable. We still find ourselves tempted to believe that what we see is all there is: in Rosi Braidotti's words, 'the primacy of sight' is still maintained as 'a site of legitimation of knowledge' (2002: 27). Sexuality in cinema does not just exist in the transplantation of a visual reckoning of sexual activity from our idea of it in 'reality' to a recognisable representation on the screen. The 'parameters of visual form' that Rose asks us to consider draw our attention as much to what is *not* shown as to what *is*. Nevertheless, *Chloe*'s 'updating' of *Nathalie . . .* threatens to confine a reading of the two films to a linear assumption of the visible's predominance over the invisible. As Rose insists, the relationship between image and sexuality can neither be purely imposed from the outside as it is by the mandatory reading of *Nathalie . . .* in the context of more recent advances in lesbian visibility, nor can it be left unnoticed. Instead, our engagement with what we might call the anticipatory pre-sexual image emphasises the sexuality of that image '*in potentia*' (Rose, 2005 [1986]: 231).

It is what remains untouched, unsaid, between Catherine and Nathalie that presents a queer register of desire. What alerts us specifically to this queering in *Nathalie . . .* is not only the potential of the unsaid but its radical saying in the later film. A pivotal scene from *Nathalie . . .* proves to be the source of an irresistible re-write. The women dance together in a busy nightclub. They face one another and then simultaneously throw their heads back, exposing their necks and opening their bodies (see Figure 2.7). The voyeuristic gaze we

Figure 2.7. Frame grab from *Nathalie . . .*
Nathalie and Catherine dance.

Figure 2.8. Frame grab from *Nathalie . . .*
An unnamed 'hôtesse du bar' (Prudence
Maïdou) laughs as the 'patronne du bar'
(Évelyne Dandry) serves.

must occupy as spectators matches the earlier statement of Catherine's own voyeurism on her first visit to the bar in which Nathalie works: she sits on a seat looking out at the bar, a mirror behind her, and in a close-up shot from her point of view we see the arched-backed bodies of sex workers standing at the bar, the camera contemplating their bare necks (see Figure 2.8). The repetition of this pose in Catherine and Nathalie's dancing scene reminds us, through a recollective visual grammar, not only of the foundational eroticism of the bar, in which the women's poses are professionally seductive, but also of Catherine's gradual initiation into Nathalie's world. It is this world, far removed from domesticity, that becomes the foremost space of the film (whereas in *Chloe*, the domestic realm remains necessarily dominant in order to shore up the paradoxical demands of the thriller). One of the most intimate scenes in *Nathalie . . .* then occurs between Catherine and Nathalie in a taxi on the way home from this night of dancing. Catherine puts her head on Nathalie's shoulder and closes her eyes. If we view this scene with what has been called the 'future anterior' (see for instance Berlant and Edelman, 2014: 14) – in this case the anticipatory mode of the future remake – we notice that *Chloe*'s almost identical shot-for-shot and word-for-word replication of this taxi ride occurs not after dancing, but after the sex scene that is missing from the first film. With this anticipation of the future anterior, we might recast the taxi scene in *Nathalie . . .* as even more intensely erotic, and the dancing scene as one that incorporates the potential and expectation of its future 'remade' replacement, the sexual act.

In Fontaine's film, Nathalie's stories of her fabricated sexual encounters with Catherine's husband are fictions both visually and narratively: the encounters between her fantasised alter-ego and Bernard are only projected – to Catherine and to the film's audience – by her verbal narrations of them. Catherine fabricates a name and an occupation, and chooses clothes and accommodation, for Nathalie, a character with whom she can experience desire for her husband through a play on the other woman's sameness to herself. We imagine Catherine playing both roles. Together, Catherine and Nathalie create and occupy a space of queer recollective eroticism that is premised on, but not inhabited by, the man. In a model of spectatorship that undermines the rigid distinction between lesbian and straight, we can see a queering of female spectatorship through this eroticisation of identification. In Egoyan's film, that potentially homoerotic space is immediately precluded by the visual reiteration of Chloe's (otherwise fabricated) sexual encounters with David. 'I can become your living, breathing, unflinching dream . . . and then I can actually disappear', says Chloe in her opening voice-over. This potential for simple disappearance is precisely what is at stake in the overt signification of *Chloe*'s erotic situations as unambiguously sexual, what is lost in the remake's process of making graphic. The problem with *Chloe*'s updating of *Nathalie* . . ., in the wake of an unprecedented increase in lesbian visibility on-screen between 2003 and 2009, is that it hinges on a need for visibility to work in relation to the visible.

Chloe is not only pictorially but also generically less ambiguous. The lesbian becomes an object of burdened recognition; in the thriller, this recognition precisely depends on the capacity for the revelation of lesbian sex to act as a twist. Surprise is a generic inevitability that is premised on the predictability of invisibility (we will only be surprised if we never saw it coming). *Chloe* sharpens the visual evidence of desires that remain at the level of suggestion in *Nathalie* . . . *Chloe* fixes desire in the language of 'the sex scene', falsely leading us to assume that what we are witnessing in the move from original to remake is a linear progression from the invisible to the visible. If it is desire that is lost in the move to make sex the visible object of sexuality's representability, this lost desire has been rendered already queerly ambiguous in *Nathalie* . . . It is formed not only through heterosexual acts, but also through homoerotic gazes and a queer spatialisation of desire. In *Nathalie* . . ., desire is revealed to hold within it the complexities of identification, impersonation and vicariation. The image of desire is, moreover, revealed by the *mise en scène* to be itself an imitation, a fantasy. This chapter has instituted my use of queer as a way of thinking outside of the dominant paradigm of sex as evidence of sexuality and eroticism. In the chapters that follow, I continue to observe the triangulations that trouble our conceptions of the singularity of lesbian desire.

My argument in these first two chapters has explored how these films expose the contradictory relationship between absence and presence in cinema's production of lesbianism, troubling the ease with which sex can be read as the visual evidence of sexuality. The subsequent three chapters move from psychoanalytically informed studies of the cinematic coding of lesbian fantasy to an investigation of the affective, spatial and temporal registers of desire and eroticism that have provoked recent debates in feminist theory.

These chapters consider the ways in which the in-between and expectant modes of subjectivity and sensation that characterise adolescent sexuality coincide with, and accent, lesbian desires in *Water Lilies* (Céline Sciamma, 2007), *She Monkeys* (Lisa Aschan, 2011) and *Circumstance* (Maryam Keshavarz, 2011). Chapter 3 continues the project of the first two chapters in examining the masquerade of visibility involved in screen figurations of lesbianism while pointing to the focus in the remainder of the book on the relationship between intense desires, abject longing and the ambivalence surrounding sexuality's coherence as the endpoint of adolescent growth. Interrogating the film's projection of a desire for urban space to bear the utopian possibility of a sexual and political liberation ostensibly evidenced in US cultural imports, the chapter explores how *Circumstance* constructs the desire for identity as a fantasy through the negotiations of private and public space.

CHAPTER 3

Anywhere in the World: Circumstance, *Space and the Desire for Outness*

The scene in *Circumstance* (Maryam Keshavarz, 2011) that has become the most frequently cited ambassador for the film's blend of youthful frivolity, political commentary and uncompromising drama is one in which four young Iranians dub the gay rights biopic *Milk* (Gus van Sant, 2008) into Farsi in a screening room at the back of an illicit video store in Tehran. In this scene, which intervenes in *Circumstance*'s ultimately tragic narrative, layers of comic incongruity unfold in the form of a bid to produce the dubbed *Milk* as a black-market double bill with the *Sex and the City* movie (Michael Patrick King, 2008). As the camera pans hesitantly left and right across three awkward faces staring beyond the frame at the sexual images whose sound effects they must translate, several fantasies overlap: of escape to the utopian USA of the movies they dub; of the radical potential (and humorous incompatibility) of the sexualities available through those two contrasting narratives; and of the film's own profession of cultural identity beyond the diegesis.

Circumstance was directed by Maryam Keshavarz, an American-Iranian graduate of New York University. It was filmed in Beirut as a stand-in for Tehran and co-produced in Iran, France and the USA. The dubbing scene gestures to the world beyond Tehran, creating the fantasy of a universal space linking nation states via the illusory and contradictory sexual politics of North American cinema. B. Ruby Rich's account of the 'explosion of lesbian filmmaking' at the 2011 Sundance Film Festival uses the scene in order to exemplify the film's expression of a 'desire to be somewhere else' (2011: 63). For Patricia White, whose essay on *Circumstance* also begins with this evidently irresistible scene, it 'functions as a canny commentary on the film's positioning within global cinema networks' (2018: 159). White's chapter focuses on these feminist circuits and the film's positionality as a diasporan product of cross-cultural contemporary lesbian possibilities. And for Rosalind Galt and Karl Schoonover, who use the dubbing scenario to set their world stage in their book *Queer Cinema in the World*, *Circumstance* offers a way in to thinking about the paradoxical and sometimes even uncomfortable tropes that determine how we theorise the queerness of the world, the queerness of world cinema and the 'worlding' of queer cinema (2016: 5).

Figure 3.1. Frame grab from *Circumstance* (Maryam Keshavarz, 2011). Atafeh (Nikohl Boosheri) and Shireen (Sarah Kazemy) dance through the streets of Tehran.

Set in a recent Tehran under the presidency of Mahmoud Ahmadinejad (2005–13), *Circumstance* follows two teenage girls, Atafeh (Nikohl Boosheri) and Shireen (Sarah Kazemy), whose rebellion against the oppressive authority of the morality police begins with drug taking and underground partying and culminates in a love affair. Atafeh comes from a wealthy liberal family and occupies the familial domestic sphere in T-shirts watching American television programmes; her father Firouz (Soheil Parsa) longs for 'one day' when his wife Azar (Nasrin Pakkho) and daughter can shed the veil to join him in the water at the seaside. Shireen – as far as we know, so little back story are we provided with – is the orphaned daughter of political rebels. She is brought up by an uncle (Fariborz Daftari) who is unnamed, barely glimpsed and reduced to his insistence on the arranged marriage that provokes the film's unambiguous stance against gender inequality. Progressive beliefs and modest rebellion are affiliated with Atafeh's bourgeois family; desperate concession to the Iranian regime's oppressive policies is associated with Shireen's. This balance shifts within the film's timeline when Atafeh's drug-addicted brother Mehran (Reza Sixo Safai) returns as the prodigal son and imposes on the family his new ties with religious fundamentalism and the morality police. A stark division is thus created between the two young women, insinuating the film's ideological positioning: a religious and cultural binary performed by these contrasting families exemplifies a call for tolerance of female sexuality (and by extension homosexuality) within Islam. Comparison can be made here with the work of another diasporan filmmaker, Canadian-Indian Deepa Mehta, whose film *Fire* (1996) provoked outrage in India for its depiction of lesbianism and its condemnation of homophobia (see Desai, 2002; Gopinath, 2002). A more recent film making political interventions in diasporic narratives, *Margarita with a Straw* (Shonali Bose and Nilesh Maniyar, 2014), is described by Sophie Mayer (2016: 170) as having a 'confident sense of home turf' as it intertwines, in a narrative crossing from Delhi to New York, 'love, justice and togetherness' (Ibid.: 171). The arguably unnuanced condemnation of religion in *Circumstance*, in contrast, reveals a stance for which Keshavarz, with what is perceived to be her indubitably Western gaze, has been rigorously critiqued (see Rastegar, 2011).

In the very first scene of Keshavarz's film, the words whispered by an anonymous voice-over – 'If you could be anywhere in the world, where would you be?' – are joined by the sounds of a tambourine and then a fantasy sequence in which Atafeh performs on stage, watched by Shireen. The film itself participates here in a masquerade of cultural identity. The Farsi calligraphy that adorns the screen with its English translation is also part of a fantasy of the film's own production context: the screenplay for *Circumstance* was written in English by its writer-director Keshavarz and then translated into Farsi, and most of the actors are North American nationals who were taught to speak 'authentically' by a dialect coach. In her reading of the film, White argues that its opening waves the 'veil of orientalist seduction' (2018: 169) whilst it self-consciously 'jam[s]' those very codes (Ibid.: 167). The film simultaneously employs orientalism for aesthetic appeal and critiques it. White suggests that Keshavarz, an American-born, Iranian-American-identified filmmaker, employs her diasporic status in a way that speaks to wider networks of contemporary global women's cinema. The opening dream sequence creates another world for this orientalist 'veil' and then abruptly deposits its actors in a schoolyard line, the stark reality of institutional boredom, banality and inequality. Here is foregrounded the more severe detention that might await them. The global is conjured not only through the characters' fantasy of escape (America) but also through the film's own fantasy of the homeland (Iran): one is sensationalised while the other is bound by institutions first mundane and then devastating. This opening scenario provides just one in a series of fantasies that construct the world of which Atafeh and Shireen dream. These might all be set in Dubai, the professed focus of their immediate escape, but they are stylised in the form of the American culture that infiltrates the film from all sides. If, as Robin Cohen (2001: 180) argues, typical taxonomies of diaspora include a recurring devotion to an ideal of the homeland, this functions as a reverse devotion in which the new (home)land (Keshavarz's USA) is that which is idealised through fantasy.

The spatialisation of cultural idealisation is evoked intensely by *Circumstance*'s narrative of adolescence in a non-Western, Islamic state. In particular, the domestic arena becomes increasingly compromised by Mehran's fanatical leanings. The city is also depicted through the illusion of opportunity: hope is premised upon a familiarity with or desire for global queer and youth cultures.

Circumstance's humanist message is announced in its tag line: 'Freedom is a human right.' However, at the heart of the film's supposed subcultural or underground political appeal is a process of spatialisation that charts, embraces and highlights the paradoxical inconsistencies of identity that the external marketing strategy must advocate. Space becomes the film's stand-in for the 'contested realms of identity' (Vidler, 1992: 164) that market its universality as a romantic narrative capable of transcending political and geographical borders. The girls' romance is set against the competing spaces of domesticity and urbanity, both of which commence as guarantors either of freedom or of oppression but are ultimately found to be complex and inconsistent.

In Chapter 2, through a consideration of the spatialisation of desire, I argued that fantasy in *Nathalie* . . . (Anne Fontaine, 2003) offers lesbian potential through heterosexual disruption and vicarious desire, disturbing a ubiquitous hunger for visibility as stand-in for political progress. I used the work of Jackie Stacey (2010, 1994) and Teresa de Lauretis (1994) to foreground those unlikely or contradictory moments of identification that are yielded even within what we think of as fixed or incontestable identities. In this chapter, I explore the desire for identity through its conflation with the desire for sexual liberation. I analyse the ways in which cinematic constructions of fantasy provide hopeful sites of selfhood in the face of identity's seeming impossibility. In particular, I address *Circumstance*'s display of the tussle between urban and domestic space. I consider the city as a phantasmagoria of urban freedom through its role as shorthand for transnational identity, contrasting a generic variant of the traumatic domesticity that haunts *Chloe* (Atom Egoyan, 2009). The physical spaces in *Circumstance* are rivalled by fantasy spaces that palpably generate the promise of the film's tag line. *Circumstance* projects a desire for urban space to bear the utopian possibility of a sexual and political liberation divergently evidenced in *Milk* and *Sex and the City*, the two films they choose to dub together on a black-market DVD.[1] Yet, as a film that gives a diegetic platform to questions about the gaze, the screen and the projection of the image, *Circumstance* reveals all of these idealised spaces as, precisely, fantasy. This chapter explores how *Circumstance* simultaneously epitomises and ironises the desire for sexual liberation – or sexuality *as* liberation – and asks how the film constructs this desire as fantasy through the negotiations of private, public and virtual space.

ANYWHERE BUT HERE

The Tehran of *Circumstance* is a city that buzzes with colour, silliness, adventure and the headiness of risk in the face of the constant threat of criminalisation. As a site both of fear and of fun, it situates a broader paradoxical tension – about subcultural pleasure and identity politics – in spatialised terms. The city visually embraces Atafeh and Shireen, as a montage follows their outbreak from the grey-clad schoolyard. In one shot, they blend into their surroundings as they pass in front of a coloured mural that precisely matches their outfits (see Figure 3.1). In comparison to the comparatively bland colour scheme that adorns the film's interior shots, colour is produced by the urban setting as Atafeh and Shireen dance through the city streets in quick edits that are timed to a pulsing hip-hop beat. Whilst interior shots are slow and static (with an increasingly ascetic palette as Mehran returns to the fold), the city is presented as visually and aurally playful. Here, *Circumstance* echoes other films about urban adolescence, from *Times Square* (Alan Moyle, 1980), a landmark film for the representation of urban space as sexual, queer and rebellious (see Halberstam, 2006: 189); to Alex Sichel's *All Over Me* (1997), which has remained a cult lesbian drama in the twenty years since its release; to Dee Rees's *Pariah* (2011), in competition at Sundance in the same year as *Circumstance* and paired with it by Rich in her festival roundup (2011). The threat in all these narratives is that the city will be taken away from its queer inhabitants, politicised further in *Times Square* through a narrative of New York gentrification. The tag line of *All Over Me* articulates sexuality (and more) through preposition: 'In a world that expects you to fit in, sometimes you just have to stand out'. *Pariah*'s title, and the dictionary definition that accompanies it on the film's poster, comments on what it means to be a pariah, outcast, *cast out* (see Bradbury-Rance, 2016). The characters of *Circumstance*, *Pariah*, *Times Square* and *All Over Me* seek escape in spatialised terms from the family, from poverty, from racism, from the closet (see also Keeling, et al., 2015). At the thresholds of physical encounter, the adolescent girls in these features are both within and without, their positioning mediated by reflective surfaces, dreamlike *mise en scène* or handheld mobile camerawork. City streets are spaces of colour; they are spaces of fun and of risk; they are spaces in which to try out identity; and they are spaces of opposition.[2]

Where do we find the 'oblique world' in which queer bodies are said to reside (Ahmed, 2006: 161)? Is it somewhere in the polarised relation between what is frequently characterised as the private domain of normativity and the urban space of queer potential (see Weston, 1995; Rubin, 1993; Halberstam, 2007)? In *Beyond the Hills* (Cristian Mungiu, 2012), set in the Romanian orthodox church, the space itself, filmed in overbearingly dark tones, becomes an oppressive obstacle to desire, only the film's title gesturing to what might exist beyond them. The original title of *Show Me Love* (Lukas Moodysson, 1998) – *Fucking Åmål* – highlights adolescent frustrations associated with growing up in a small town (Åmål) in which there is seemingly nothing to do and nobody to love. In *In Between* (Maysaloun Hamoud, 2016), the juxtapositions of closeted lesbianism, devout religion and overt female sexuality among the members of a female collective must force them into liminal spaces already fraught by a Palestinian existence in Tel Aviv. In *The Edge of Heaven* (Fatih Akin, 2007), the need for political and sexual radicalism to be relocated across borders is evoked in the film's original title, *Auf der Anderen Seite*, meaning 'On the Other Side'. In these films, we repeatedly sense where and when the queer world is *not*.

As in *The Edge of Heaven*, the city space in *Circumstance* stimulates a frequently posed opposition between Western freedoms and Islamic moral restrictions. The non-diegetic soundtrack that provides the exuberant pace of the vibrant urban montage alternately links the city space directly to subcultural risk as the song that accompanies the girls through the streets is carried over and greets them diegetically at an illicit house party. The room is crowded; this is an animated space that combines the potential liberation of the city with the walled enclosure of the domestic. Whilst the party offers the potential for sexual experimentation, its heterosexuality goes without question. The presumptuous pairing of Shireen with a strange boy in a side room creates a literal closet: neither one is romantically interested in the other – and the boy, Hossein (Sina Amedson), is later revealed also to be gay when he instigates the dubbing of *Milk*, a film about San Franciscan politician and gay rights campaigner Harvey Milk. Standing in for the very possibility of outness as a politicised act, the citation underwrites *Circumstance*'s political platform, even as *Milk*'s narrative climax (Milk's assassination) begs the question asked by Judith Butler: 'For whom is outness an historically available and affordable option?' (1993: 19).

Circumstance's protagonists take charge of their city space by converting it into a fantasy space of transnational escape. The 'anywhere' of the opening line is ideologically positioned by the film's unfolding narrative as, instead, 'elsewhere'. Only when conjured in fantasy can this elsewhere become, really, anywhere (as in, here, in Iran). For Lauren Berlant, the word 'elsewhere' describes a fantasised space or time clung to by our expectation, optimism or apprehension; desire, for instance, 'propels you toward an elsewhere that, you imagine, will offer you a fresh start, a new horizon of possibility and fewer economic impediments' (1999: 207). However, implicit in these words is the notion that this desired elsewhere is perpetual, remaining always out of reach or somehow removed from the presently attainable. If identity's completion in adulthood is the persistent 'elsewhere' of adolescence, *Circumstance* uses its adolescent protagonists to reveal the desire for an adulthood that offers public sexuality and protected domesticity, but only through a fantasy of relocation to *somewhere else*.

In the dubbing scene that later forms the film's ideological centrefold, a postfeminist citation of *Sex and the City* looks beyond the walls of the city and the home to a fantasy of social and sexual citizenship. Unlike other runaway films such as *Gasoline* (Monica Lisa Stambrini, 2003) and *The Fish Child* (Lucía Puenzo, 2009), *Circumstance* allows its protagonists to escape through popular cultural citation. What they thus encounter is a politics of self-improvement that functions largely through consumerism.[3] As they run away from the party, which has been raided by police, Atafeh and Shireen break a car window, steal the bag within and share a fleeting kiss. In this moment the film gestures towards what Dereka Rushbrook argues is the perhaps incongruous notion of a queer consumer cosmopolitanism (2002: 188). The diasporic context of production and its cultural worlding of the experience of Iranian teenagers adopts a cosmopolitan reach from the USA to Tehran and back again. *Circumstance* in this way matches the register of American films in which girls claim the spaces of the city through marginalised practices that are also tied up in a corrupted form of consumption as a process of becoming.[4] In both *Thirteen* (Catherine Hardwicke, 2003) and *The Bling Ring* (Sofia Coppola, 2013), drugs and theft are ways to occupy the space that is not one's own. Dominating the streets in open-top cars or shoplifting on LA boardwalks, the girls in both these films try to take charge of the urban space whose publicity gives them freer rein than the closely monitored family home. In the latter film – Sofia Coppola's true-crime portrait of a group of middle-class teenagers who steal vast collections of expensive goods from Hollywood mansions – the inevitable symbolic publicity of the celebrity homes creates a space that bleeds into the public character of the city itself. *Circumstance* highlights how, in the Iranian context, the stakes of transgression are heightened. Sexual liberation as an exported American value system is accomplished through dreaming in this postfeminist language. However, the political and moral consequences of the apparently nebulous but nevertheless dangerous terms of lesbian sexuality under an oppressive regime can be compared, but only uncomfortably, with the legal and moral consequences of stealing as a form of US consumerist girl power.[5]

Paired in the dubbing scene, *Sex and the City* and *Milk* together occupy a space of hope for the guarantee of an identity in adulthood enabled by sexual liberation (see Ashby, 2005; Gerhard, 2011; Genz, 2010). David Alderson suggests that, paradoxically, 'queer cosmopolitanism' has 'produced a conformity of style whose very function is to be recognisable *despite* cultural differences' (2005: 76, original emphasis). This is an ideological horizontalism of presumed universal experience. The guaranteed queerness of *Milk*'s gay liberation narrative is asked to occupy a transnational significance, just as *Sex and the City* seems to circulate effortlessly across contemporary American texts such as *Girls* (Lena Dunham, 2012–17) and *Appropriate Behaviour* (Desiree

Akhavan, 2014).[6] Gay liberation and female sexuality are conflated in an illusion of what can be made available in the 'anywhere' (else) of the film's opening line.

White observes that the poster for *Circumstance* relies on an exoticism of lesbianism as the elsewhere of romantic genre, selling the film on the basis of 'an arthouse history of lesbianism as signifier of sexual novelty and thus a kind of foreignness in and of itself' (2018: 162). 'If you could be anywhere in the world': these words, repeated throughout the film, are the platform upon which *Circumstance*'s desire for outness rests. This need not be located in a specific city but rather an abstract fantasy scene; indeed, the 'anywhere' imagined by both Shireen and Atafeh remains at the level of fantasy, instituted through the film's display of technological mediation to create a virtual 'world' of possible desire. The hope for the security of Atafeh and Shireen's relationship is figured not in the (hetero)sexualised margins of the party, nor even in the city streets whose montaged appeal provides a visual template for liberated urban practices. The hope for a queer world is figured instead in the elsewhere promised in the form of (literal or metaphorical) transnational escape. In answer to Butler's question: outness is promised as available and affordable but only by fantasising the shedding of national difference. *Circumstance* plays with the complications of presenting Tehran as an enabling space of non-normative sexuality: the urban montage is expectant but cannot be sustained. The visual seeds of Atafeh and Shireen's relationship are planted in the city streets of a turbulent Tehran, but they are not allowed to remain there. Oppression is compensated for by citational fantasy, metaphorising the desire for *out* sexuality to be not anywhere but always elsewhere.

PROMISING WORLDLINESS

Circumstance's discursive construction of sexual liberation as elsewhere functions to posit the possibility of identity in the form of the liberal possibility for *out* sexuality. For Eve Kosofsky Sedgwick, the term queer refers to 'the open mesh of possibilities, gaps, overlaps, dissonances and resonances, lapses and excesses of meaning when the constituent elements of anyone's gender, of anyone's sexuality aren't made (or *can't* be made) to signify monolithically' (1993: 8, original emphasis). Here we see spatial orientations becoming metaphors for sexual orientations. In the middle of a film almost entirely constructed around this disjuncture between public and private space, the dubbing scene offers one way in which to understand queer as a term working to offer us non-normative identity whilst also shattering the fallacy of identity itself, both 'lapse' and 'excess' of normative meaning at once. The idea to dub *Milk* comes from Hossein, a visitor to Tehran from the USA who befriends

Figure 3.2. Frame grab from *Circumstance*. Atafeh, Shireen, Joey (Keon Alexander) and Hossein (Sina Amedson) dub *Milk* (Gus van Sant, 2008) into Farsi.

Atafeh, Shireen and their friend Joey (Keon Alexander). In the process, the USA from which Hossein hails comes to stand in for the endpoint of that hope for change, a symbol of the desired elsewhere that Tehran cannot be. He is frustrated with his friends for not trying to 'change your circumstances'. The subtext of this command, belonging to the film as well as to the character, is for them to allow themselves the freedom of the visible, to 'lay claim to identity through visibility' (Feldman, 2017: 13). Amid moderate teasing, Atafeh reassures Hossein that 'we knew you were gay', revealing the privilege of assumption whilst situating this American elsewhere as precisely the site of 'having come out' that neither she nor Shireen is able to attain. If the desire for identity comes from the desire to be linked, in Zeena Feldman's words, to 'narrative history, to a linear story about "us"', this 'us' here becomes attached, unavoidably, to the (US)A (Ibid.).

The dubbing scene is introduced by a shot that imposes the amateur actors' heads in front of a screen upon which is projected a gay-rights march at the heart of *Milk* and then Sean Penn as Harvey Milk delivering a rousing speech (see Figure 3.2). The projected film is in bright colour, in contrast to the black silhouettes of the Iranian viewers in the foreground. However, with the sound delivered to the characters through headphones, *Milk*'s provocative protest scene is silenced. The parodying voice of childish Joey is what takes its place, smothering the soundtrack with his campy imitation of Penn as Milk. Gay rights are made urgently present by the dynamism of this figurehead of the 1970s movement (the only aspect of the *mise en scène* visible in colour is Penn, highlighted in a bright red jersey). Yet they are simultaneously made inaccessible (the speech is silenced except by mocking mediation). 'Radicality isn't romantic,' chides Shireen. Political protest (a crime for which, we are led to believe, Shireen's parents have long since paid with their life) is only endorsed by success in fantasy: Harvey Milk of the gay liberation movement is witnessed speech-giving but not dying for the cause, before he is swapped for the postfeminist sexual liberation of *Sex and the City*'s (mostly straight) women. The parallel silencing of the actual terms of the radicalism of Shireen's parents' political activism contrasts awkwardly with the strident naming of Milk's white American fight. Queer possibility is enabled through this whiteness, the screen on which Hossein and his friends project their hopes mimicking what Melanie Kohnen advises is a 'closet-as-screen' that 'appears as a blank surface – a *white* screen upon which queer images are projected' (2016: 12, original emphasis). This is a screen that simultaneously projects some and 'screens out other facets of queerness' (Ibid.). The politics of race and of nation overlap here, one screening out the other. Just as it is possible to assume Hossein's gayness from his American coding ('we knew you were gay'), it is possible to situate human rights more broadly as something to be achieved in and by this American context (see Hesford, 2011; White, 2015).

In the middle of the frame, the projector draws attention to *Circumstance*'s narrative use of cinema as that which projects a contradiction. Roland Barthes describes the cinema's 'absence of worldliness' as he gestures to the 'urban dark [in which] the body's freedom is generated' (1989 [1984]: 346).[7] The dubbing scene in *Circumstance* provides an urban closet for these adolescent characters. It is a private space which is within, but hidden away from, the public realm and in which the darkness yields an absence of other worldly markers of location. Symbolically, however, this scene is also the film's most present and vivid offering of the desire for awareness of the world beyond Iran's borders. This is exaggerated by the film's dispassionate abandonment of the plotline that would see the dubbing scene's promised outcome, a black-market DVD, make the characters not only consumers but producers. Instead, the scene is left in the unresolved heterotopia of the cinema (see Foucault, 1986 [1967]). The promise of worldliness, and of a tangible connection to a space beyond, remains in the closet of the cinema's interior. Where, then, do we find Ahmed's 'oblique world' (2006: 161)? Is it in fantasy, in reflection, in transit, on the streets? What would it mean to admit to finding the queer world in the closet? The cinema and the dream act as promissory creators of 'worlds' of non-normative inhabitation. The queerness of lesbianism in *Circumstance* resides in the spatialising of desire onto fantasy spaces enabled by the cinema itself. Is there no desire beyond the image? As geographers Kath Browne and Eduarda Ferreira write, 'sexual and gender liberations are constructed in relation to the place where they occur, that is place matters to how we do politics, how we create our identities, relationships, desires and communities' (2016 [2015]: 2). Yet, the construction of 'place' cinematically – and through identification – complicates this very attachment.

In an early scene, Atafeh, on hearing a favourite song, declares that 'this song is orgasmic' and exhales with the sexual tones of the music with delight. This potential for 'orgasmic' sexual pleasure resides in the girls' relationship to a cultural fantasy of sexuality – the song, rather than the sensation, is experienced as pleasurable. Later, when Atafeh and Shireen proceed from *Milk*'s political oratory to a *Sex and the City* sex scene, the noises they perform seem to threaten the alpha male Joey. His mocking and over-the-top impersonation of Milk, which reduces politicised homosexuality to exaggerated campness, is replaced by the sign of discomfiture on his face. Exaggeration on Atafeh and Shireen's part – female sexuality reduced to sex – proves to be too much to bear. It is in this precise moment that the scene brings to the fore the erotic soundscape that has been lacking from the sexual reveries of the rest of the film. The hypersexualisation of the dubbing scenes exposes the alternative. As in *Nathalie . . .*, diegetic fakeness as such can, through enactment, still provide the representational platform for sexuality's visualisation. Shireen and Atafeh are not really making these noises during sex, not really touching each other – indeed, the *Sex and the City* scene that they imitate/perform is heterosexual. Their excessive performances of these audibly erotic sounds highlight and emphasise, by contrast, the hushing of their 'real' sex scenes. *Sex and the City*'s imitated erotic soundtrack maintains the aural transition into the immediately subsequent scene, in which they sit in the back of a taxi cab jokingly replicating the very sounds they made during dubbing. Flying in the face of restrictions on female outness – not of homosexuality specifically but simply of emergence into the urban sphere without male accompaniment – the girls are, as a consequence of this taxi ride, arrested by the morality police. This marks the tragic shift of the film: what awaits is prison and then patriarchal discipline. This is not a direct or literal consequence of the sexual sound-making, but its juxtaposition marks sexuality as dangerous at the level of plot progression. There is a clear link made between sexual liberation and punishment, just as there is in *Friend* (Wanari Kahiu, 2018), *My Days of Mercy* (Tali Shalom-Ezer, 2017) and *Disobedience* (Sebastián Lelio, 2017), three recent films that have delivered critiques of (Christian and Jewish) religious doctrines. The unrestrained sexuality projected by *Sex and the City*'s international reputation is mediated by Atafeh and Shireen and becomes in turn a raw evocation of their own sexual desire for one another. Culture is mediated by their imitating performance, which in turn shapes their sexual expression. The result of their sexual verbalisations here is punishment by the morality police – sexual physicality is, in this moment, forcibly contained within

Figure 3.3. Frame grab from *Circumstance*. Atafeh and Shireen are watched performing Americanness.

make-believe or imitation. Sexuality is given representation by the colour schemes and music of these erotic scenes, but ever mediated by the confinement of its potential to spaces of fantasy.

VEILING AND SURVEILLING

Circumstance manages a contradictory register of the promise of outness and its threat through a commentary on spatialised sexual identity. The sexual potential of Atafeh and Shireen's relationship might begin in urban fantasy but becomes both pleasurable and threatening when it comes into contact with the domestic. This threat is accentuated by the imposition of technology into the domestic realm. Having returned to the family home after a long absence, Mehran begins to take his place as patriarchal regulator of family life. This regulation increasingly takes the form of an uninhibited voyeurism, the first hint of which appears when a shot of Atafeh and Shireen dancing in Atafeh's bedroom to *American Idol* (Simon Fuller, 2002–) converts to a point-of-view shot, followed by a second shot revealing the POV's owner: Mehran, in the doorway (see Figure 3.3). Mehran's desire to prohibit and control the expression of sexuality – via other kinds of pleasure – in this way becomes mapped onto space. As I will argue in this section, it is significant, moreover, that this is a scene in which an American programme blares a cultural promise into the home through televisual technology.

Whilst in narrative terms *Circumstance* follows the romantic drama, aesthetically it summons other genres in which space intervenes more readily into the representation of desire. Mehran's surveilling gaze is enabled by space, echoing Michael Winterbottom's dystopian science-fiction film *Code*

Figure 3.4. Frame grab from *Circumstance*. The film takes on an aesthetic of surveillance.

46 (2003), in which, as Stacey writes, 'the desire for absolute control of sexuality' is 'mapped onto the regulation of mobility through surveillance in a zoned world' and 'the threat of the outside is given geographical location and physical presence' (2010: 158).[8] Surveillance increasingly takes hold of *Circumstance*'s aesthetic, setting the tone for patriarchal control of sexuality and instituting the visual zoning of space. As Shireen, Atafeh and their friends enter the barber's that is the front for the video store where they will decide on a pair of black-market films to dub, the light shining from within the building through the horizontal blinds against the dark foreground gives off a televisual effect that again reminds us of these young characters' vulnerability to surveillance (see Figure 3.4). As silhouettes, they look into the shop as if into an oversized television screen. They too are implicated, captured in the shot's wider framing. Moments such as this one invoke the capture of the still frame in which, as in Figure 3.4, the production of the gaze is isolated in a carefully constructed *mise en scène*. Our response to a shot that replicates the external production or reception of the film as cultural product (we are suddenly made aware of the technology that generates and disseminates the image) is to pause on what Laura Mulvey calls the 'there-ness and then-ness of the film's original moment, its moment of registration', which normally remains hidden by the '"here-and-now-ness" that the cinema asserts through its affinity with story-telling' (2006: 183). *Circumstance*, of course, continues to tell a story, of the hazards that face two young lovers whose cultural circumstances prevent their relationship. This moment allows for a shift in consciousness that highlights the ways in which technological mediation is adopted to construct the terms of this particular narrative. Increasingly, digital culture creates ways of understanding the mediation of sexuality through technology, a development that has itself been captured on film: in *Young and Wild* (Marialy Rivas, 2012),

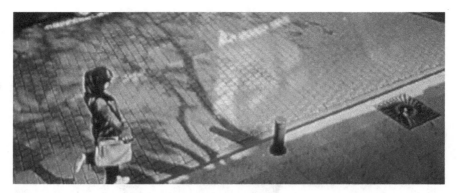

Figure 3.5. Frame grab from *Circumstance*. The source of the surveillance aesthetic is revealed.

the central character explores the mediation of her explicit sexual encounters through social media, while the protagonist of *Spider Lilies* (Zero Chou, 2008) is a 'web cam girl' who broadcasts her image across the Internet. The surveillance aesthetic of *Circumstance* functions to construct strict zones in which sexuality is made ostensibly available to Shireen and Atafeh but in which public disclosure remains an aesthetically insinuated menace.

The intimacy of the private sphere is dismantled by Mehran's paranoia. Like other films analysed in this book, *Circumstance* is instituted here into the mode of the family melodrama, in which, in films likes Douglas Sirk's *Written on the Wind* (1956) and *Imitation of Life* (1959) and Elia Kazan's *East of Eden* (1955), the home itself takes on a status of threat. As D.N. Rodowick writes of the melodrama's aesthetic, it does 'not so much *re*produce as *produce* the inner turmoil of the characters' (1991: 274, original emphasis). Eventually, this threat literally takes the form of a single image. Mehran's surveilling gaze is accentuated with gradually more and more extreme impositions. A crucial turning point in *Circumstance*'s narrative occurs when the flattened and distorted shots that have randomly appeared throughout the film are proven to be, in fact, actual CCTV. Re-working the melodrama, these mysterious shots give the domestic space itself a kind of paranoia. A visual metaphor becomes sinisterly realised. Mehran's imposition of technological surveillance reconstructs – and thus, in cinematic terms, constructs – the space of desire as one of paranoia. The melodrama's 'extreme compartmentalisation of the frame', as Rodowick puts it, serves to oppress the characters in their self-enforced locational isolation (Ibid.). The literal compartmentalisation of the frame in *Circumstance*'s CCTV footage represents Mehran's agony but imposes it onto Atafeh and Shireen, indexing the irreconcilability of social obligation and inner turmoil. The repetition of this aesthetic framing device turns the home into a space of public surveillance, leaving us pondering a further sinister question: just how many spaces have actually been under Mehran's watchful eye? Even public freedom is ambiguously threatened with precariousness. The distorted CCTV images cause confusion when they appear to have captured not only the family's home but also supposedly inaccessible spaces like the city's streets (see Figure 3.5). The private is made semi-public and the public is made sinisterly accessible in Mehran's voyeuristically enabled illusion of privacy. This blurring of lines between public and private distorts our perception of Atafeh and Shireen's sexualities as 'out'. This is not the hopeful outness projected onto American film (*Milk*) or fantasy of escape but a controlled publicity forced by patriarchal surveillance. Technology brings another culture into a domestic world (*American Idol*) and becomes a tool of punishment, used to restrict the freedom that the other culture promises (CCTV).

Shireen becomes the film's focal point for conflict between the inside and the outside. In a plot development that itself feels unbearably abrupt, Shireen escapes the threat of more serious punishment by the morality police by agreeing to marry Mehran. This is quite directly a punishment for both girls. The marriage exposes Shireen's spatial vulnerability as she is moved from the house of her uncle to the house of her husband. It is a newly incarnated site of cruelty, as the marriage becomes a space for Mehran's paranoia to take the form of horrific sexual violence. Of course, this is also vicariously the house of Shireen's lover, Atafeh, who still lives in the family home: ironically, the tragic imposition of heterosexual marriage brings them all under one roof. The household space becomes a violent one but it also, as Gayatri Gopinath writes of a series of films including Mehta's *Fire*, 'unwittingly generates homoeroticism' (2005: 15).

From the very beginning, Shireen is continually framed as the passive recipient of other characters' movements, appearing still in the frame while others explode into it. Repeatedly the bearer of the gaze, but only clandestinely, Shireen watches goings-on in both domestic realms through cracks in doorways. In one shot, Shireen, detached from the playful antics of Atafeh's liberal family, is filmed standing in the doorway with her hair blending into the dark room behind her so that all we can discern of her figure is a bare outline (see Figure 3.6). It is not a literal veil that affects our reading of Shireen's capacity for vision in this shot. The space *itself* veils her. The cinematic apparatus is revealed to be participating in a masquerade. Mary Ann Doane writes that the close-up of the veiled woman, in films from Josef von Sternberg's *Dishonoured* (1931), *The Scarlet Empress* (1934) and *The Devil Is a Woman* (1935) to Ridley Scott's *Blade Runner* (1982), is 'a site where the classical film acknowledges the precariousness of vision and simultaneously seeks to isolate and hence contain it' for 'the veil functions to visualize (and

Figure 3.6. Frame grab from *Circumstance*. Shireen is veiled by the *mise en scène*.

hence stabilize) the instability, the precariousness of sexuality' (1992: 46). In *Circumstance*, the literal veiling of Shireen marks her in contrast to Atafeh, for whom the veil is not necessitated by her home surroundings or familial hierarchy: both girls must tolerate and obey the restrictions of urban space, but in the home, Shireen's family requires her to wear the veil, while Atafeh's does not. The veil comes to represent the tussle over the right to freedom that the film's tag line announces. In a film whose conditions of production subject it to a particular set of problematics relating to appropriation and censure, Shireen's veiling is a potent symbol. The term itself is metaphorised by the titles of *Three Veils* (Rolla Selbak, 2011) and *Unveiled* (Angelina Maccarone, 2005); the latter's original German title *Fremde Haut* means 'Strange Skin'. The English translation of Maccarone's film draws attention to the process of veiling and unveiling through which the protagonist Fariba (Jasmin Tabatabai) sheds the veil when she is forced to leave Iran after her lesbian sexuality is discovered, and then dons another kind of veil, drag, when she enters Germany using a man's passport (see Aaron, 2012). *Unveiled* simplifies the notion of the veil as signifier of Islamic oppression, its choice of English title 'leveraging a colonialist representational history of white male desire to "life the veil" on Muslim women', as Galt and Schoonover write of the film's American marketing strategy (2016: 52). This becomes an aesthetic argument in relation to *Circumstance*. Doane writes that in classical films by von Sternberg and others, the veil mimics 'the grain of the film', allowing for the woman to be 'revealed as no longer simply the privileged object of the gaze in the cinema but the support of the cinematic image' (1992: 72). In *Circumstance*, the reverse happens: the grain of the film mimics the veil. Just as *Mulholland Drive* plays with the absence and presence of the figure of the lesbian, as I argued in Chapter 1, here we see again a consistent process of revealing and withholding. The film's complicated play of vision and outness is isolated and contained by this very image.

STYLISED FANTASIES OF ESCAPE

In the opening scene of *Circumstance*, the words, 'If you could be anywhere in the world, where would you be?' are accompanied by the anticipatory percussive rings of a tambourine and the composition of Farsi script against a black screen. The guitar riff that increases the intensity of the opening and brings light onto the screen is joined by close-up shots of the body of a dancer, spotlights accentuating a belly button, a hand, a mouth and the sequins of a skirt. The voice on the vocal track is finally attributed to the dancer, Atafeh. Re-watching the scene with hindsight, we are made unsure whether Atafeh is really singing: the centrality to the film of dubbing (*Sex and the City*) and lip-syncing (*American Idol*) prepares us for yet more simulations. Such a perversion of our suspension of disbelief in the authenticity of the female voice highlights the film's presentation of a masquerade of the feminine image through which, as Doane has famously written, 'womanliness' is revealed to be 'a mask which can be worn or removed' (1992: 25). The masquerade's 'exaggeration of femininity' (Ibid.) functions not only through clothing and demeanour but also through multiple levels of cultural appropriation: the mask that can be put on and taken off is a performance of a performance. The face we see in full in *Circumstance*'s opening scene is not that of the dancing Atafeh but of Shireen, whose posture is nonchalant as she holds a cigarette casually in her hand. If her metaphorical veiling through the apparatus in Figure 3.6 is a symptom of her interstitial positioning in the doorway *and* in the family, it emphasises not only what can be seen *of* Shireen but also what she is entitled to see. By contrast, in this fantasy scene beginning the film, she is allowed to evoke a *film noir* protagonist taking in the exquisite beauty of the *femme fatale* for the first time. Both characters over-perform their roles in the gaze structures set up by the sequence of shots that shift from one to the other: Atafeh in close-up, Shireen in medium shot. The abstracting shots of Atafeh's body are captured by a desiring and even fetishizing gaze (she is reduced visually to a sequence of body parts). However, this gaze is, unusually, female, instituting a 'tension between conventional framing and radical desire' that, as Mayer writes in her review, 'characterises the whole film' (2012: 97). The radicality of desire is highlighted by a kind of double masquerade on the part of both Atafeh (singer) and Shireen (voyeur), both of whom occupy not only particular roles of femininity but also particular relationships to space that they are unable to attain beyond the fantasy. Shireen is the less privileged of the two girls, her character arc seeing her forced into marriage

Figure 3.7. Frame grab from *Circumstance*.   **Figure 3.8**. Frame grab from *Circumstance*.
Shireen gazes . . .   . . . at Atafeh.

by familial and financial demands. She is most consistently the film's object of desire, subjected to the desiring gazes of both Atafeh and Mehran. The fact that it is Shireen who watches and Atafeh who dances further disrupts conventional assumptions of to-be-looked-at-ness and the coding of female subjects and objects. This tension is what defines the film's use of space, too, where domestic and institutional zones interact with the radical reclaiming of the city. Dreams such as this one are an extension of frequent mirror sequences and of the dubbing scene, all of which chart the girls' 'desire to be somewhere else' (Rich, 2011: 63).

What propels Shireen and Atafeh out of the masquerading, imitating space of the fantasy – orientalist performance meets Hollywood *noir* – is again the soundtrack, on which the music is smothered by the roll call of names anticipating the abrupt re-placement of Atafeh and Shireen into the grey-and-black tones of the schoolyard. But it is in this shot following that of Shireen's gaze (the immediate shot-to-shot juxtaposition of which can be seen in Figures 3.7 and 3.8) that Atafeh, erstwhile *femme fatale*, returns the gaze. Albeit across disparate shots, we now get the sustained image of Atafeh's face that was missing from the opening. The erotic red tones of their fantasy (Shireen's red lipstick, the colour filter) find remnants in the origami crane that, in close-up, passes discretely between their fingers in the school line. This momentary shift from one girl's gaze to the other's marks this as one of the most radical sequences of the film, an observation and claiming of the role of fantasy in lesbian representation. It is fantasy – precisely film *as* fantasy – that constructs, through the apparatus, the returned gaze to which desire's achievement is bound.

Later, another stylised fantasy of escape is juxtaposed with Shireen and Atafeh's giggling erotic play in the real world of Tehran. Their fantasy is initiated by Atafeh's desire to be a contestant on *American Idol*: 'the young can dream', mocks Shireen, and with her words is generated a dream sequence that is formed by the promise of the aesthetic, if not the literal location, of *Idol*'s version of American culture. The girls lie on their backs against a deep red sheet, and the camera swirls above their heads as they dream in verbal evocations of escape. Their words replicate the opening scene's disembodied dialogue, continually relying on the familiar stock of their elsewhere fantasy. The bar space that replicates the opening scene then shifts into a hotel room with floor-to-ceiling windows looking from a height over the sea, in which Atafeh and Shireen undress against a backdrop of a pale-blue ocean and white furniture. Unlike the Beirut location that is shot to look as much as possible like gritty Tehran, this is an anonymously pristine space. The smooth, groomed bodies of the girls are shot at the slow and seductive pace of a prettified Hollywood sex scene. Both Mayer and White have referred to the film's use of the stylised aesthetic of *The L Word* (Ilene Chaiken, 2004–9), a show that has been criticised for its glossy presentation of affluent middle-class West Hollywood: even as a landmark lesbian text, it offers a postfeminist version of the lesbian lifestyle based on consumption, the disintegration of class and gender politics and the disavowal of sexual activism (see Chambers, 2006). Allusion to the show is thus bound to be critiqued as shorthand for aestheticisation at the cost of representation. *Circumstance* draws here on a postfeminist economy of the image through which the prettification of Atafeh and Shireen's fantasies of sexual consummation into pristinely whitewashed spaces maintains the film's presentation of a sexual elsewhere. The possibility for out sexuality is defined by white role models (Sean Penn as Harvey Milk, Sarah Jessica Parker as Carrie Bradshaw). The return to the red sheets of the 'real' bedroom presents a contrastingly cluttered frame, highlighting a move away from the fantasy's depoliticising reach. The fantasy hotel demonstrates a de-cluttering of visual space as metaphor for a whiteness that is both sexually and spatially liberating. In 'reality', the girls are fully dressed as they kiss, and jerky camerawork abruptly dismantles the smooth transitions of the hotel-room fantasy. Awkward giggles and Shireen's joking words – 'Do you feel embarrassed?' – coincide instead with the noisy car horns of the city streets whose juxtaposition emphasises all the more the extent to which that fantasy really is 'elsewhere'.

As I explored in detail in Chapters 1 and 2, for psychoanalytic film theorists such as de Lauretis (1994), lesbianism must always be presented in cinema as part of a fantasy. Moreover, the predictability of surprise that attaches itself to lesbian desire in mainstream genre cinema is part of lesbianism's signification of 'sexual novelty' (White, 2018: 162). In the spatial terms of this chapter, lesbianism is always constituted in relation to an 'elsewhere'. Fantasy spaces become stand-ins for the sex that cannot occur in real space and time. It is only when Atafeh views her own encounter with Shireen on the CCTV footage of her brother's computer that their 'real' scenes actually *become* a kind of mediated fantasy, and all moments of intimacy threaten to have been technologically mediated all along. As Atafeh positions herself as voyeur, the film's networks of surveillance become distorted; just as Atafeh and Shireen over-perform their roles in fantasy, Atafeh here over-performs the paranoia of the gaze through the eye of the camera. She watches Shireen but cannot touch her even if she wanted to; in this moment, the apparatus of Mehran's voyeurism stands literally between them.

The tensions in the cosmopolitanism of *Circumstance*'s culture-shifting cinematography are evidenced in scenes of dreams, dubbing, lip-syncing and surveillance. This world-making also produces a fantasy of universality that calls for dominant visions to be drawn upon, confirmed by the postfeminist image economies of *Sex and the City* and *The L Word*. This is also the direct bid that filmmaker Shamim Sarif makes with *I Can't Think Straight* (2008) and *The World Unseen* (2007). The virtual worlds of *Circumstance* slip into the spaces between the seemingly prevalent concrete dichotomies between inside and outside, public and private. Indeed, part of what *Circumstance* offers is a citational lifestyle fantasy. The phrase with which the film starts – 'If you could be anywhere in the world, where would you be?' – is mobilised throughout, repeated at intervals first in fantasy (in the imagined bar/club), then in 'reality' (in Atafeh's bedroom), then in recording (as Mehran watches CCTV footage) and finally in a revengeful reprisal (as Mehran jadedly repeats the words to his wife as threat). The phrase is thus deployed as a marker that moves through the different spatial realms of *Circumstance*, enunciating a contradiction at the film's heart, the desire to substantiate an out lesbian world.

This chapter has explored how the city streets, and all they suggest (rebellion, freedom, lack of borders), accomplish *Circumstance*'s expression of sexuality while at the same time shoring up the identity politics that it depends on for its universalising humanist message. While queer promises to reside in the margins, the world it creates necessarily invokes identity elsewhere in a time yet to come (adulthood) or other space (USA). Throughout *Circumstance*, the cinematic apparatus is revealed to be participating in a masquerade of femininity, of spatial consistency and of sexual legitimacy. The film's central dubbing scene both mocks and pays tribute to the fact of sexual identity's cultural production. The film plays with the relationship between visibility and outness, isolating this tension in singular images in which the *mise en scène* veils Shireen or in which the characters participate in a televisual, then surveilling, aesthetic. Sexuality and its cultural promises are mediated through cultures of the elsewhere. The city *cannot* be sustained as the space of queer promise. The film's offer of 'freedom' for its characters as a 'human right' is constructed through a series of fantasy spaces and is thus simultaneously revealed to be itself a fantasy of a time beyond adolescence or a space beyond the nation. A fantasy of sexual identity as legitimately public is what is mobilised in signifiers of lesbian eroticism that move from *The L Word* to *Circumstance* via

the consumerism of *Sex and the City* and the politics of *Milk*. No such citational markers exist in *Water Lilies* (Céline Sciamma, 2007) and *She Monkeys*
(Lisa Aschan, 2011), the films that I explore in the next chapter, in which
I consider those lapses in identity and knowledge produced by adolescent
bodies in a precarious state of desire's discovery. In these films, what distorts
the assumptions of sexual identity is the shifting into a queerly ambiguous
(and ambiguously lesbian) potential. I explore the lingering 'unsaid' of queer
eroticism in terms of affective potential, arguing that desire is produced by
the ambivalent intimacies that reside in the spaces between touch and speech.

CHAPTER 4

In-between Touch: Queer Potential in Water Lilies *and* She Monkeys

The adolescent protagonist of *Water Lilies* (Céline Sciamma, 2007), Marie (Pauline Acquart), strikes a deal with Floriane (Adèle Haenel), the captain of the local synchronised swimming team. Marie will avert parental suspicion by playing chaperone to the older girl's prohibited sexual rendezvous, in return for the opportunity to accompany the team in the pool for training sessions and on the bus to competitions. *Water Lilies* combines the spectacle of performance (its opening is accompanied by the extravagant 'Dies Irae' from Giuseppe Verdi's *Requiem* [1874]) with the comedy of adolescent inadequacy (Marie tries to build up her muscles to join the team by lifting boxes of laundry detergent) and the muted disappointment of unrequited desire (Floriane's reciprocation only occurs in moments of strategic necessity). In the first of a pair of scenes that evoke the sensory intensity of this unspoken desire, Marie is granted permission to try on a sparkly 'synchro' costume in Floriane's bedroom. Jokingly donning the costume over her clothes in a reverse striptease, she falls onto the bed giggling with Floriane. The promise of attainment (of the costume, of its connotations of inclusion in the group and of parity with Floriane) is sabotaged by silliness. In the immediately subsequent scene, Marie, willing to do anything for attention and proximity, steals a rubbish bag that Floriane has just deposited in a bin. As Marie returns to her own bedroom and draws out a series of Floriane's discarded objects, the impossible physicality of her desire unfolds through sight, touch, taste and smell. The camera tilts in close-up from Marie's inhalation of the scent of a makeup-stained piece of cotton wool, to her gentle caress of a scrunched-up note, to a perishing apple core held tentatively in her hands. The camera moves with the apple back up to Marie's mouth. In a prolonged close-up shot, she chews, winces and then brings the back of her palm up to her mouth as if to retch. Marie's desire for Floriane holds within it both appreciation and disgust, experienced here on a multi-sensory level. The juxtaposition of these two scenes evokes first spectacle and playfulness and then abjection and misguided intimacy.

Friendships unfold as transaction; infatuation coexists with narcissism. In *She Monkeys* (Lisa Aschan, 2011), Emma (Mathilda Paradeiser) and Cassandra

Figure 4.1. Frame grab from *She Monkeys* (Lisa Aschan, 2011). Emma (Mathilda Paradeiser) is seen watching intently.

Figure 4.2. Frame grab from *She Monkeys*. Cassandra (Linda Molin) balances atop a horse in a display of mastery and balance.

(Linda Molin) are rivals for a coveted place in an equestrian vaulting team, in which challenging gymnastic movement is made all the more precarious upon a moving horse.[1] From an early scene in which newcomer Emma contemplates the performance of star gymnast Cassandra, to a final reversal in which a wounded Cassandra must watch her protégé in the limelight, the desire for sporting and sexual triumph is sustained through competition. Desire meets and is confused with other affects such as envy and disgust, all of which attach, sometimes simultaneously, to objects that do not always seem to recognise or permit them. The film's languid scenes reveal desire's potential but rarely its achievement. Its long shots of wide-open Scandinavian landscapes and brawling musical score set the scene for Western showdowns rather than close-up sporting montages. The film's director, Lisa Aschan, has remarked that she 'wanted every scene to be a duel' (in Swash, 2012), and the film stages the girls' relationship as a series of competitive encounters in which interactions are amplified in their intensity but precarious in their intimacy. In *She Monkeys*, the desire for sporting inclusion and success veils an ambivalent desire for the love object, with potentially abject results. In this chapter, I explore the erotic potential of those ambiguous intimacies that reside in the spaces between bodies, asking what happens to that potential when it is generated but immediately contained by the negotiations of control.

Water Lilies and *She Monkeys* are two in a series of transnational, female-directed films released within a ten-year period in which we see a mode of filmmaking that is saturated by desire but not defined by desire's labelling. In *Thirteen* (Catherine Hardwicke, 2003), girls urge each other to push boundaries on the surface of the skin. In *Mosquita y Mari* (Aurora Guerrero, 2012), a close friendship is eroticised in moments of *almost* touching. In *The Falling* (Carol Morley, 2015), eroticism cuts across coded practices, as dispersed affects rather than object-oriented desires pass between adolescent schoolgirls through the 'fainting spell' that inexplicably swells into an episode of mass psychogenic illness. In her expansive reading of *Water Lilies*, Emma Wilson writes that Sciamma's film 'has its own sensorium and this is tightly aligned with the perspective, the point of view, the corporeal sensation and affective state of its protagonist Marie' (2014: 212). Coming into desire is described here by Wilson as a process that transpires through sensory abundance. Katharina Lindner, in her reading of *She Monkeys*, considers the film's 'sense-ibilities' through a theorisation of queer processes of cinematic embodiment (2017b: 122). Lindner highlights the apparent clash of registers that are brought together by the film's queer tactility. Both Wilson and Lindner powerfully re-centre the body by theorising desire through affect. Whilst I make the comparable claim in this chapter that the queerness of lesbian desire can be evoked as a series of affects outside of figurative norms, the interiorised identifications generated by such affects also call to be read through psychoanalytic language that moves beyond the testimony of the physical. In this way, I consider the potentially fraught and uncomfortable notions of ambivalence, attachment and envy that have been investigated by queer theorists such as Lauren Berlant (2012b) and Eve Kosofsky Sedgwick (2007). The chapter engages the affective ambiguities that occur when tactility is compromised while other sensory monitors, such as the gaze, are intensified. Here we find the queer affects produced by moments and movements in-between touch.

In Chapter 2, I addressed desires conveyed on-screen through space and fantasy rather than through the notion of sexuality as defined by sexual activity. In Chapter 3, I argued that the figuration of lesbianism is evoked in *Circumstance* by shifting adolescent desires but is left as a possibility to be found in a fantasy of 'elsewhere' beyond adolescence and the nation state. *Water Lilies* and *She Monkeys* make no such promises or gestures, the age and status of their characters forging instead transitory modes of meaning. The cultural and social projects of gay and lesbian liberation movements could be articulated as the desire for desires to be taken seriously. *Water Lilies* and *She Monkeys* divert this call for seriousness, refusing to offer a discernible movement from the closet to outness, a coming-of-age narrative to cling to with the optimism of romantic satisfaction or identity formation.[2] The precariousness and unpredictability of *Water Lilies'* and *She Monkeys'* homoerotic drives – their erratic visibilities – threaten to re-figure the lesbian in the discourse of the passing phase, a form through which, as Whitney Monaghan argues, 'queer girls are temporalised' in popular culture (2016: 5). However, an erotics of friendship need not supersede nor dissolve an erotics of lesbianism, the need for whose 'sexiness' remains politically charged but so often theoretically overdetermined.[3] In *She Monkeys*, intense gazes are abundant but frequently unreturned; touches are insistent in their brief moment of contact but then found to be all too fleeting. Slowness and interruption build up a throughline of possibility that is erotically, if frustratingly, charged with suspense. The film thus exhibits a homoerotic, or, following my argument in Chapters 2 and

3, we might now say queer, affect. This chapter allows the films to remain in the conceptual space between lesbianism and queerness, acknowledging the political and theoretical tensions that arise in the slippage between those terms and their connotations. Eroticism is found here in the intertwining of identification, idealisation and desire. Heightened in these registers because of its uncertain execution in the diegesis, it is always left in anticipation of a narrative guarantee by what Annamarie Jagose calls the 'structuring mechanisms of lesbian invisibility' (2002: 2).

The discipline of the sports genre is made unruly and unpredictable by its juxtaposition with undercurrents of childishness and animalism that resist narrative impulses towards growth and seriousness. By gesturing towards the sports genre but infusing it with the capriciousness of adolescence, the worlds of *She Monkeys* and *Water Lilies* temper discipline with play. We cannot depend on the consistency of either one, any more than we can force an uncomplicated reading of the film through the tropes of lesbian cinema: desire and attachment are stubbornly infused with frustration and disappointment. In both cases, physicality produces not result but potential. Thereby troubling the notion of seriousness as a requisite of a triad of possible generic affiliations – sports, teen, lesbian – the body in these films is a site not only of discipline but of play; not only of sexuality but of violence; and not only of attachment but of ambivalence.

BODIES IN MOTION

The sports film often thrives on the closeted eroticism of the changing room: overt lesbian films in the genre such as *Thin Ice* (Fiona Cunningham-Reid, 1995) or *Signature Move* (Jennifer Reeder, 2017) are marginal and rare, and the pleasures for lesbian viewers of *A League of Their Own* (Penny Marshall, 1992), *Bend It Like Beckham* (Gurinder Chadha, 2002) and *Whip It* (Drew Barrymore, 2009) are induced by vicarious modes of spectatorship (see Kabir, 1998; Whatling, 1997). The competitiveness that characterises the team cultures documented in these films does not just dilute, but rather has the potential to augment, the homoeroticism that is also a feature of those spaces. The quintessential lesbian sports film *Personal Best* (Robert Towne, 1982), on the other hand, is structured around the inevitability of competition between two female lovers competing in the same athletic discipline. The romance between Tori (Patrice Donnelly) and Chris (Mariel Hemingway) begins with an arm wrestle in a now-famous scene of foreplay whose sweaty, erotic potential seems to predominate, in critical recollection, over later sex scenes (see Ellsworth, 1988; Straayer, 1984; Williams, 1986). In some ways, this coheres with heteronormative wishful thinking. *Personal Best*'s trailer makes no reference to the romance at the heart of the film. Yet, reading such a marketing strategy against the grain, we can see that what the film's trailer foregrounds is the competition between the two women, which, as suggested by this arm-wrestling scene, is what in turn provides the eroticism that does not need to be accounted for by sex.

She Monkeys merges these competitive tropes of the sports film with the gendered performance of balletic movement (see Lindner, 2011). In the voyeuristic opening scene, we watch the vaulting team rehearse. The heavy breaths of the balancing young gymnasts are synchronised with the pounding hooves of the horse as it circles the barn. Two girls, with identical postures in uniforms of grey and red, hold on to one another so that their bodies become entangled and seem to create a single shifting figure. Emma stares from the sidelines as Cassandra stands atop the horse with her partner's hand on her waist and her own arms outstretched (see Figures 4.1 and 4.2). Janet Wolff writes of classical ballet that it has emphasised 'in its commitment to line, weightlessness, lift and extension an ethereal presence rather than a real corporeality' (1997: 95). Cassandra's figure in the opening scene captures this same weightlessness: she is literally lifted by the moving horse, and by the camera, which disengages the performer from the ground below her. This necessary ethereality – the body made so light and delicate as to be lifted into the air – codes the movements in this film as conventionally feminine, just like those of synchronised swimming, the only Olympic sport to be restricted to one gender in competition. Moreover, in *She Monkeys*, dance mirrors the controversial 'phasing' of lesbian desire. The dancers are never rooted to the floor, just as the film can never be grounded in the reliable physicality of sexual consummation.

Negotiating the interplay between the ethereal and the corporeal, *She Monkeys* meditates on the ambivalence that is produced through the unattainability underpinning the fascination with the star. In another early scene, shortly after the girls have met, we witness their first proper exchange. Cassandra pushes Emma's thighs into the splits: 'Focus!' she shouts. In the next frame, as they proceed with their exercises, Emma is the other girl's slightly belated mirror, her body moving only in accordance with Cassandra's command. This silent regime will continue throughout the film. From the start, Emma and Cassandra's friendship is forged through instruction and discipline, first physical and then emotional. The narrative proceeds tentatively from scenes of competition and aggression to those of suspended affection – and then back again. The anticipation of touch is just as tentative; the bodily control associated with gymnastic feats requires a hold that is given then withdrawn.

The significant tension that defines my interest in these films is brought about through this almost simultaneous generation and control of potential, be it sexual or sporting. While *Personal Best* presents an almost constant spectacle of physical prowess, both *She Monkeys* and *Water Lilies* put their isolated scenes of athletic performance into tension with everyday activities. Seeking to champion the failure that 'allows us to escape the punishing norms that discipline behaviour and manage human development', Jack Halberstam argues that success is tied up in the regime of growth towards a 'serious' adulthood (2011: 3).[4] Demonstrations of muscular physicality find space alongside interludes of mundane adolescent summer play. Throughout *Water Lilies*, Marie's friendship with her best friend Anne (Louise Blachère) signals a nostalgia for childhood, from Anne's insistence that she buy a Happy Meal at McDonald's to their comically apprehensive discussion, in the same scene, of the relative sizes of their breasts. In *She Monkeys'* dusty, brawling *mise en scène*, figuratively colourful interludes come from Emma's little sister Sara (Isabella Lindquist). Sara, clownish and endearing, is dismissed from her swimming class for wearing just bikini bottoms and for leaving her undeveloped chest bare; the necessity for concealment secures the body as a staging of inappropriateness (indicating that there is something to conceal). She is subsequently intent on wearing clothes for older girls, insists on wearing a fake tattoo on her arm and misunderstands the affection of her babysitter. Such encounters unsettle not just the biological imperative towards reproductive maturity but also the social imperative to grow into maturity as seriousness.

Sara stands for childish, undisciplined discoveries of tactile pleasure. Emma and Cassandra's relationship, meanwhile, is infused with the 'punishing norms' that deliver us in Halberstam's words 'from unruly childhoods to orderly and predictable adulthoods' (Ibid.).[5] Yet, unpredictability lurks even in their highly disciplined interactions. Speech is often entirely abandoned in favour of other sensory expressions; desires remain unspoken. This is markedly distinct from the verbal wit of Ellen Page's titular protagonist in *Juno* (Jason Reitman, 2007), for instance, about which Sciamma has remarked that 'everyone talks in the same clever way [. . .] and I didn't believe that this girl was sixteen' (in Oumano, 2010: 53). *Water Lilies* leaves us pondering these inarticulate desires through non-verbal affective states: the intensity of verbal silence is made apparent by the aural dominance of Para One's musical score and the background chatter of nameless girls, while the few very brief adult speaking roles are reduced to a 'trace element' (Palmer, 2011: 34–5). These traces extend into other films of this period. When Ginger (Elle Fanning) of Sally Potter's *Ginger and Rosa* (2012) visually explodes with ugly tears as she cries 'I'll explode if I say it', we understand her articulation of the dual possibility of both the verbalisation and containment of difficult feelings:

in this case, her father's affair with her best friend, movingly explored by Sophie Mayer in her account of 'British Cinema as a Runaway Girl' (2016). In *Attenberg* (Athina Rachel Tsangari, 2010), two friends' devotion to nature programmes instils in them a bizarre tendency to use their bodies to create animalistic shapes and noises, the tactile but pre- or anti-verbal a way of surmounting desire's excess, of writing it on the body. In *Dogtooth* (Yorgos Lanthimos, 2009), carnal, animalistic behaviour is a mechanism to deal with familial imprisonment. In *She Monkeys*, the family dog subjected to Emma's formidable training whistle demonstrates yet another domain of control. The monkeys used as metaphors in the film's peculiar title are, on the other hand, animals that are routinely classed as erratic; playful smiles guard misread signs of anxiety and fear and precursors to violence.[6] They share Halberstam's 'wondrous anarchy of childhood' (2011: 3), a space and time the film opens up to tease and resist the disciplining and reining in of desire by the narrative's central premise. Juxtaposing the animal, the child and the adolescent, *She Monkeys* and *Water Lilies* remove us from everyday cycles of obedience and hierarchy; rejecting the classroom as the primary space of adolescence, the films' summertime settings extend instead a temporal and spatial dreaminess. Like in *Porcupine Lake* (Ingrid Veninger, 2017) or *My Summer of Love* (Pawel Pawlikowski, 2004), whose title announces its temporal register, the experience of first love and attachment is rendered out of sync by its withdrawal from the regimes of classroom experience.

The cinematic conditions of adolescent life are reduced to an irrational, emotionally realist but socially fantastical 'sensorium' (Wilson, 2014: 212): desires are in high definition whilst everything else fades into irrelevance. What makes *She Monkeys* and *Water Lilies* remarkable is a refusal to allow the resolution to structure the film's narrative journey. In her essay 'Lesbian Minor Cinema', Patricia White reads two films, *Flat Is Beautiful* (Sadie Benning, 1998) and *Portrait of a Young Girl at the End of the 60s in Brussels* (Chantal Akerman, 1994), that allow for 'representations of the juvenile that mark the marginalization of lesbian in relation to a series of terms including gay, women, feminist, queer' (2008: 415). White reads as full of potential what could otherwise be read as failure: lesbians have 'deployed the *minor* in a range of culturally successful ways', she writes (Ibid.: 425). Like 'minor', 'queer' is another term that, for White, 'inflects rather than opposes the dominant' (Ibid.: 411). Through the usage of these two terms in alignment, White does not pit the lesbian against queer, but rather gestures at lesbianism's queer potential. Thus, she lays out the grounds for a mutual, rather than merely substitutive, relationship between the two terms. Queerness here rejects both the 'phase' *and* the coming-out narrative, refusing 'predictive narratives in favour of an unrealized potential' (Ibid.). Not 'predictable', but 'predictive'. White's choice of term here is critical. Not only do we see a refusal of the singular moment of identity enunciation, but also a refusal to predict it. Unruliness and unpredictability: these are the terms that, for Halberstam and White respectively, unite the queerness and childishness that characterise *She Monkeys* and *Water Lilies*. The films both finish in the lingering uncertainty of either romantic or sporting triumph. Where adolescence meets competition, a space emerges that holds off potential, resists heteronormativity, heightens the 'phasing' of desire as a provocative risk.

Nothing but a Mirage

Coming into desire is a process that transpires through sensory abundance. Wilson observes of *Water Lilies* that 'we enter [Marie's] world at a moment of heightened receptivity, as Marie knows desire for the first time viewing Floriane emerging from the pool water' (2014: 212). This 'heightened receptivity' is what provides our entry as spectators into the scene of desire. This is enforced by the multi-sensory drama of the film's first scene, which jolts us from meditative observations of girls changing and chattering to the abrupt and jarringly loud opening of Verdi's 'Dies Irae'. Aurally besieged, Marie's gaze is lifted and we follow it as the soundtrack is adapted to the flirty dance of a synchronised swimming routine. The spectacle of the scene conjures the set pieces of Busby Berkeley-choreographed musicals such as *Gold Diggers of 1933* (Mervyn LeRoy, 1933) and *Footlight Parade* (Lloyd Bacon, 1933).[7] In *42nd Street* (Lloyd Bacon, 1933), as Lyn Phelan observes, Berkeley's choreography produces 'a curious intensification of both female fleshiness and abstract uniformity' (2000: 169). With precisely this effect, *Water Lilies* matches the rhythm of the music with the dolphin-like dives of the swimmers, the flash of flesh against water and the sharp movements of their angular limbs. The film's spectacular scenes of synchronised swimming routines, reminiscent of Berkeley's choreography, connect the figurative and the abstract in shows of pattern and flesh.

The film's audience is aurally aligned with the diegetic audience in the pool, the acoustics of the swimming pool reducing Verdi's foreboding 'Day of Wrath' to the soundtrack's echoey recording of scratchy strings and synthesised vocals. But when Marie's eyes widen in close-up, a shared soundscape is subordinated to her fixed gaze on a singular figure emerging from the pool. Floriane is glorious in bright red and orange, with tightly slicked hair and an arm waving straight up in the air. As the object of the film's first break from the ensemble shot, she is the sole focus for several seconds of screen time (see Figures 4.3 and Figure 4.4 and note their almost exact replication of the gaze structures of Figures 4.1 and 4.2).[8] The water beads that glisten on

Figure 4.3. Frame grab from *Water Lilies* (Céline Sciamma, 2007). Marie (Pauline Acquart) applauds as if on behalf of the whole audience.

Figure 4.4. Frame grab from *Water Lilies*. Floriane (Adèle Haenel) receives her applause.

Figure 4.5. Frame grab from *Water Lilies*. Marie tastes the water that is her connection to Floriane.

Figure 4.6. Frame grab from *Water Lilies*. Marie finally shares the space of the shower with Floriane.

Figure 4.7. Frame grab from *Water Lilies*. Marie watches on as Floriane and François (Warren Jacquin) frolic in the shower.

Floriane's flesh give her an other-worldly sheen and bring the physical texture of water to the fore. Focused here by the voyeuristic gaze of Marie at just one of the performers, what Barbara Creed calls an 'excess of beauty' in the musical genre heightens but then condenses desire (2009: 92). In the changing room, the multiple chattering girls are homogenised by a swathe of colour, but through Marie's gaze they become singularly objectified via Floriane. Moving beyond the realm of desires in fantasy that I charted in earlier chapters, here desire is an affective trace left in the watery space between touch.

As Marie showers following her first invitation into the pool for the synchro team's practice, she sticks her tongue out to taste the water that drips down, as if tasting her connection to Floriane (see Figure 4.5). Later, when Marie and Floriane share this same shower (Figure 4.6), the spatial and textural consistency recalls the more obvious sexual potential of an earlier scene in which Marie has watched Floriane kiss a boy in this very spot (Figure 4.7). The lesbian potential of Marie's desire is non-sexual, even disappointingly so, but remains affectively powerful. Wilson describes the way in which, 'with whatever abrasion, Floriane opens Marie's world and reorganizes her senses' (2014: 213). Significantly, Wilson is willing to acknowledge this abrasiveness even as sensory reorganisation signals something that we might read as deeply romantic.

She Monkeys' opening scene, introduced above, is almost exactly replicated in the gaze structures of Sciamma's film. Lifted above the ground and the rest of the team, Cassandra is set up, from the voyeuristic opening scene, as Emma's singular object of desire (see again Figures 4.1 and 4.2). Ethereal and seemingly weightless as a dancer, her body is lifted into air not only by the requisites of the sport in which she participates but by the film's framing of her. Created partly *by* desire, moreover, she is a 'mirage, a shaky anchor' (Berlant, 2012b: 6). The illusion referenced here by Berlant's metaphor for desire's form becomes, on the screen, optical. It is only Emma's voyeurism that constructs Cassandra as a desired object. Produced by the cinematic sequencing of Emma's gaze, Cassandra does not exist *outside* of Emma's desire for her. This object of desire is established through a spectacle of physical prowess, but also through the star's isolation within the team and her unattainability: she is an object of voyeurism but not of touch.

Insistently playing with the (shaky) anchoring of desire in the body and in the gaze, both films explore the tensions that arise when voyeuristic idealisations are not satisfied corporeally or, when they are, are infused with painful affects. If we must all discover that our object of desire is really nothing but a mirage, *She Monkeys* and *Water Lilies* evoke precisely the frustration that is thus produced. Berlant writes of desire that it

> describes a state of attachment to something or someone, and the cloud of possibility that is generated by the gap between an object's specificity and the needs and promises projected onto it. This gap produces a number of further convolutions. Desire visits you as an impact from the outside, and yet, inducing an encounter with your affects, makes you feel as though it comes from within you; this means that your objects are not objective, but things and scenes that you have converted into propping up your world, and so what seems objective and autonomous in them is partly what your

desire has created and therefore is a mirage, a shaky anchor. Your style of addressing those objects gives shape to the drama with which they allow you to re-encounter yourself. By contrast, love is the embracing dream in which desire is reciprocated: rather than being isolating, love provides an image of an expanded self, the normative version of which is the two-as-one intimacy of the couple form. (Ibid.)

My discussion of the films' regimes of competition, silliness and unpredictability has begun to demonstrate the affective and theoretical 'convolutions' that are produced by *desire*'s dissatisfying refusal to be represented *as love*. What follows in this chapter's second half examines this refusal in dialogue with works that theorise envy, attachment and the ambivalent pathways to development that characterise the phasing of queer/lesbian adolescence.

She Monkeys affectively occupies the space of what Berlant calls that 'cloud of possibility'. The film presents as contradictory, frustrating and painful those needs that accompany desire and its 'promises'. Emma's entry into the vaulting team is the entry into a world of desire. Yet, this is a 'sensorium' – to re-quote Wilson's term (2014: 212) – not just of desire, but of frustration and ambivalence. Cassandra and Emma by turns tease, trick and physically hurt each other. Their interactions are abundantly physical from the start, and yet outbursts of feeling fall flat, as if muted by what Catherine Wheatley observes in the film's 'pale half-light that makes everything spectral' (2012: 76). A sole utterance of the words 'I love you' remains unanswered, taking place in the shallow water of a beach at dusk. The barn in which they train, and thus its world of discipline, is evoked by this sandy beachscape. The importance of space in the representation of desire and sexuality means not only the coding of *particular* spaces, but also the cinematic rendering of those spaces as erotic through the structuring of the *mise en scène*. The sand of the barn, for instance, is not inherently erotic, but evokes a motif of colour and texture whose repetition across space and time generates an affective charge. The mystical half-light shrouds this scene in a disorienting dreaminess. This is an aesthetic and narrative state that characterises the temporal disjunctures of *Summertime* (Catherine Corsini, 2015) and *Lovesong* (So Yong Kim, 2016), both of which pull their (adult) protagonists out of everyday cycles of responsibility and into the affective reach of desire. In both of these films, the rural landscape provides this potential for both disorientation and escape. In *She Monkeys*, the fairytale ambience of the Swedish coast meets what Fiona Handyside calls the beach's potential for 'radical and transformative encounters' (2014: 5). But this particular beach scene provides, rather than the pleasure of encounter, the pain of it: the verbal promise of romance ('I love you') is met with the induction of physical repulsion, as Cassandra pulls away from the vulnerability of her words to place a slimy jellyfish in Emma's hands. The animalistic unpredictability discussed in the last section permeates even a prospectively romantic scene such as this. The desire for, and fear of, intimacy is countered by the pain that always threatens to have been held within it.

Cassandra's touch has strictly been one of discipline until the arrival on the beach of Jens (Adam Lundgren), one of two boys invited for a double date that is provoked by Emma's playful banter and derailed first by Cassandra's indifference and then by her sabotage. When Emma's liaison with Jens promises – or rather threatens – to become sexual, Cassandra instructs Emma to humiliate the boy, stealing his clothes and abandoning him. His brief appearance serves only to reveal the potential for jealousy to provide the evidence of desire. Running from the beach to a roadside bus shelter, the girls sit side by side and hold hands, the frenzied aftermath of Jens' humiliation inducing more proximity. It is the first time the girls' hands have touched on-screen outside of the regimes of sport. As if to announce the inappropriate-ness of this moment of undisciplined contact, the scene quickly departs from the potential of intimacy to the bluntness of transaction, as Cassandra hands over half of the cash that she has retrieved from Jens's wallet. The potential for Emma's heterosexual liaison has been both enabled by Cassandra and curtailed by her. To paraphrase Berlant, Cassandra has become the prop for Emma's world (2012b: 6).

Yet, Cassandra cannot maintain the affirming role that makes this world a pleasurable one in which to reside; her professions of love turn quickly to punishment. *She Monkeys* makes desire precarious. Toying with its pro-tagonist's potential defences, it questions the capability not only to generate but to sustain desire. First, the film depicts Emma's excessive idealisation of Cassandra, who is exalted as a singular figure of excellence in the frame. Emma will thus defend against the possibility of envy through a voyeuristic enhancement of Cassandra's position: how could she be compared with one so radiant?[9] Even a desiring gaze signals a painful gap between voyeur and spectacle, between subject and object of desire. And yet, of course, idealisa-tion all too easily tips over into envy. Cassandra becomes in Melanie Klein's terms a '"persecutor", and on to her is projected the subject's envious and critical attitude' (1987 [1956]: 217–8). Finally, Emma's voyeuristic desire transitions into the sense that Cassandra has something she wants; she thus finds the 'envious impulse' to 'take away' or 'spoil' what Cassandra has – her success, her role in the team (Ibid.: 212). This is the attitude that puts the violent phantasies of Kleinian theories of child development onto the screen in the form of painful affects of competition.[10] Envy becomes a ward against excessive feeling.

Such a relationship seems surely impossible to sustain. Just as Berlant warns (2012b: 6), the drama of desire is performed as a mutual encounter but revealed to be an isolating dream which has preoccupied many on-screen narratives of adolescence. In *Heavenly Creatures* (Peter Jackson, 1994), the jealous and competitive relationship between teenage girls is given shape in a dream world through which Pauline (Melanie Lynskey) and Juliet (Kate Winslet) share their erotic and violent fantasies. *Highly Strung* (Sophie Laloy, 2009) turns the school arena into a stage of obsessive competition and artistic sabotage whilst *Breathe* (Mélanie Laurent, 2014) is about the unsustainability of competitive friendship without violence. For Sedgwick, the 'Kleinian infant experiences a greed whose aggressive and envious component is already perceived as posing a terrible threat both to her desired objects and to herself' (2007: 633). This infantile experience gets played out again and again in adult relationships and, as Sedgwick tells us, through affect; in *Water Lilies* and *She Monkeys*, as I argue, this affect is what creates the foundation of the film. But if, for Sedgwick, 'the resulting primary anxiety is an affect so toxic that it probably ought to be called, not anxiety, but dread' (Ibid.), how does the film weather the storm of this affective toxicity and still leave room for desire?

DISAPPOINTING EVIDENCE

In discourses of lesbian representation now familiar from previous chapters, sex becomes a structuring presence even in the form of notable absence. In *Water Lilies*, sex as 'sex scene' becomes a transaction of necessity. Every scene of physical intimacy between Marie and Floriane is juxtaposed with a subsequent scene in which Marie watches Floriane with François. In one shot, the girls' hands and wrists are in the frame, touching for the first time as Floriane writes her address on Marie's palm. The close-up produces an intense affect of potential intimacy made erotic not only because of the framing of skin on skin, but also because of the absence in the frame of any social indicators of separation that distinguish the rest of the film. Even here, their hands touching as they lie on the bed, the frame divides them and creates a visual obstacle to diegetic intimacy. In the two-shot that follows, their hands no longer touch. In the very next scene, Marie must wait alone for Floriane in a long shot of a bleak grey car park that emphasises the abrupt suspension of close-up affection. The transaction they have made – for Marie to be allowed into the team as resident voyeur but only if she chaperones Floriane's dates with François – is put into stark relief as the physical intimacy of their touching hands is superseded by Marie's lonely waiting. Later, again, physical intimacy between the girls is vicarious, produced only in conversations they have about boys: Floriane's verbalisations of her sexuality produce temporary and short-lived physical manifestations of erotic potential.

Floriane is figured as the film's object of desire through the gaze of Marie, the gaze of the viewer and the gaze of the boys who remain silent and sidelined except as verifiers of Floriane's desirability. It is the twist of the film when she reveals that she is in fact still a virgin and that her reputation for sexuality as activity is an affectation. Rather than an act of desire, sex becomes for Floriane a necessity for the maintenance of this façade. 'I want you to be the first. I want you to remove it for me. Then it would be real,' Floriane demands of Marie. Her request heralds Marie's first visualisation of her desire for Floriane. Tracing with her finger the outline of lipstick from a much earlier mocking kiss Floriane has planted on the glass of Marie's window, Marie then kisses the same spot on the other side of the glass to fashion two kisses, left slightly out of sync. The kiss itself endures only as an illusion. Even once realised, the sexual transaction remains unnamed: the scene in which it is initiated is introduced by Marie's obscure agreement to do 'what you wanted'. The girls go through the motions of the breaking of the hymen, itself an antiquated and irrelevant token of virginity, and then make the bed with quaintly patterned sheets. The ring of the doorbell sounds the disruption of Marie's attempt to turn this into a scene of further intimacy and re-introduces François, the absent third term of the triangulated procedure. Marie's best friend Anne remains sidelined by the promise and beauty that Floriane holds for Marie. This scene is cruelly juxtaposed with the arrival of François at Anne's house in order to use her for the sex that we are led to believe has again been withheld by Floriane. Marie and Anne are paralleled as unrequited lovers, both perfunctorily utilised by their objects of desire. It is together, as friends holding hands on the bed, that they consummate the intimacy they have both sought elsewhere. Thus, just as in *Foxfire* (Annette Haywood-Carter, 1996) and its remake (Laurent Cantet, 2012), female friendship is used to defend against male bullying and interference, even if within it are created chronic systems of competition and control (see Kearney, 2002).

Even as these films rest on the intensification of touch, the critical task here is to avoid submitting to either the promise, or disappointment, of sex as the evidence of desire. We are always left just out of reach of the consummation of desire that we cling to as the narrative convention is resisted. *She Monkeys* eschews altogether the necessity for narrative climax in the form of sexual climax. Midway through the film, and in a transitional point of the narrative, we witness an embrace that we might habitually presume will lead to sex. Spending the evening together, without parents, at Emma's house, the girls lean into each other's arms. The scene's prelude combines the humour of Sara's childishness with the tension of Emma and Cassandra's competitiveness, the force of discipline and the seeking of tactility, the flippancy of giggles and the anticipation of arousal. A precarious moment with a

Figure 4.8. Frame grab from *She Monkeys*. Cassandra prepares Emma for sleep.

shotgun is a false alarm but hints at violent potential. Sport, dance, play and threat all take their place. The girls' embrace in an unexpected slow dance is but a temporary tender punctuation in a scene of childish play; swiftly, they leave each other's romantic hold to wrestle in a fit of giggles so feverish that Emma wets herself. Desire in this moment is made grotesque just as it is made explicit. Following this first breakdown of bodily control, Emma must then endure another: as if on demand, she throws up at the precise moment that Cassandra asks her if she feels sick. Just as in training she was the belated mirror of Cassandra's poise, here her physical breakdown is instructed by Cassandra. In the slow movements that follow, there is something ritualistic about the way in which Cassandra takes Emma's clothes from her, silently preparing her for sleep; the dark and brown chiaroscuro lighting evokes the religious solemnity of a Caravaggio painting (see Figure 4.8). With equal gravity, the anticipation of touch, gaze and speech is followed by withdrawal rather than relief. When Emma's breathing quickens, her stomach stirs with Cassandra's touch in close-up before the camera pulls out to reveal the whole of her body. She is presided over by Cassandra as if in the replication of another renaissance motif: the *pietà*. When they kiss, their faces are obscured. They move together and, as they kiss, the shadows they cast immerse them. Then, Emma suddenly and wordlessly stops responding to Cassandra's touch. The affective relief of tenderness is thwarted as she tortures Cassandra with a flattening of erotic affect through stillness and silence. As Berlant writes, 'an object gives you optimism, then it rains on your parade' (2012b: 13). Desire provides both pleasure and pain in its possibility and immediate disappointment (brought together here into the same frame). Yet, as Berlant continues, 'that is never the end of the story' (Ibid.). 'Never the end of the story': this is precisely the affective register within which this narrative lingers.

Emma and Cassandra have initiated a friendship that combines the mutual competitiveness of teammates, the identification of resemblance and the desire for physical prowess. Cassandra has helped to train Emma's physical flexibility. She has used the negotiations of bodily discipline to exert power over Emma, as well as to engineer physical proximity. Choreographing and then dismantling the meeting with the boys on the beach, she has also inaugurated Emma's sexualisation. Emma now yearns to reverse the imperative transformation initiated by desire. Her shattering of erotic potential in this scene is payback for Cassandra's control over the friendship, and for her introduction to desire's disorienting world. Emma's withdrawal of touch and of voice here (still and silent as she is gently seduced) is as powerful as Cassandra's initial insistence of it (to do the splits, to 'Focus!'). To consummate the visual and aural pairing of desire and control, the immediately subsequent scene returns to the training room, with the sound of the crack of the whip alongside the interpolations 'Cassandra' and then 'Emma'. Intimacy and control become intertwined through editing, through the aural interruption of physical potential. The sound of the whip, which occurs at infrequent but clearly defined moments in the film, also brings us back into the realm of the gymnastic performance. Once again, *She Monkeys* negotiates this tension between the ethereal and the corporeal. Stagings of desirability as spectacle and to-be-looked-at-ness become insubstantial, while moments in which the characters are brought into the corporeal presence of the other are infused either with extreme discipline and control, as in the first training scene, or abjection, as in the scene above in which it is only losing control of one's bladder and then one's stomach that creates a space for desire as care.

DESIRE AND ATTACHMENT

Desire itself is, in Berlant's words, a 'state of attachment' (2012b: 6). As Cassandra incarnates for Emma both the rebuke and reward of the friend who must also be tutor, parent, child and lover, she thus becomes invested with the potential – and then disappointment – of Emma's demands for attachment. The film thus manifests the pushes and pulls, the strategies that compensate for overwhelming need. The 'excessive submissiveness' of the ambivalent subject described by John Bowlby is a way of avoiding having to process painful affect, having 'to feel and resolve the pain of separation and loss' (in Holmes, 1993: 79). As an object of desire, Cassandra becomes over-burdened as the potential caregiver and role model. Knowing she might fail Emma, might always be unreachable, Emma clings to her image – and then rejects it – in order to control the way in which she produces her care. Simultaneously, Emma makes herself unreachable for her little sister Sara, who wears her desire for intimacy on her frequently bare skin and in her literal reaching for physical comfort. In contrast, touch is intertwined for the older girls with a power relationship in which intimacy is offered, but always taken away again. Here we see the film's presentation of the relationship between eroticism and the potential for physical intimacy. The latter does not disappear when the former is withdrawn; indeed, rivalry and dissatisfaction are actually productive of erotic potential (even if clung to in the form of what Berlant [2012a] calls our 'cruel optimism').

The dreaminess of the pace of *She Monkeys* gestures at violent climaxes but pulls back before they reach the generic demands of a thriller. In a late scene of violent revenge against unwanted desire, and with the result of rendering her unable to compete, Emma strikes Cassandra in the knee. The film ends with a shot largely reminiscent of the one with which it begins, once again muting the erotic register of the relationship between Emma and Cassandra. At the film's conclusion, which returns to the training room as site of competition and desire, Cassandra now looks on alone, bandaged and with crutches. Isolated in her voyeurism, she takes Emma's place as sideliner, whilst Emma is uniformly figured as part of the team from which Cassandra has been ousted. Rather than the tension and satisfaction of the duel and its victory, this final scene provides instead a discomfitingly unremarkable substitution. Such a star-reversal brings to mind the 'intra-feminine fascinations' in *All About Eve* (Joseph Mankiewicz, 1950) and *Desperately Seeking Susan* (Susan Seidelman, 1985) as theorised by Jackie Stacey (1987: 57). Emma is framed exactly as Cassandra was in the original scene, in close-up from waist to head with arms outstretched and the appearance of detachment from the horse, the ground and the other girls who make up the joint effort of the team.

Queer potential must reside here in the in-between: forced – or we might say *allowed* – to remain *as potential* by these films' unhurried narrative tempos. In Berlant's terms, identity 'teaches you to renounce your desire's excess and ambivalence so that you can be intelligible under the discipline of norms that make hierarchies of social value seem natural by rooting them in the pseudonatural structure of hetero-sexualized sexual difference' (2012b: 52). What comes first: the renunciation of excess, or of ambivalence? Or do they always come together: one (excess) producing not overwhelming pleasure, but rather the other (ambivalence)? It is precisely desire's 'excess and ambivalence' from which conventional teen films such as *Bring It On* (Peyton Reed, 2000) and *Mean Girls* (Mark Waters, 2004) ultimately seek to protect their protagonists in the name of that naturalisation of social hierarchies as they strive to produce pleasure in their spectators (see Colling, 2017). In such films, envy and idealisation come into tension at points of narrative climax but are swept aside for the sake of closure. The 'phase' – as the antithesis of the kind of identity

Figure 4.9. Frame grab from *Water Lilies*. Marie and Anne (Louise Blachère) play together in the pool in the film's final sequence.

Figure 4.10. Frame grab from *Water Lilies*. Floriane dances alone in the film's final sequence.

formation that Berlant writes is triumphantly promised by heterosexuality – is inherent to the cultural positioning of lesbianism, in which in Judith Roof's words it is 'unfixed, mediated, and [. . .] impossible to sustain' (1991: 26). We might argue that desire's excess is precisely what makes it unsustainable in these heterosexist terms.

She Monkeys provokes the frustration and even banality of closure's refusal. The queer affects that take the place of articulated desires are unfulfilled moments in long summers of childish unproductivity. Within the film's running time (which, of course, is all we know) the girls do not live happily ever after, nor do they consummate their relationship with the sexual act we are trained to read as inevitable. Beginning as a literalised mirage of the spectacle of the gymnastic performer suspended and made weightless by the camera, Emma's desire for Cassandra's star to become substantialised is frustrated and ultimately leads to banal conclusions (despite violent gestures). *She Monkeys* actively compresses the feelings of seriousness and pleasure that we might want to have guaranteed under the new terms of a sanctioned lesbian visibility. Despite hints of sex and violence, the film's mood is typically as flat, muted and unremarkable as its beige colour palette. Emma is left in her final scene fully occupying the affective female space of competition, aspiration and desire but separated from her object of desire/love. Such spatial negotiations provide on the one hand frustration and, on the other, enduring potential.

In *Water Lilies*, the spectacle that Floriane promises as object of the gaze of the boys around her (an almost identical earlier scene has rewarded her desire for attention) is juxtaposed with the childishness of romantic indifference (Marie and Anne have chosen each other for platonic intimacy instead). The star shapes that Marie and Anne make in the water are like propulsions back to childhood. By uniting both shots in the shared haze of a blue filter, this emphasises, like the pair of scenes with which I began the chapter, the encounter between these two modes of adolescent bodily inhabitation (see Figures 4.9 and 4.10). In this final scene, the swimming pool is where Marie wipes off the lipstick from the kiss that she has received, at last, from Floriane. The refusal to allow this kiss to point towards individual or romantic growth (Marie ends up more childish than she began) signals an indifference to sexuality rather than the consummation of it.

This chapter has argued that the arena of competition – literalised in a quasi-sporting film like *She Monkeys* or *Water Lilies* but evident across many cultural narratives of girlhood – amplifies the intensity of interactions whilst making intimacy painfully precarious. Intense physicality might yield sex, or violence – or a reconciled flatness (see Stacey, 2015; Duschinsky and Wilson, 2015; Berlant, 2015). Unable to depend on the consistency of either playfulness or seriousness, we are forced to reckon with the body's simultaneous sexuality and violence, attachment and ambivalence. Where jealousy provides the provocation for flirtation; where desire is demonstrated through disciplinary transaction; where control is confused with care, the terms of sexual visibility become unpredictable and even unruly. Queer affects are defined here not only by the cinema's traditionally erotic structures of gaze and spectacle, but also by their disruption. *Mise en scène* might privilege the interrelationships between friendship and desire, even where no lesbian figure is discernible. Queer affect is enabled and made apparent by the opening up of the senses, by the excessive physicality of sporting worlds; it is induced by desire's state of attachment but not confined to it. In Chapter 5, I will explore the ways in which *Blue Is the Warmest Colour* delivers a spectacle of overwhelming desire that *is* materialised through sex but that, instead of reinforcing a path to sexual orientation, *disorients* us in a queer time and space. The chapter asks how we might complicate conventional readings of *Blue Is the Warmest Colour* as dependent on and derivative of existing conventions for the image of the lesbian. The chapter considers the film's setting up of a series of orienting structures of recognition in light of the ways in which it breaks them down in disorienting turns of temporal and spatial play, arguing that it formally queers desire in a way that unsettles the over-privileging of sex in the characterisation of lesbian sexuality.

CHAPTER 5

The Politics of the Image: Sex as Sexuality in Blue Is the Warmest Colour

Twelve minutes into *Blue Is the Warmest Colour* (Abdellatif Kechiche, 2013), a teenage girl, Adèle, crosses a busy urban intersection. In close-up, the focus on her face evolves as she catches sight of another young woman who is new to us and to her: a stranger with vibrant blue hair, a self-possessed glance and an arm casually draped across the shoulders of a female companion. We track the approach of this blue-haired stranger until she crosses the path of our protagonist. The camera then swivels along with both figures in a single sweeping take as they contemplate one another, each contorting her body to keep the other in sight (see Figure 5.1). In the aftermath of a wordless, touch-less encounter, fast pans and jump cuts accompany the beeping horns of impatient cars surrounding Adèle in a disorienting haze of traffic, colour and movement. By this moment in a three-hour film, we have been made familiar with three recurring locations: the classroom, the playground and the home. We might call this a lesbian *bildungsroman* – all of the features are there in place for Adèle to make her way to adulthood through the requisite spaces of development.[1] Lifting us out of such recognisable generic locations, the scene yields an abrupt sense of disjuncture not only for its central character but also for its viewers. This is the moment at which *Blue Is the Warmest Colour* begins its delivery of a spectacle of overwhelming desire that, instead of providing us with a journey towards clarity of sexual orientation, *disorients* us in time and space. Here we see, instead, sexuality itself *as* disorientation. If it is a point of transition in a *coming-of-age* narrative – the protagonist meets the person with whom she will fall in love – it is not the reassuring transition from innocence to experience that is promised by the teleological semantics of that genre.

Blue Is the Warmest Colour, a film of intense drama and explicit sexual detail about the romance between two young women, won the prestigious Palme d'Or at the Cannes Film Festival. Both actresses, Adèle Exarchopoulos (Adèle) and Léa Seydoux (Emma), shared the prize with Abdellatif Kechiche in an acknowledgement of their crucial contribution to the film's 'synergy' (see Pulver, 2013).[2] In the aftermath of its success at Cannes, *Blue Is the Warmest Colour* received extensive and sustained attention in the press. It was released in fifty-two cinemas in the UK – significantly more than many

Figure 5.1. Frame grab from *Blue Is the Warmest Colour* (Kechiche, 2013). Emma (Léa Seydoux) and Adèle (Adèle Exarchopoulos) set eyes on one another.

lesbian films, and indeed more than many non-Anglophone films, but 500 fewer than the major earner for the same opening weekend, *The Hunger Games: Catching Fire* (Francis Lawrence, 2013; see British Film Institute, 2018). *Blue Is the Warmest Colour* was discussed in forty-three features – reviews, articles or commentaries – between May 2013 and October 2015 in *The Guardian* alone. *Mulholland Drive* (David Lynch, 2001), earning slightly more at the UK box office and almost three times as much globally, has been discussed in the same newspaper just half that amount in all the years since its release (see Box Office Mojo, 2018). Tim Palmer writes of Kechiche's film that it is 'already a twenty-first-century cause célèbre' (2018: 3).

Blue Is the Warmest Colour's triumph at Cannes marked an international landmark in lesbian cinematic history; no other film about a lesbian relationship had won the Palme. It also signalled a point of convergence between screen visibility and political progress (or one version of it, at least); in the same week, gay marriage was legalised in France, the film's country of production. A gay pride rally featured in the film gestures to the politics it hopes to wear on its sleeve. Even so, Steven Spielberg, the chair of the 2013 Cannes jury, expressly stated that 'politics was not a companion in our discussion; it was not in the room' (in Pulver, 2013). Such a high-profile award undeniably indicates an increase in public and critical acclaim for lesbian narratives. However, another jury member, Lynne Ramsay, insisted that 'it was just a love story, and it didn't matter if it was gay or straight' (Ibid.). The question we are left with by Ramsay's characterisation of the Cannes jury's decision is one that has haunted all of the readings in this book: is this a 'gay' film, or just a film (neither 'gay' nor 'straight')? Can we use these same words to describe some of its images (but not others)? Are the images themselves 'gay' (not straight), or rather the acts depicted in them, or the characterisations that traverse them?

For the Cannes jury, *Blue Is the Warmest Colour* is not *just* a lesbian love story. For many critics, it is not a *lesbian* love story at all. The (authorial) authority on the question is repeatedly accorded to Julie Maroh, the writer-illustrator of the graphic novel from which it was adapted (2010), who has written on her blog that 'it appears to me that this was what was missing on the set: lesbians' (2013). The film is criticised for its explicit sex scenes on the one hand and lauded as a universal love story on the other; it slots into a narrative of political progress for some and is just another misogynistic appropriation of the female body for the rest. In an essay on art cinema and *Lianna* (John Sayles, 1982) written over thirty years ago in 1986, Mandy Merck reads 'the love scene' as holding a 'particularly symbolic function: the ability to represent "lesbian experience"' (1993: 167). The questions and contradictions demanded by *Blue Is the Warmest Colour*'s critical reception seem to reduce the discourse on lesbian film to just this: the representability of 'lesbian experience'.

In the last chapter, I analysed the ambiguous intimacies generated by the competition that permeates desire in *Water Lilies* (Céline Sciamma, 2007) and *She Monkeys* (Lisa Aschan, 2011). While their erotics are established through the spectacle of performance and the idealisation of physical prowess, I argued that these films present meditations on desire's affect rather than a narrative of its journey. I posited a queer filmic affect that resides, contrary to expectation, in the spaces between bodily exhibitions of sexuality. And yet, the sexual act insists on framing any perception of sexuality in the visual field. Even in *Water Lilies*, whose erotic affects disturb the presumptions of sexual activity, the act's pared-down gestures still hold the weight of climactic transaction – of power, if not of pleasure. As I argued in Chapter 2, *Chloe* (Atom Egoyan, 2009) ostensibly enhances the traces of desire borrowed from *Nathalie . . .* (Anne Fontaine, 2003) *only if* we understand sex as the visual register through which sexuality is perceived.

Blue Is the Warmest Colour is the only one of the films discussed at length in this book to have received an '18' certificate from the British Board of Film Classification. Accordingly, popular writing on the film has almost entirely focused on the controversy over its extended explicit sex scenes.[3] The BBFC's classification is explained by a simple shorthand indicator of explicit content: 'strong sex and very strong language' (2013). It is the association with this label – 'strong sex' – that, I argue, initiates a process of conflation in which the explicit obscures the affective or implicit. Sexuality is manifest every-where in *Blue Is the Warmest Colour*, affectively infusing the three-hour film in between and beyond the sex scenes that make up only a small fraction of its overall running time. And yet, the film is insistently announced by the discursive sphere surrounding it rather than on its own aesthetic terms. Moreover, this discursive preoccupation with sex, and in particular 'strong sex', makes the film beholden to questions about more than *just* explicitness. Critics everywhere, from national newspapers to lesbian popular culture fan pages, have focused their attention on *Blue Is the Warmest Colour*'s status as a 'lesbian film'. On one website alone, the lesbian pop-cultural hub AfterEllen, this response takes the form of a video of 'lesbian reactions' to the film (Bendix, 2013); an article that measures the cast's 'convincing' queerness (Rosenblum, 2013); and a review that asks, straightforwardly, 'is *Blue Is the Warmest Colour* a "lesbian film"?' (Bianco, 2013). The questions asked of the film's lesbianism thus parallel the criticisms of its explicit sex scenes, framing together, as if seamlessly aligned, the two halves of the popular and critical discourse in which the film's reputation has been embedded. This chapter considers how one critical preoccupation – with the explicitness of the sex scenes – becomes the only lens through which a second preoccupation – with the film's status as 'lesbian' – can be addressed. It is because of the definitional hold that 'sex' has on the discursive construction of identity that *Blue Is the Warmest Colour*, more than any other film of the past two decades, is asked to account for the authenticity of its representation of lesbianism.

As I argue in this chapter, *Blue Is the Warmest Colour* perhaps paradoxically reveals the limits of the representability of sex; the limits of the sexual encounter as a definition of sexuality more broadly; and the limits that the sexual *as* sexual encounter places on our ability to perceive anything else. I argue that the 'anything else' that sex obscures is, in *Blue Is the Warmest Colour*, the radical set of spatial and temporal disorientations that boldly convey sexuality's complexity. Positioned against its director's auteurial investment in cinema's political responsibility for social commentary, *Blue Is the Warmest Colour* ambivalently positions the stakes of its projection of desire, gesturing to a political scene of civil rights whilst making its representations of lesbian experience wholly particular. The film's indeterminate space, time and incident sit in contrast to the demand to represent lesbian experience as an essence. The explicitly sexual withholds rather than confirms the reconcilability of image, politics, identity and development.

WITHHOLDING THE ESSENTIALS

Tim Palmer (2018) reads *Blue Is the Warmest Colour* as a descendant of what he has termed the '*cinéma du corps*' (2011: 57), following in the footsteps of films such as *Trouble Every Day* (Claire Denis, 2001), *Irreversible* (Gaspar Noé, 2002) and *In My Skin* (Marina de Van, 2002). Long sex scenes – which Hila Shachar

Figure 5.2. Frame grab from *Blue Is the Warmest Colour*. Adèle baths in sea water in a frame that expresses ecstasy.

(2018) also argues distract from myriad other features – are only part of the film's corporeal emphasis, which also heightens the visceral experience of eating, laughing and crying. The camera lingers on Adèle's open mouth as she slurps spaghetti; she is presented as a character who, in the first chapter of her life, is brimming with sensory pleasure. The experience of love and heartbreak is turned into a texture that lingers far beyond the explicit scenes that grabbed critics' attention to such an extent. In a shot used to conclude the film's trailer, Adèle lies on her back in a turquoise ocean that seems to envelop her (see Figure 5.2). In this frame, Adèle's eyes are closed and her mouth is slightly open in what we perceive to be a pleasurable state. In the frame that follows, it is made clear from the angle of her eyes and her smudged mascara that she has been crying. Her open mouth is a feature that figures her voluptuousness, sexiness and hunger throughout the film. It is this complex blend of ecstatic love and desperate heartbreak, and the blurriness of the lines between them, that characterise the film in its totality. The *mise en scène* of this aqueous cocoon signifies desire (Adèle's open mouth, her red lips) and its disruption (the optical trick that shifts her look from bliss to despair from one frame to the next). It gestures to the freedom of the love that marks the film (the water's potential liminality) and its suffocation (our perception of the water's solidification). Adèle's prostrate body speaks to her openness to sexuality. At the same time, the water around her conjures baptism, conversion and cleansing, all of which are figured in the narrative as a whole by the central consuming relationship that becomes everything to the protagonist: in the unmarked second chapter, Emma is friend, lover and mother to Adèle, the rest of whose life folds away the moment she is subsumed by desire. The lighting in this frame also gives Adèle's hair a bluey gloss, simulating Emma's

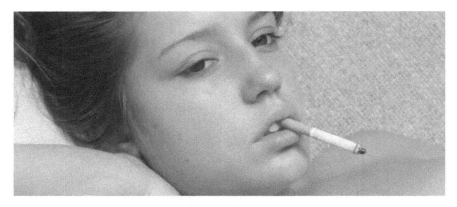

Figure 5.3. Frame grab from *Blue Is the Warmest Colour*. Adèle as the artist's muse.

dyed blue hair and punctuating the visual similarity of the two young women in a narrative that is an incessant struggle of sameness and difference. When they first meet, Emma's hair identifies her as different from Adèle but it is illustrative, or generative, of a colour that comes to unite them, an apparent sign of uniqueness creating, in the end, visual homogeny.

This single shot characterises the film's overall texturing of desire. It is echoed in various others: the water seems to resemble a mattress, and Adèle's pose mimics another scene in which, at the same close-up level, she lies on a blue sheet in her blue-tinted bedroom and masturbates, thinking of Emma. In yet another, she lies naked on a sofa shrouded in blue cloth with a cigarette dangling from her mouth, modelling for Emma in her inaugural pose as the artist's muse (see Figure 5.3). In the graphic novel, entitled in French *Le Bleu Est une Couleur Chaude*, the diegetic narrative is almost entirely drawn in black and white with only flashes of a single colour: blue. Blue *is* Emma, signifying not only youthful rebellion but also the standout feature of her erotic appeal. This is a visual motif that Kechiche adapts in his film by making the blues of the palette rich and intense. Blue, rather than the ubiquitous red of passion, makes desire not universal but particular. A single person, figured in desire's 'cloud of possibility' (Berlant, 2012b: 6), can overwhelm the entire *mise en scène*. Found in fabrics, props, costumes, landscapes and decorations, the colour blue is, throughout, the reminder of desire, just as in *Three Colours: Blue* (Krzysztof Kieślowski, 1993) it submerges Juliette Binoche's protagonist in an inescapable reminder of grief. Blue is a colour of extremes, insistently converted to a superlative in the English translation: *Le Bleu Est une Couleur Chaude* (*Blue Is a Warm Colour*) becomes *Blue Is the Warmest Colour*. What Carol Mavor calls that 'paradoxical colour' – signifying purity, obscenity, eternity and fatality all at once – is what underpins an ecstatic and tragic chronicle of overwhelming emotion (2013: 10).[4]

B. Ruby Rich writes that Kechiche took Maroh's work and 'expanded' it into an 'epic: his *Blue* demands viewers' attention for a full 179 minutes of measured, deliberative observations of a young woman's adolescence, erotic awakening, and maturation' (2014). These 'full 179 minutes' do indeed advance on a grand scale, forcing the viewer to endure notoriously long sex scenes (up to ten minutes long), a fight scene and a fifteen-minute post-break-up scene. The 'contours' of the film's world are conjured by 'camera work and performance', Rich writes, 'with everyone in close-up and nothing essential withheld' (Ibid.). I love Rich's evocation of the film's expansive scene of desire. However, I read the film as withholding *everything* essential – if by essential we mean the transparency of narrative markers and placeholders that choreograph the coming-of-age drama and its stages of development.

The film's original French title is *La Vie d'Adèle: Chapitres 1 et 2* ('The Life of Adèle: Chapters 1 and 2'). Different again from the novel and the English translation, this version of the title bespeaks a linearity of movement from one stage of life to another. However, even a cursory look at the film's narrative arc disrupts the promise of destination.[5] In an unnamed city in northern France, Adèle is studying for the *baccalauréate littéraire* with an inseparable group of friends, a new boyfriend Thomas (Jérémie Lahuerte) and a devoted family. Early on, Adèle identifies the dissatisfaction of sex with Thomas as a symptom of her desire for women and, following a disappointingly fleeting kiss with a friend (Alma Jodorowsky) who rebuffs her the next day, enters into a relationship with Emma, an art-college student. Following their meeting, which is received with disapproval and a homophobic verbal attack by her friends, Adèle's social life almost entirely melts into irrelevance as she is consumed by her relationship with Emma. Fast forward several years to the second chapter of the film's French title, and Adèle is now a teacher, living with Emma but dissatisfied with Emma's focus on her art work and her preoccupation with her intellectual friends. Following Adèle's admission of an affair with a male colleague, Emma abruptly breaks up with her, and she descends into depression.

Initially, *Blue Is the Warmest Colour* follows an unremarkable trajectory. The film's timeline sporadically chronicles a move from the school where Adèle occupies a stable position in her group of friends, to the bar where she and Emma have their first proper meeting, and onwards to the various apartments they share in the film's second chapter. The first few scenes of the timeline thus comfortably establish the daily routines of Adèle's home and school life: repeated sequences of morning commutes and family mealtimes. The recurring dish, spaghetti bolognaise, is mundanely familiar by its third outing. Adèle's slurping scenes show a voracious character but in essence are simple and lacking in extravagance. In this way, the film finds common ground with social-realist dramas, taking interest in its characters' daily eating habits; Kechiche's *Couscous* (2007) also finds common food to be at the heart of a small community's way of life. *Blue Is the Warmest Colour* also operates within a French tradition of *lycée* films that include *The Party* (Claude Pinoteau, 1980), *Good Old Daze* (Cédric Klapisch, 1994), *The Class* (Laurent Cantet, 2008) and Kechiche's *Games of Love and Chance* (2003).[6] In these films, the school is neither a mere supplementary location to the home, nor the marker of education's role as stepping stone, but rather a central character. In *The Class*, the camera resides only in the school's classrooms, halls and playground. Similarly, throughout *Blue Is the Warmest Colour*, these two location templates – school and home – remain prominent. Of the seventy-seven scenes in a three-hour-long stretch, over twenty-two – a quarter – take place at school, while twenty-one take place at home. No other location is privileged to the same extent.

The school location provides an ensemble ready-made: Adèle's gossipy friends share almost equal screen time with Adèle in the film's first act, and even speak the film's first words. However, these initially vital friends are at odds with the film's lesbian storyline, which disrupts the continuity of these locations rather than secures it. When Adèle is surprised to find Emma waiting for her at the school gates after a single meeting, she walks away with her, ignoring the summons of her friends. Afterwards, just one final school scene occurs in Adèle's diegetic adolescence. Her friends speculate on Emma's 'gouine' (dyke) image, which becomes immediately transferred onto Adèle herself in an aggressive naming of her identity: 'tu lécheras pas ma chatte, sale gouine' (you won't lick my pussy, you dirty dyke), shouts one of the girls. It is a scene that recalls the exuberant chatter of earlier playground gossip but with the hard edge of homophobic condemnation. This space is significant as the only site of the verbal interpellation of either girl's sexual identity; if to come of age is, traditionally, to *come out*, no such arrival occurs here. This pessimistic homophobic episode instead expedites Adèle's transition from this stage of her life; her friends are now silenced by screen absence. The reliability of repeated and prolonged returns to spaces like the classroom is narratively served by Adèle's role as a teacher in the film's second chapter. However, this is an illusion of familiarity within difference. As *Blue Is the Warmest Colour* progresses, not only do these initial orienting locations and characters increasingly disappear from the story, but the rapidity with which we are introduced to new locations and new people intensifies.

From this point, what counts is a different kind of pedagogy. An early date is a picnic in which extreme close-ups follow the flickering of Adèle and

Emma's gazes from mouth to eyes and back again. Adèle's sexual curiosity maps on to a familiar pedagogical model of lesbian cinema reinforced in a classic trio of lesbian films: *Lianna*, *Personal Best* (Robert Towne, 1982) and *Desert Hearts* (Donna Deitch, 1985). It continues across genres and periods, most recently in *Imagine Me and You* (Ol Parker, 2005), *Itty Bitty Titty Committee* (Jamie Babbit, 2007), *The Four-Faced Liar* (Jacob Chase, 2010) and *Kiss Me* (Alexandra-Therese Keining, 2011). In *High Art* (Lisa Cholodenko, 1998), produced at the tail end of the New Queer Cinema, this very tendency is mocked; when the ostensibly straight protagonist Syd (Radha Mitchell) hesitantly asks Lucy (Ally Sheedy) in their first sexual encounter, 'Is this hard enough?' Lucy responds with a teasing retort: 'Is this soft enough?' In Maroh's graphic novel, the relationship between Clementine (Adèle) and Emma involves a kind of induction into lesbian community via sexuality; the words, 'Are you ready?' preface their first sex scene. Learning lesbianism is premised on a foundational innocence, on knowledge to be attained. The question whose variant is so often posed in these coming out films – 'When did you first know you liked women?' – is in *Blue Is the Warmest Colour* framed by Adèle not through knowledge but through sensation – 'When did you first taste a woman?' It is through their mouths and eyes, to the exclusion of the rest of their bodies, that they first exhibit desirability. This is not only a sexual lesson: throughout the film, it is through taste that the young women try out each other's social and cultural differences. Gaps in experience are not only sexualised but classed, marking out mealtimes (from spaghetti bolognaise to oysters) and cultural curiosities (from Bob Marley to Jean-Paul Sartre). Sexual fluency translates as cultural and culinary fluency.

With these lessons, *Blue Is the Warmest Colour* from this point on conveys a temporal dislocation in which Adèle's overwhelming desire for Emma interrupts growth almost literally. From one 'chapter' to the next, Emma's blue hair becomes blonde, depriving her of her main signifier of youth; Adèle's face and hairstyle remain noticeably unchanged. In the film's second chapter, which arrives abruptly and without announcement, Adèle has grown up and is working as a teacher. We are denied witness to her final schooldays with her friends; we do not see evidence of her graduation. It is striking to perceive how young she looks as she conducts a classroom of children, having so recently – in terms of screen, rather than diegetic, time – sat amongst her peers for her own schooling. Adèle is never given, diegetically, the opportunity to follow the process of growing up awarded for instance to Mason (Ellar Coltrane) in *Boyhood* (Richard Linklater, 2014), a film whose production methodology guarantees it.[7] *Boyhood* reliably includes at least one scene from every annual cycle of its measured twelve-year scope. In that film, we witness the protagonist's early childhood, adolescence and approach to adulthood;

the promise of the narrative's endpoint is confirmed by the regularity and linearity of progress towards it. In contrast, if the first half of *Blue Is the Warmest Colour* serves to orient us, then the second chapter takes the seeds of that orientation and disperses them, throwing us into a time and space of uncertainty.

DESIRE IN CLOSE-UP

Rather than contextualising wide-angles of global or even local scale, the majority of *Blue Is the Warmest Colour*'s shots are close-ups, with occasional medium and very few long shots (the exceptions, contrary to all acceptable convention, are in the sex scenes, which I will explore in a later section). The sight of the front door of Adèle's childhood home, while familiar through repetition, is never contextualised within a long shot of the city at a larger scale. In comparison to the home spaces of *Circumstance* (Maryam Keshavarz, 2011) that are in constant negotiation with the public sites of the city, *Blue Is the Warmest Colour*'s intimately shot city streets, while filmed 'on location', could, to the uninformed eye, be anywhere. Rather than offering a simulacrum of a well-known capital city as *Circumstance* does (filming in Beirut as stand-in for Tehran), *Blue Is the Warmest Colour* eliminates any particularising markers. The film's tempo follows the immediacy of Adèle's desire rather than the framing lifeline around it; the textures we come to know are those of Adèle's skin rather than the city in which she resides. Mary Ann Doane writes that, 'of all the different types of shots, it is the close-up that is most fully associated with the screen as surface, with the annihilation of a sense of depth and its corresponding rules of perspectival realism' (2003: 91). Here, the texture of Adèle's skin is reminiscent of what Doane calls 'an image rather than a threshold onto a world. Or rather, the world is reduced to this face, this object' (Ibid.: 90). *Blue Is the Warmest Colour*'s world is reduced to close range, to the intimacies of Adèle's immediate conditions of life.

Blue Is the Warmest Colour's concentration on a denseness and closeness of scope also shuts out wider social contexts. It refuses the even temporality of *Boyhood* or of *52 Tuesdays* (Sophie Hyde, 2013), a film that tracks a young woman's relationship with her trans father over the course of his transition. Sophie Hyde's film is set – and was filmed – one day a week for a year, and marks each of the '52 Tuesdays' of its narrative trajectory with a title frame, each of which is accompanied by news footage of current events from the particular day in the year of production. *Blue Is the Warmest Colour* resists the kinds of nods made to world events by *52 Tuesdays*'s title cards or the psychedelic period gestures of the coming-of-age comedy-drama *20th Century Women* (Mike Mills, 2015), which intersperses (autobiographical) fiction with style and content borrowed from the experimental documentary *Koyaanisqatsi*

(Godrey Reggio, 1982). These hallmarks are more than just stylistic flourishes: they situate their protagonists' chronologies in space and time.

Intersectional questions about *Blue Is the Warmest Colour*'s sexual sphere
– such as those framed by class and pedagogy, by nation and outness, or by
gender and objectification – demand to be answered as, precisely, *political*
questions, even as they contrast with its apparent emotional solipsism. On the
international arthouse circuit, Kechiche is a director known for the politicisation
of cinema (see Nonrindr, 2012). The shipyard setting in the French coastal town
of Sète and its links to Tunisia are crucial to the political force of the narrative
in his film *Couscous*. Kechiche dedicated *Blue Is the Warmest Colour*'s Cannes prize
'to the youth of France' and the revolutionary youth of Tunisia, where 'they
have the aspiration to be free, to express themselves and love in full freedom'
(in Pulver, 2013). The political accenting of the film's success in the director's
words is quite clear. However, the pride march that signals an investment in
the politics of sexual orientation is reduced to a festival of colour and romantic
sentiment – here is joy but not anger. The scene's twin, a workers' rights march
attended by Adèle and her school friends at an earlier stage of the film, evidences
the political invocations of injustice that are lacking in recent divestments of
pride's political agenda (see Chasin, 2001). Kechiche thus gestures, in his own
commentary on the film's reach, to a wider scene of gay (and other) civil rights,
endorsing the fight to 'love in full freedom' (and implicitly exposing the many
places where this outness is still not a possibility). There is a sombreness to both
these scenes in their original form in the graphic novel: depleted grey tones make
them unremarkable, but also insistently and unambiguously *serious*: the rainbow
of colour does not exist in the text as a signifier of pride's celebration, as it does
in the film. Here we have a revival of the distorted promise of outness discussed
in Chapter 3. If Kechiche celebrates the individuals of his film for whom, as
Judith Butler demands that we continue to ask, 'outness [is] an historically available and affordable option' (1993: 19), their politics threaten to become visually
and narratively compressed by the immediacies of their desires. The anger of the
workers' rights march feels disjunctive next to the pride of the gay rights march,
as if one must be swapped for the other. The playground scene described above,
in which Adèle is called out for her association with the 'dyke' Emma, is the
only scene in which identity is explicitly named; while both sets of parents make
appearances, and two sets of introductory dinners take place, they produce
awkwardness but not confrontation. The film withholds the coming-out scenes
– tragic or otherwise – that characterise so many films of lesbian adolescence.

The same film is heralded for its universalism by some, and condemned
for its lack of lesbian specificity by others. Ramsay's account of *Blue Is the
Warmest Colour*'s universal love story – in the Cannes's jury's decision 'it didn't
matter if it was gay or straight' – mirrors responses to *Brokeback Mountain*

(Ang Lee, 2005) that are condemned as the embodiment of the de-politicisation of 'universalizing mass public spheres' (Herring, 2006: 93). Lee's film is cited several times by queer theorists as the universalising text *par excellence* (Miller, 2007), its display of unmarked whiteness another dubious gesture towards universal recognisability in its bid to be 'nothing but' a love story (White, 2015; McBride, 2006). However, Lisa Henderson writes of *Brokeback Mountain* that it nevertheless elicits a 'distinctly queer effect': 'its image of sexual and emotional urgency and its raw and tender physicality between two men perilously in love' (2013: 102). *Blue Is the Warmest Colour* undoubtedly exhibits this 'raw and tender physicality'. But without the coming-out scenes, those standard encounters of 'queer' particularity, how can we understand Kechiche's call to love?

With its resistance to conventional markers of growth and an accentuation of the intensity of desire in isolation from everyday experience, *Blue Is the Warmest Colour* refuses the linear narrative drive implied by any cursory synopsis. Elizabeth Cowie writes that cinema 'selects and excludes. It is therefore, even without the spoken or written word, an utterance or enunciation, an *organised* presentation of reality which presupposes an intelligibility of the utterance; it is organised for understanding' (1997: 26). Rather than organising, or arranging 'into a structured whole' (OED, 2018), *Blue Is the Warmest Colour dis*organises its reality into a whole that lacks all of its parts. With these gaps in our knowledge (the details of Adèle's teacher training, her final departure from her family, her move-in with Emma) the film cannot be organised, in Cowie's words, for understanding; it is instead organised (or *dis*organised) for misunderstanding, for a failure to understand correctly on the basis of what is selected for utterance. What we thus fail to 'understand' are precisely love's broader implications, including the 'perilous' everyday that defines so much lesbian experience. While it withholds the essentials of the *bildungsroman*'s narrative procedure (graduations, goodbyes), the film magnifies, in epic proportions, the essential scenes of first romance: sex and fights take the place of what Emily Apter calls the epic's requisite 'wars and revolutions' (2010: 4). *Blue Is the Warmest Colour* stretches and compresses, hinting at epic time but refusing the expectations of that scope. Desire throws the characters, while desire's disorganised diegesis throws us, into a state outside of the temporal logic of teleology, just as the film's offering and withdrawing of familiar spaces dismantles the spatial logic of continuity.

THE RIGHT IMAGE

What exists here is a conflicting set of multiple realisms: emotional, social, sexual. Not all can be satisfied at once: the archetypal social realism of the

French school genre is compromised when desire takes hold, taking over the *mise en scène* with the warmest colour blue. As I wrote in the book's introduction, queer theory has become axiomatically attached to politics in a way that was historically always the domain of lesbian feminism (see Hesford, 2013). Here, the defiance of 'perspectival realism' in the close-up (Doane, 2003: 91) registers the emotional realism of desire's disorganisation but inhibits the representability of politics as progress. And, as I will demonstrate in the next section, sexual realism might be *too close* to the real to be comfortably perceived. In an essay entitled 'The Woman's Image – A Woman's Imaging' that begins her collection *Representing the Woman*, Cowie writes:

> We will be moved by images in ways which we neither expect nor seek nor want. And it is through the images and narratives of representation that we can find ourselves spoken in a way which we take to be *real*, or wish to be true. However the demand by feminists – or by other groups – for images which are felt to be *real* and true can never be met in any absolute sense. For images are not already 'truthful', they become so only at the point at which they produce identification in the spectator-subject, when she or he 'finds' them true. The demand and desire for identity in the image as the right image at the same time raises the difficulties of difference, and especially the difference of the other's desire, and some of the fiercest debates within feminism have involved the issue of identity, its definition and its images, giving rise to disputes over lesbian versus heterosexual desire, the use of pornography, and the pleasures of sexual fantasy. (1997: 5, emphases added)

Cowie writes of 'the demand and desire for identity in the image *as the right image*' (emphasis added). Of course, there is never *one right image*. Indeed, there is never a *real* image at all, since, as I have explored throughout this book in dialogue with a corpus of texts dwelling on the construction of sexuality in fantasy, the 'pleasures of sexual fantasy' cannot be separated from the pleasures of *sexuality*.

In an early scene, we observe Adèle and Thomas (the boy with whom she has a short-lived relationship) in a dark cinema auditorium. From the vantage point of the cinema screen, we look inwards at the members of the audience, the glow of the moving image dancing on their faces. The scene is immediately juxtaposed with a shot of Adèle, filmed in the same dark light that allows only for a reddish glow of softly illuminated skin. Alone in her bedroom, she is lying awake and thinking not of Thomas but of the as-yet unnamed girl she has passed in the street. As she touches herself, the camera cuts from close-ups of her skin to close-ups of Emma's mouth and hands, her blue hair swathing Adèle's body. In Maroh's graphic novel, this fantasy is illustrated by dismembered hands painted a vibrant blue (see Figure 5.4). In the film, a solitary close-up of Adèle cuts to an almost identical close-up in

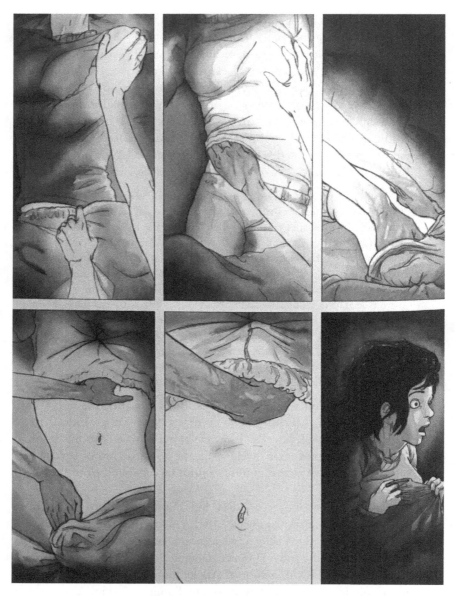

Figure 5.4. A panel from the graphic novel *Blue Is the Warmest Colour* (Maroh, 2010).

which the unmistakeable blue of Emma's hair signals her presence. Among its many functions, the colour comes to figure the augmentation of desire in fantasy. This scene is the first in which we are forced to confront our relation to the gruelling intensity of the film's sexual realism: are we as shocked when

Figure 5.5. Frame grab from *Blue Is the Warmest Colour*. Adèle and Emma gaze at women gazing at each other.

Figure 5.6. Frame grab from *Blue Is the Warmest Colour*. Adèle looks at Emma and back at herself.

'the sex scene' is part of a fantasy within what is already a fantasy? In *Sex, or the Unbearable*, Lee Edelman writes of Lydia Davis's story 'Break it Down' (2009) that it 'parses the problem of defining an encounter – of determining whether or not it takes place and of knowing precisely in what it consists – by reducing it first to a finite number of delimited sexual acts' (2014: 74). In this scene, the 'encounter' is precisely not delimited because Emma both is and is not there. Only the conventions of narrative storytelling tell us that Emma's presence in Adèle's masturbation scene is merely a fantasy – they have not yet formally met or exchanged words, and Emma has not been present in this scene until this moment. In terms of her cinematic presence, she is every bit as 'there' as Adèle is. It is only *sequence* that tells us this sex scene is enacted solo, yet it is also sequence (in the form of repetition as described above) that harnesses familiarity and then distorts it.

Like the diegetic cinematic spaces in other films discussed in this book that produce, in Roland Barthes's words, 'an absence of worldliness' (1989 [1984]: 346), these spaces must do different queer work. James Williams writes that in Kechiche's work, 'different kinds of space are put into play at a range of levels, from the physical and intertextual to the theatrical and cinematic' (2013: 189). Intertextuality here is about *spatial* allusion to a genre like the *bildungsroman* (through the classroom for instance); the 'different kinds of space' that Williams cites are 'put into play' as the film utilises them to provide familiarity and then withdraws them to shake up our spatial and temporal frames of reference. Thus, we are reminded of the film's enduring preoccupation with the image *as image*. The creation of a reality effect is again compromised. After the cinema provokes fantasy as a site of desire's discovery, the film makes the art gallery the site of desire's nurture as Adèle and Emma meet there on their first date. The camera pauses on Adèle gazing at Emma gazing at one woman in a painting gazing at another (see Figure 5.5). Adèle and Emma simultaneously create the framing to the nude painting beyond and become framed within it. This brings to mind Kenneth Clark's definitive distinction between nakedness and nudity, the first defining simply a lack of clothes and the second defining the coming into being of a piece of art (1956). In *Blue Is the Warmest Colour*'s scene of multiple looking, women are the agents of the look as well as the objects of it. Positioned against the figures in the paintings behind them, Adèle and Emma are revealed to us as figures whom we will be asked to look at, in later scenes, as nudes. The process of looking and its photographic capture are accentuated when Adèle's gaze at Emma is magnified by a sheet of light between them that reflects her gaze back inwards at herself (see Figure 5.6). In the masturbation scene, Adèle's own hands become Emma's through fantasy's articulation in the visual field. Adèle's gaze makes her both object and subject, her reflection replicating Emma's desire through the cinematic image.

Emma's blue hair, matching the flashes of teal in the paintings around them, is a mark both of aesthetic cohesion and social rebellion. Blue is the visual focal point around which the film's colour palette can cohere; if it is rebellious, it also becomes familiar. Emma's skin, moreover, is as white as the nudes in the paintings they contemplate, even as white as the alabaster sculpture that follows in the next shot. Whiteness is the assumed colour of nudity. Just like *Mulholland Drive*'s projection of whiteness as transparency, as a metaphor for cinematic invisibility, here whiteness is precisely that which goes without comment and yet which is part of the film's corporeal texture. Rosalind Galt writes of the role of colour in art history that 'purity has helped construct the white body as transparent, rational, and modern, linking fleshly corruption and racial otherness to excess colour' (2011: 68). In cinema, Galt writes, something similar happens, 'where the simple, pure qualities of the captured moment place heavily racialized and gendered attributes on the correct or unruly forms of the image' (Ibid.). In *Blue Is the Warmest Colour*, this 'fleshly corruption' of Adèle's slightly darker (though still white, European) skin arrives with the 'excess colour' of Emma's blue hair.[8] As if through the desiring gaze, Adèle's skin becomes lit according to her own desire and desirability. In the middle third of the film it has a sweaty sheen, a glow initiated in the bar in which she first meets Emma and seamlessly carried through to their first sex scene. Premised through this first date in the gallery, the signification of their domestic commitment and the next stage of Adèle's life are also introduced through the gaze as Adèle herself becomes the object of Emma's artwork.

SEXUALITY'S SYNECDOCHE

In Chapter 1, I explored cultural anxieties associated with the simultaneously singular and doubled conceptualisations of lesbianism on-screen. The psychoanalytic film theories that I drew on articulate tensions between sameness and difference in these cinematic figurations. If *Mulholland Drive* draws on a cinematic history of female homoerotic identifications, *Blue Is the Warmest Colour* accentuates the cinema's debt to the aesthetics of fine art. Its alleged objectifications of the female body find antecedents not only in the pornographic reconstruction of lesbian sex, but also in a history of art dominated by men. This provokes readings of the film based on Laura Mulvey's theory of the gaze, as Linda Williams has observed and contested (2017). The film announces these debts at a narrative as well as at a visual level. Spaces such as the home and the school, realist in their quotidian repetition, are interrupted and then overtaken by the heightening of the image in the cinematic construction of desire.

The spectrum of adjectives used by film critics to describe *Blue Is the Warmest Colour* is rife with contradictions. While Stephanie Theobald in *The Guardian* (2013) sees the sex scenes not only as 'long and relentless' but also as 'muted and unsweaty', Tim Robey in *The Telegraph* (2013) points to the 'fleshy abandon' of these very same scenes. Manohla Dargis in *The New York Times* (2013) writes that Adèle's 'hunger is contained, prettified, aestheticised', while Jonathan Romney in *Sight and Sound* (2013) suggests that the film 'achieves a sculptural tactility in catching the detail of the heroines' bodies, their fleshiness, and the porousness of their skin, blotchy or not'. Many of these terms measure the film's corporeal qualities – 'sweaty', 'fleshy'. Sexuality and desire are, indeed, *reduced to* corporeality. In the context of the broader arguments of these critics' reviews, all of these terms are used to convey the film's figuration of lesbian desire, which is read by turns as either not accurate enough or too accurate – as 'lesbian life painted so that straight people can understand it' (Theobald, 2013) or as 'direct' and 'non-mystificatory' (Romney, 2013).

The oxymoronic consequence of these conflicting reviews points to an uneasiness with how to talk about a film whose depiction of lesbian sex is unmediated through the metaphorical devices we are used to in, for example, the 'sexy and silly crosscutting between breaking bread and spreading thighs' that Henderson (1999: 60) recollects in *Go Fish* (Rose Troche, 1994).[9] One evident backdrop to *Lesbian Cinema after Queer Theory*'s main argument is a cultural field in which explicit sexual images (as well as those of violence) have become increasingly common on cinema, television, computer and mobile screens. The amateur footage shot on smart phones that enables so-called citizen journalism is characteristic of the new platforming of graphic images without editorial guidance; no longer is the availability of viewing determined solely by certifications in theatrical or broadcast arenas. Netflix algorithms publicise Kechiche's film alongside both more mainstream and more marginal fare. Pornography is no longer the sole domain of the naked body; sexuality need not take metaphorical form to be legitimately viewed. If Rich argues that reductions of explicit sex scenes to the language of pornography are 'underlined by a poverty of vernacular' (2014), this poverty is increasingly evidenced in a changing visual world. The BBFC's justification for *Blue Is the Warmest Colour*'s certification employs 110 words to detail the film's 'strong sex', measuring length, nudity, the 'sight of genitals', 'range of positions' and strength of 'references to "eating pussy", for example' (2013). Of course, this available vernacular is plagued with double standards: *Fifty Shades of Grey* (Sam Taylor-Johnson, 2015), for instance, a film whose narrative is *entirely* premised on the sex between the two (heterosexual) central characters, is far less explicitly described, the summary of its sex scenes just a third of the length, at thirty-five words (British Board of Film Classification, 2017).[10]

Blue Is the Warmest Colour, deplored by Maroh for its lack of any lesbians on set, provides, in her words, merely 'a brutal and surgical display, exuberant and cold, of so-called lesbian sex, which turned into porn, and made me feel very ill at ease' (2013). What stands out here is the suggestion of 'so-called' lesbian sex. So-called: that which masquerades but deceives, that which is inappropriate. What is implicit in Maroh's statement is the assumption that 'lesbian sex' could not *itself* be 'brutal and surgical', 'exuberant and cold', or even 'porn[ographic]'; that it must, in fact, follow a different set of rules to be *called* 'lesbian sex'. Accordingly, Susie 'Sexpert' Bright famously acted as a technical advisor (read: authenticity advisor) for the neo-*noir* cult film *Bound* (Lana and Andy Wachowski, 1996), a favourite on lists such as AfterEllen's 'Best Lesbian/Bi Movie Poll' (2012). The sex scene in *Bound* has become famous for its lesbian authenticity, even as it draws on the mechanisms of representability enabled and warranted by the (neo) *film noir* genre (see Kessler, 2003; Merck, 2000).

With a contrasting set of antecedents, *Blue Is the Warmest Colour* fits within the scope of the European art film, which has historically been read through its eroticism, a status exemplified by the infamous nudity of Brigitte Bardot in Jean-Luc Godard's *Contempt* (1963). This quintessentially male tradition has freely expressed lesbian sexuality, as Andrea Weiss has written citing films such as *The Conformist* (Bernardo Bertolucci, 1970) and *May Fools* (Louis Malle, 1990) which 'convey through images what the Hollywood cinema conveys through absence' (1992: 109). But the art film has also been readily appropriated, as Weiss discusses, by lesbian filmmakers such as Chantal Akerman in *Je, Tu, Il, Elle* (1974) and *The Meetings of Anna* (1979), Ulrike Ottinger's *Madame X* (1978), Diane Kurys's *Coup de Foudre* (1982) and Léa Pool's *Anne Trister* (1986). Against this context, there emerge several potential counter-arguments to Maroh's accusation. The first states that *Blue Is the Warmest Colour* should not be read as pornographic at all. Linda Williams has dulled the conviction of Maroh's argument on this point by comparing *Blue Is the Warmest Colour*'s sex scenes to typical pornographic fare (in terms, for instance, of the imagery of genitalia and of particular sexual acts) and concluding that the film itself is 'actually rather chaste if we only consider what we actually see rather than what we *think* we see' (2017: 469, original emphasis). A second counter-argument states moreover that explicit sex, whether technically pornographic or not, can and should be part of a feminist visual politics without triggering the prohibition of its description as either legitimately feminist or as legitimately lesbian (see for instance, Ryberg, 2013). Here we might point to films such as *Intimacy* (Patrice Chéreau, 2001), *In the Cut* (Jane Campion, 2003) and *Grand Central* (Rebecca Zlotowski, 2013). The last is a film that, for Sophie Mayer, indicates a 'mainstreaming of [Catherine] Breillat's Brechtian approach, a return of explicit eroticism to European women's cinema' (2016: 178). Such examples surely meet both the conditions of twenty-first-century visibility *and* the call to move beyond the exploitation of sex as a device to titillate.

Perhaps counterintuitively, the *mise en scène* of Kechiche's film evokes, for me, Akerman's *Je, Tu, Il, Elle*. Part of what is striking about *Blue Is the Warmest Colour*'s sex scenes is that, unlike the close-ups of the film's remainder, they are frequently filmed using medium shots. This marked contrast appears as a concerted decision to force us to reckon with the explicitness of sex. Doane's argument about the close-up suggests its link to universality rather than to particularity. She writes that the close-up 'has been seen as the vehicle of the star, the privileged receptacle of affect, of passion, the guarantee of the cinema's status as a universal language, one of, if not *the* most recognizable units of cinematic discourse' (2003: 91). While the close-up thus universalises the image because it strips it of particularities, it also safeguards against the unambiguousness of the particular. In both Akerman's film and Kechiche's, two women embrace on a bed in a medium long shot that leaves open their readability: instead of cutting up – by way of cutting closer to – the figures' moving bodies, the shot lets them speak for themselves. What provokes an uncomfortable reaction to the graphic nature of *Blue Is the Warmest Colour*'s 'so-called' lesbian sex scenes is, as in *Je, Tu, Il, Elle*, the longer, more distanced take that, over the course of several minutes instead of seconds, lingers for an awkwardly long time before cutting to close-up for the relief of abstraction.

The controversially explicit sex scenes of *Blue Is the Warmest Colour* refuse to provide relief from the static and distanced shot, recalling the excruciating bareness of Akerman's film, whose sex scenes intensify the immediacy of the sexual by refusing techniques such as slow-motion montage and atmospheric music. In most feature films, music is used to orient us, to orchestrate the way in which we read what we see on-screen, just as the montage of the art film's avant-garde love scenes closes down ambiguous legibility even as it masquerades *as art*.[11] Music not only reflects the characters' interiorities but also commands our reading of them. While *Desert Hearts* famously eschews musical accompaniment in its climactic sex scene, it otherwise operates along familiarly orienting lines. Rhona Berenstein (1996: 132) writes that its 'sexiness is produced in large part by [. . .] slow pacing, romantic lighting, and gentle gestures'; the same goes for *The Hunger* (Tony Scott, 1983), Berenstein writes sardonically, 'even in the case of a vampire attack'. These are the ingredients of the 'spectacle' that Merck writes is 'disturb[ed]' by the loud volume of *Je, Tu, Il, Elle*'s sex scenes (1993: 175). In both *Blue Is the Warmest Colour* and *Je, Tu, Il, Elle*, we hear every intake of breath and passionate sigh. Without music for much of the film but most notably for the sex scenes, *Blue Is the Warmest Colour* provokes a disjuncture between what we see and how we are compelled to regard it.

Of all the films that Lucille Cairns analyses in her broad study of Francophone lesbian cinema, *Je, Tu, Il, Elle* provides, she argues, 'by far the most explicit mediation of lesbian sex' (2006: 161). What is striking about Cairns's assertion in this context is her use of the word 'mediation'. For what makes both *Je, Tu, Il, Elle* and *Blue Is the Warmest Colour* remarkable is a (perceived) *lack* of mediation. And this is precisely what elicits the (so-called) threat of pornography and its particular conditions of representation; Richard Dyer writes that 'what makes watching a porn video exciting is the fact that you are watching some people making a porn video, some performers doing it in front of cameras, and you' (2004: 102). Amongst the buzz that *Blue Is the Warmest Colour* has elicited is the surprise, bafflement, scepticism and amusement aroused by the use of prosthetic vaginas worn by both actresses during the sex scenes (see Oler, 2013). We might ask what is at stake here – the actresses' 'real' touching of each other's genitals or the spectators' 'real' viewing of them?[12] In a discussion about the 'unsimulated' sex of John Cameron Mitchell's *Shortbus* (2006), Nick Davis points to the unavoidability of the 'hypermediated apparatus of filmmaking, which works precisely to simulate any object or event in its path' (2008: 623). Of course, even a film's elicitation of the *perception* of a lack of mediation is, precisely, mediated.

Thus we might ask, as Davis parses, 'what precisely is "real" about "real" sex' (Ibid.: 624)? If the 'lesbian' sex scenes of *Blue Is the Warmest Colour* are derided as 'pornographic' (a derision whose ideological assumption is that the latter cannot possibly capture the reality of the former), they are condemned in their inability to serve the (again, ideologically assumed) aim of lesbian cultural production: to be reflective of something *real*. The call for visibility as a call for realism relies on a version of 'lesbian experience' that is at the very least a misrecognition. Chris Holmlund writes that the femme is 'most visibly a lesbian when making love with another woman' (2002: 39); particularly for the lesbian whose gender presentation does not conform to stereotype, then, the visibility of sex is a determinate of more than sexual *behaviour* but rather sexuality itself (see also Harris and Crocker, 1997: 2). And Rosi Braidotti writes that 'in pornography, sex is represented through the spectacle of organs interpenetrating each other, but that proves a very unsatisfactory image for the act itself. There is always something more to experience than the image can show' (2002: 25). In the case of *Blue Is the Warmest Colour*, sex is asked by its critics not only to be a satisfactory image of 'the act itself', but also of lesbian identity more broadly: of the film's legibility as lesbian. When sex is cut into pieces, into singular images of genitalia, we are left with an 'unsatisfactory' image of the lesbian as legible. The explicitness of *Blue Is the Warmest Colour*'s sex scenes provide tension with a gesture to a further version of realism, a communally understood notion of what is legitimately lesbian: the images we 'want' and 'seek' to be 'moved by' (Cowie, 1997: 5). Paradoxically, the explicitness of the film's sex scenes becomes the foundation for an argument against its status as a lesbian text. If its reviews induct *Blue Is the Warmest Colour* into a discourse that, as Merck writes, 'privilege[s] the body, particularly its sexual functions, as a source of truth about social relations in general' (1993: 167), they not only ask who can speak for whom but also to what extent can we see part of that speech (sex) as the synecdoche for the whole (lesbian experience)?

LINGERING JUST TOO LONG

What potentially gets lost here is the fact that all of the arguments presented above are premised on a limited understanding of what might constitute one of *Blue Is the Warmest Colour*'s 'sex scenes'.[13] One late scene, occurring after Adèle and Emma's relationship has ended following a climactic fight, radically disrupts any argument that can be made about the turning of sex into a decorative spectacle. Over the course of fifteen minutes, Adèle sits across a table from Emma at a bar, the frame unoccupied by anybody else until the final few seconds that pull out of a suffocating close-up. The film's longest by far, this scene is rarely mentioned in reviews. Revealing her enduring desire for Emma, who has begun a relationship with another woman, Adèle spends much of the fifteen minutes on-screen with her face sodden with tears and snot, the public culmination of countless antecedent scenes of her physically manifested misery. After seven minutes of conversation, Adèle clasps Emma's hand and brings it to her lips, sucking on her fingers and then on her fist. The shots in this climactic moment shift between various close-ups: of Adèle's open mouth, her teary eyes, her desperate and almost ugly kissing of Emma's lips and her grasp of Emma's hand at her crotch. The presence here of the abject – alongside its absence in the media discourse that contrives the film's potential for controversy

– reveals a prevalent inclination towards smoothing over such ambiguous framings of desire.

The sequence of shots of Adèle in the water that I discussed in an earlier section of this chapter offers a moment of tension between passion and despair that characterises the film's broader exploration of the intensity of first love. The water around Adèle has a bright sheen to it that confuses our perception of its surface and depth. In the image we can see Adèle's skin beneath the surface but the water seems to congeal around her. This play extends to the film's attention to its characters' surface affects, the tears that signify despair and the sighs that signify passion always shielding a deeper interiority that is both hinted at and withheld, consistently confusing our notion of access to the characters' emotional depths. In his book on space in French cinema, in which he cites Kechiche as a pivotal auteur, James Williams addresses cinema's ability to evoke interiority – not only through point-of-view shots, of which *Blue Is the Warmest Colour* actually yields very few, but also through the 'exclusive close focus on one character moving through screenspace' (2013: 3). However, such devices – which can offer the 'illusion of unboundedness', as Williams writes – have the potential to be disrupted or disturbed, such as when 'the apparent promise of spectatorial identification and unstoppable access into a character's subjective space is peremptorily thwarted by the film's withdrawal into another type of subjective space' (Ibid.). *Blue Is the Warmest Colour* creates an illusion and then breaks it down. Adrift in an urban intersection in the shot with which I began this chapter (see Figure 5.1), Adèle's subjective space is thwarted as we lose our hold on her as the stable thread of our focus; momentarily, our subjectivity as it has been created by the film shifts to the object of her desire. In the notable moments in which the camera films in the face of direct sunlight, the residue of light that creates red rings around the frame is captured and celebrated through a lingering regard rather than closed down. The young love that is thrust upon us in high definition requires a feat of stamina, and a three-hour running time, because it brings with it all the awkwardness, explicitness and toughness that comes with lingering in these moments just too long.

Incessant graduations from one similar space to another give *Blue Is the Warmest Colour* a forward momentum but also a cyclical repetitiveness. The *bildungsroman* theme of progression is stalled by repeated returns to the same spatial signifier of childhood, the classroom. The film exhibits both sides of the sensation of what Julia Kristeva calls 'women's time': on the one hand cyclical, defined by repetition, and on the other hand a 'monumental temporality, without cleavage or escape, which has so little to do with linear time (which passes) that the very word "temporality" hardly fits: all-encompassing and infinite like imaginary space' (1981 [1979]: 16). The film begins at sunrise and ends at sunset, the final *mise en scène* referencing the very first with a medium shot of an urban street through which a solitary Adèle walks with her back to the camera. This scope could represent many years or just a single day, and the film juggles these two temporal registers of epic scale and intense immediacy.

Blue Is the Warmest Colour familiarises its viewers with particular locations, shots and characters before throwing these orienting frames of reference into disorder. Just as certain spaces become familiar but are then withdrawn or disrupted, so too the film withholds the essential markers of chronology that emphasise the coming-of-age genre's theme of progression. The film flourishes the politics of identity before deflecting their pursuit. A relationship begins in a site of collective identity – the lesbian bar – but promptly leaves it behind. Gay and workers' rights and grievances are celebrated and protested, but the political stakes of these collective endeavours are dissolved into the close-up of desire's intensely immediate setting. The counter-pedagogical question – 'When did you first taste a woman?' – seduces rather than defers, and from that point on the film's sexual affect takes hold, extending far beyond what are officially categorised as 'sex scenes'. Linda Williams summarises an apparently commonsensical alternative critical response to the film's sexual abundance: 'Since sex exists in life, then why not, proportionally so, in movies?' (2014: 10). In contrast to the normative requirements of *the* (singular) sex scene (see Finlay and Fenton, 2005; Gupta, 2013), it is precisely *because* sex in *Blue Is the Warmest Colour* becomes heightened, prolonged, even narratively excessive, that it has any chance of representing some version of sexual realism (if it must) – in its abjection and its sublimity. These scenes encapsulate the endurance required of the film's potential generic allies, the *bildungsroman* and the epic, but with the 'essentials' reorganised.

Popular critical debates about *Blue Is the Warmest Colour*'s sex scenes produce a demand for lesbian legibility, obscuring the exciting indeterminacy of the film's generic, spatial and temporal registers. The imperative trope – narrative climax in the form of the sex scene – also urges us towards a theoretical climax. We must reach a definitive conclusion, celebrating the film as defiantly lesbian or denunciating it – defiantly – as anything but. The solipsism of its sexual representation seems to screen out the problematic conditions of its production; of course, to defend it – for accusations of either absurdity or offensiveness – is discomforting. On another level of argumentation, however, the film's sex scene (for it is repeatedly reduced to just one), as framed within and then by the film's critical reception, *must* be read as a paradox, indeed as *the* paradox of lesbian representability in an age of extreme visibility: as either unable to represent lesbian experience because it is pornographic (and thus cannot be real), or as being the very thing that makes *Blue*

Is the Warmest Colour a lesbian film more than anything else (because the sex comes to stand in for lesbian experience *par excellence*). My response to the film must also accommodate my own ambivalence. I can but remember the way it submerged me in a haze of blue. Here was an emotional realism, for me.

If in *Blue Is the Warmest Colour* we are delivered sex as excess, the film I discuss in the next and final chapter, *Carol* (Todd Haynes, 2015), forces us to retreat, accustoming our desiring gaze to the seemingly endless anticipation of touch. No defence is needed for the adaptation of Patricia Highsmith's classic novel, already overdetermined in its lesbian status. In contrast to the excessive centrality of physicality, Haynes's film cites cinema's historical relationship to lesbianism through the look. And yet, *Carol* matches *Blue Is the Warmest Colour*'s affective register, producing the drifting headiness of an erotic, if not sexual, affect that saturates a *mise en scène* filtered through the colours of desire's evolution and loss.

CHAPTER 6

Looking at Carol: *The Drift of New Queer Pleasures*

Bringing this book's case studies together as one corpus has revealed the frequently and even inherently imitative structure of desire's figuration. Erotic identities are constituted through identification. The lesbian finds herself mediated through culture, her sexuality defined only through a depleted patriarchal vernacular, a performance of a sexual role or a culturally imagined style. The cinematic image, even as it promises to provide 'evidence', always threatens to reveal itself as that which has been an illusion. In *Blue Is the Warmest Colour* (Abdellatif Kechiche, 2013), Emma's sexuality first takes form in Adèle's mind as masturbatory fantasy before any acquaintance has been made and is then reduced to the iconic image of her blue hair that figures desire on her behalf for the rest of the film. The ensemble switch in *Mulholland Drive* (David Lynch, 2001); the titular character's death in *Chloe* (Atom Egoyan, 2009); the surveillance aesthetic in *Circumstance* (Maryam Keshavarz, 2011): these are all ways in which, through a constant preoccupation with revealing and withholding, each film exposes, and then threatens to shield, lesbian desire.

Studies of lesbian cinema have increasingly shifted conversations away from the intentionality of desire central to psychoanalytic film theory. In her book *Lesbianism, Cinema, Space* (2009), Lee Wallace foregrounds the spatialisation of desire, dividing up her chapters in order to account for the lesbian set, *mise en scène*, location, edit and diegesis. Conspicuous in its absence from this list is the gaze. Such a term seems to turn back time, invoking primarily the active desires belonging to the *men who look* in the classical Hollywood films forming the basis of Laura Mulvey's 1975 study of 'visual pleasure': *The River of No Return* (Otto Preminger, 1954); *To Have and Have Not* (Howard Hawks, 1944); *Only Angels Have Wings* (Howard Hawks, 1939); *Morocco* (Josef von Sternberg, 1930); *Dishonoured* (Josef von Sternberg, 1931); *Vertigo* (Alfred Hitchcock, 1958); *Marnie* (Alfred Hitchcock, 1964) and *Rear Window* (Alfred Hitchcock, 1954). When Linda Williams reviews the 'afterlife' of Mulvey's article, she begins by stating that, 'in the early years of feminist film studies, it was difficult to write anything that did not cite' it (2017: 465). Continuing in the next paragraph, Williams advises that 'those were simpler days' (Ibid.).[1]

Figure 6.1. The original motion picture soundtrack for *Carol* (Todd Haynes, 2015), scored by Carter Burwell, depicting Carol (Cate Blanchett) and Therese (Rooney Mara).

Still, the writers most consistently cited in *Lesbian Cinema after Queer Theory* – Teresa de Lauretis, Jackie Stacey and Patricia White – are all scholars who have, in different ways, put the gaze at the heart of their readings of cinematic lesbian desire in the twentieth century, giving life to theories of spectatorship in the study of lesbian representation. Processes of looking continue to lay the groundwork of lesbian representability in twenty-first-century cinema. The gaze intensifies desire, even if it does not produce it. Atafeh watches Shireen through a CCTV camera, a vicariously produced system of lesbian voyeurism; Emma and Marie watch as their idols perform and, through performance, become objects of desire; Adèle becomes an artist's living muse. We are reminded of Mulvey's poignant articulation of the way in which the woman's 'visual presence tends to work against the development of the story line, to freeze the flow of action in moments of erotic contemplation' (1975: 11). Contemplation provides the space for desire to take shape; desire is shaped within *and by* the image. These are no simple, uninterrupted processes of looking: fantasy remains the pivotal screen onto which desire is projected. Desire is mediated if not altogether distorted by a screen (metaphorised in water and mirror, window and canvas) as it '"positions" and obscures simultaneously' (Mayne, 1990: 41). We are made aware of these processes of voyeurism even as we take pleasure in the illusory identifications and desires that they grant to us.

And so it follows with *Carol* (Todd Haynes, 2015), a film that demands to be read as a narrative of looking. Therese (Rooney Mara) is a budding photographer who begins the film half-heartedly occupying a cold Manhattan apartment and a cold relationship with Richard (Jake Lacy). Meeting Carol (Cate Blanchett) across the counter of the department store in which she works, Therese falls into desire with the seductive woman who confidently invites her for lunch and then for a departure from New York. Together, they escape the mundanity of a heterosexual relationship going nowhere whose end has pathetically few consequences (Therese) and the severity of a divorce whose plausible consequence is the tragic loss of a custody battle (Carol). The film diffuses desire across a sweeping affective repertory: misty windows, sheets of rain and saturations of city light; lingering musical themes; the revival of celluloid grain. It signals its tribute to the 1950s with 16mm film and an aesthetic nod to the imagery of Saul Leiter's New York; beyond set design, costume or narrative detail it is *photographically* a period piece (see Lachman, 2015). Breaching the logic of visibility's progression, moreover, *Carol*'s erotic and romantic potential is largely generated from a series of looks and fleeting touches. First audacious gazes precipitate first tentative words. Once they do speak, meet, speak and meet again, dialogue is often punctuated by adamantly silent moments of intense looking. Chapter 5 captured the excesses of visual pleasure and the extremes of the uncompromising image. Chapter 6 returns us to visual sidelines and reservations. In contrast to the furore surrounding *Blue Is the Warmest Colour*, reviews of *Carol* barely if ever mention its sex scene. And there is no reason to: no rules are broken, representability remains within the confines of acceptability. The grainy, almost painterly image from the scene functions on the album cover of the soundtrack to announce two elements together: arty abstraction and sweeping musical orchestration (see Figure 6.1). The film's preoccupations seemingly lie elsewhere. Affect lingers long beyond visible acts. *Carol*'s erotic register draws on the suspended terms of mid-twentieth-century cinematic homoeroticism.

The film was adapted from Patricia Highsmith's bestseller *The Price of Salt*, a novel first published under a pseudonym in 1952. Hollywood films of the time were released under the auspices of the mid-twentieth-century Motion Picture Production Code, which censored explicitly homosexual images on-screen. Unlike these films and its contemporaries in the world of literary and popular fiction, *The Price of Salt* left open the potential for its two protagonists to enjoy a romance beyond the final page. It was eventually re-published under Highsmith's own name and with a new title, *Carol* (1991).[2] Its adaptation was in pre-production from 1997, when it was first in preparation by screenwriter Phyllis Nagy, long preceding Todd Haynes's directorship or the stars' casting. From that point on, it became arguably the most widely anticipated lesbian film of the last two decades. Its lesbian sensibility is prefigured by Highsmith, Nagy and by Haynes's long-time collaborator, producer Christine Vachon; its queerness is given momentum by the direction of Haynes, a key member of the New Queer Cinema movement who has since devoted his oeuvre to the reincarnation of the 'women's picture' with works such as *Far from Heaven* (2002) and *Mildred Pierce* (2011). Even before its production schedule began, the expectation, anticipation and excitement of *Carol*'s (queer) lesbianism was overdetermined.

I have argued in *Lesbian Cinema after Queer Theory* that we must look back to the history of the lesbian's cinematic image in order to explore her constitution as figure in the present. This final chapter considers not only the ways in which *Carol* is indebted to cinemas of the past on a narrative and aesthetic level, but how its treatment by the discursive field surrounding it reignites the historical conditions of representability with which I began this book: the singularity of the lesbian figure and the paradoxical status of her doubled/coupled form. Two Academy Award categories endorsed the central performances in *Carol* during the 2016 awards season: Actress in a Leading Role and Actress in a Supporting Role. Lesbian cinema is revealed in this moment of nomination to be not only an aesthetic, narrative or social category but an industrial one. Paradigms of absence and presence are replicated and reinforced by institutional mechanisms. Confronting these seemingly stark figurations, the chapter proceeds to argue that, in fact, *Carol*'s sensibility queerly diffuses the presumption of both pathological singularity and normative coupling. I read this film with and through its complicated and contradictory cinematic debts – not only to classical Hollywood *noir* and re-workings of the domestic melodrama, but also to the New Queer Cinema. *Carol*'s temporality resists easy narrativisation even as its literary heritage announces a definitive optimism. I argue that *Carol* toys with us, denying our immediate satisfaction in the legibility of a new lesbian cinema but providing the intractable pleasures of queer's diffusion of desire across the screen.

ALL ABOUT THERESE

Actresses have been nominated (and occasionally won) in the Best Actress category for lesbian-themed films in the past: Annette Bening (*The Kids Are All Right*, Lisa Cholodenko, 2010); Nathalie Portman (*Black Swan*, Darren Aronofsky, 2010); Charlize Theron (*Monster*, Patty Jenkins, 2003); and Nicole Kidman (*The Hours*, Stephen Daldry, 2002). Further examples might be included here that have later been reclaimed within a lesbian film canon: Jodie Foster in *The Accused* (Jonathan Kaplan, 1988); Julie Harris in *The Member of the Wedding* (Fred Zinnemann, 1952); and Joan Fontaine in *Rebecca* (Alfred Hitchcock, 1940). However, these Oscar contenders have stood alone, figuring the lesbian in the singular even if her on-screen characterisation places her (finally) into a couple. Only four times in Oscars history have two women from the same film been nominated concurrently for Best Actress: Bette Davis and Anne Baxter (*All About Eve*, Joseph Mankiewicz, 1950); Katharine Hepburn and Elizabeth Taylor (*Suddenly Last Summer*, Joseph Mankiewicz, 1959); Anne Bancroft and Shirley MacLaine (*The Turning Point*, Herbert Ross, 1977); and Geena Davis and Susan Sarandon (*Thelma and Louise*, Ridley Scott, 1991).[3] None of these were for lesbian narratives – at least not explicitly, though *All About Eve* was of course the subject of Stacey's field-defining analysis of 'intra-feminine fascinations' in her article 'Desperately Seeking Difference' (1987: 57). Two women regularly play 'support' to male leads, so, perhaps unsurprisingly, dual nominations for two (so-called) Best Supporting Actresses in the same film are not rare; and, in *Uninvited* (1999), White writes at length about the lesbian incarnation of the supporting role itself. Since 2000 alone, five films have garnered double nominations in this category: *Almost Famous* (Cameron Crowe, 2000); *Gosford Park* (Robert Altman, 2001); *Doubt* (John Patrick Shanley, 2008); *Up in the Air* (Jason Reitman, 2009) and *The Fighter* (David O. Russell, 2010).

The issue here is not, then, that Blanchett and Mara were not nominated *at all* for their roles in *Carol*. Rather, the asymmetrical distribution of awards nominations takes the film's title at its word, reasserting a historical paradox of lesbian representability well known by readers of this book: the inevitable double must be contained within the singular figure, one name bearing the burden of lesbian figuration for two women. Awards may in themselves offer little in the way of useful analysis of the film on its own terms, but they evidence here the dependence on a historical discursive template for lesbian representation. Blanchett and Mara occupy very similar amounts of screen time in *Carol*. However, the film's nominations profile, prominently spearheaded by the Oscars, sets up an unambiguous divide between two competing constituencies – lead and supporting. Such a division of the lesbian couple into 'lead' and 'support' replicates the binary oppositions that have marked and stuck to the lesbian both with and without her consent: active/passive, masculine/feminine, top/bottom, dominant/submissive, butch/femme, leading/supporting. The first are among the duos famously characterised by Eve Kosofksy Sedgwick as contributing to the 'now chronic modern crisis of homo/heterosexual definition' (2008 [1990]: 11); the last could similarly be premised on their contributions to sexuality's polarising insistence on definition and/as differentiation.

The illusion of defined and static difference is the solution to the unbearable threat of sameness. In the cinema, this becomes a visual interplay, and one that is relied on by the majority of the publicity posters produced to market *Carol*. Two women stare out from their respective scenes, one at the top and the other at the bottom of a rectangular poster frame (see Figures 6.2–6.5). Costume, hair and makeup are repeatedly employed to define arbitrary feminised difference, as Stella Bruzzi has documented (1997). Here on *Carol*'s posters, with even the direction of their stares paralleled, the women are divided visually by costume and hair colour alone. Any presumption of difference rests, moreover, on the inability to perceive shared whiteness as sameness. This is a division that has characterised representations of white femininity in classics such as *The Birds* (Alfred Hitchcock, 1963), *Mogambo* (John Ford, 1953) and, of course, *Gentlemen Prefer Blondes* (Howard Hawks, 1953), whose face-off between Marilyn Monroe and Jane Russell is announced without ambiguity in its title; and neo-*noir* films such as *The Black Dahlia* (Brian de Palma, 2006) and *Basic Instinct* (Paul Verhoeven, 1992). *Mulholland Drive* pastiches the trope, its suspenseful drive systematically built on the sartorial and coiffured division between Betty (Naomi Watts) and Rita (Laura Harring), and on the uncanny consequences of the merging that occurs when one of them dons a wig to match the other.

In Figure 6.5, one woman is seductive, confident, her pose directed to the viewer in a display of assurance (Blanchett as Carol); the other is meek, turning her gaze sheepishly as if in surprise or uncertainty (Mara as Therese). What visually unites the two halves of the frame in every case is a word, the title of the film, a name: *CAROL*. Two women's images, gazes, directions of desire are condensed into a single figure. Played by Blanchett, the film star who exhibits mid-century glamour with a twist – gender-bending roles in Haynes's *I'm Not There* (2007) and Julian Rosefeldt's *Manifesto* (2015) queerly inflect her star persona – Carol begs to be centre stage. This assurance of her lead makes Blanchett as Carol into an almost grotesque figure; her strategies of seduction have indeed been made camp by Kate McKinnon's affectionate and hilarious impersonation in a parody at the Film Independent Spirit Awards (2016). Lexically singled out on the movie poster, Carol conjures

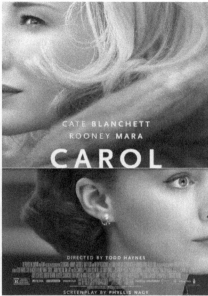

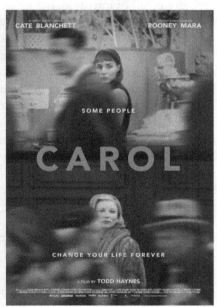

Figures 6.2–6.5. Four American posters for *Carol*.

moreover the *femme fatale* whose name so frequently graces, alone, the most famous titles of the *film noir* genre. In Otto Preminger's *Laura* (1944), Laura is the woman who, presumed dead, comes back to life, marking out the male protagonist's obsession and futile desire. Her name stands in for unknowability, deception and male impotence. In Charles Vidor's *Gilda* (1946), which was central to my reading of *Mulholland Drive* in Chapter 1, Rita Hayworth is the woman who brings the male protagonist to terms with his sordid past and the inevitability of a compromised future, the desire (for her) from which he cannot escape. Gilda comes into being in the first scene of Vidor's film through a description of her on the audio track. The famous line 'Gilda, are you decent?' characterises Gilda along with the sardonic presumption of her *in*decency before we even set eyes on her. In these classic examples of the *film noir*, the woman's name single-handedly indicates a problem. She calls to be looked at but is held at a distance. Unlike in *Mildred Pierce* – in Michael Curtiz's original (1945) or in Haynes's adaptation – there is no surname to flesh out her character or to offer biographical inscription or elaboration. Her solitary name elicits only an iconography of desire and/ or threat.

Carol is full of intention: her looks are directional, designed to seduce. In contrast, Therese might be framed – in accordance with her 'supporting' role – as a mere passive recipient: 'All I do is say yes to everything,' she moans of her own mandatory state of receptiveness in the face of Carol's assertiveness and assertion (of gaze, of presence). And yet, in a crucial allusion to a seminal narrative of voyeurism, Nagy modelled Blanchett's Carol on Grace Kelly in *Rear Window* (see Jaffe, 2016). Kelly's character Lisa is diegetically positioned in Alfred Hitchcock's film as complicit in the voyeurism of the male protagonist, helping him to solve the mystery of a murder across the courtyard of his Manhattan apartment. While Jeff (James Stewart) remains bound to a wheelchair with only camera in hand, Lisa pursues his investigation on foot. She breaks into the apartment Jeff is surveilling in order to deliver to him a series of vital visual clues (see Figure 6.6). But, by virtue of becoming his walking avatar, she is thus aesthetically positioned as the integral object of his voyeuristic gaze. The inspiration of *Rear Window* in Carol's characterisation thus constructs both subject and object of the film's gaze around the central apparatus: Jeff's/Therese's camera. The shift in vocation from set designer in the novel to photographer in the adaptation gives Therese, who is otherwise shy and unassuming, the tools with which to curate, and then to amplify, her gaze. In *Carol*, Therese's camera is even bought for her by Carol as an unsolicited gift. Carol thus invites the gaze; she willingly, indeed wilfully, becomes the object of desire. Carol *desires to be desired* – via Therese, she gives *us all* the camera through which we might gaze at her.

Figure 6.6. Frame grab from *Rear Window* (Alfred Hitchcock, 1954). Lisa (Grace Kelly) becomes object of the gaze.

Understood along the lines of this paradigm, Therese is made present only through her desire for the eponymous Carol. However, *Carol*'s tag line interpellates not only the titular lead, but she who will desire her: 'Some people change your life forever', it reads, bringing into being 'you' as Therese, who will be changed by Carol. Not only is Carol herself invoked by the singular name and its associations, then, but so is the subject of desire *for* Carol: Therese. This reverses the strategy of *All About Eve*, a film not only about Anne Baxter's Eve but also about her narcissistic identification. That film *looks at* Bette Davis's Margot Channing, but the title recognises the passive protagonism and precisely the erotic entanglement of Eve's identification. Similarly, in *Carol*, it is Therese who sets the name *Carol Aird* in script, scribbling it in her diary in a childish scrawl after they first meet. Haynes's film sits against a tangle of cinematic identifications and interpellations. It might aim its desiring drives towards Carol but it is *all about* Therese.

FANTASIES OF THE SUBJECT

By way of analogy, I return to the portrait of the ancestor through which Rebecca de Winter's absence is figured in Hitchcock's *Rebecca*. White writes of *Rebecca* that narrativity 'works to position the heroine (and the spectator who identifies with her) in relation to a desirable female object. Yet the genre enacts prohibition against their representation *together*, since one of the women is dead' (1999: xxi, original emphasis). In this way, the image of

Figure 6.7. Frame grab from *Carol*. Therese plays the metaphorical daughter.

Figure 6.8. Frame grab from *Carol*. Therese and Carol *don't quite* yet kiss.

the lesbian pre-empts absence through a spectral presence, her corporeality always uncertain. It is only once she marries Maxim de Winter (Laurence Olivier) and becomes the *second* Mrs de Winter that Fontaine's 'heroine' is awarded any name at all – one she shares not only with her husband, of course, but with his first wife. She is reduced to namelessness by the titular Rebecca; made nominally invisible, she can only support. She is but a vehicle for our vicarious, spectatorial desire for a superlative, domi-nant, exquisite object. It is of course irresistible to read *Carol* through the maternal metaphors that have dominated discussions of *Rebecca*. Neither the film's casting nor its costumes or make-up shy away from the age dif-ference between Carol and Therese, which is drawn further attention to by Carol's attentive and coddling tone: 'what a strange girl you are . . . flung out of space', she says in a peculiar act of seduction. Therese is a character with only minimal back story, her family nowhere apparent. Positioned by Carol, she is not just young but entirely other-wordly. She is frequently sit-uated diminutively next to the older woman in a direct visual parallel with Carol's young daughter Rindy (Kennedy/Sadie Heim). Therese and Rindy even share the same hairstyle – or, rather, a naïve *lack of style* (see Figure 6.7). When Carol teaches Therese to apply makeup, Therese becomes not only daughter but doll. It is also this scene of grown-up play, however, that furthers their intimacy and draws them physically together; under the guise of the application of perfume to her neck, Carol beckons Therese towards her for what visually replicates the posture of a first kiss (see Figure 6.8). The film thus invites comparison with classical melodramas such as *Now, Voyager* (Irving Rapper, 1942) in which, in Mandy Merck's words, a 'mater-nal homoerotic fantasy' is enacted 'without an explicit lesbian union by offering the female spectator and her diegetic delegate the figure of the sur-rogate mother as desirable woman' (2017). In her article, entitled 'Negative Oedipus: *Carol* as Lesbian Romance and Maternal Melodrama', Merck's close analysis makes for a convincing reading of the film through this very lens (see also Campbell, 2017: 141). The semantic equivalence of 'lesbian' and 'maternal', 'romance' and 'melodrama' in Merck's title indeed makes these terms co-constitutive.

Even as feminist film theorists draw on this maternal metaphor, however, the conflation of lesbianism and non-sexual female relationships continues to provoke defiant defences of lesbianism's sexual specificity. One might continue to fear, like Andrea Weiss in the early 1990s, that 'each lesbian image that has managed to surface [. . .] has helped determine the boundaries of possible representation, and has insured the invisibility of many other kinds of lesbian images' (1992: 1). One of these images is, of course, the 'pre-Oedipal mother/daughter lesbian relationship' (Ibid.). The framing of *Carol* in this way is simultaneously inevitable and uncomfortable, dissolving lesbian sexuality into a continuum of homosociality and homosexuality, such as that posed by Sedgwick (1985: 2) and critiqued by de Lauretis (1994: 115). Any such metaphor also threatens to dissolve the very subjectivity on which our identification is based, aligned as we are with Therese via the 'you' of a tag line announcing the 'change' of 'your life forever'. As Tania Modleski interprets the spectator's experience of watching *Rebecca*, 'both she and we are made to experience a kind of annihilation of the self' (1988: 49). In response to such a reading of *Carol*, we can, of course, seek moments in which to triumphantly argue against the female Oedipal reading. We can find a *multitude! (we say!)* of examples of Therese's own small opportunities for agency and acts of seduction. It is music played by Therese on the piano and then bought on vinyl that becomes the soundtrack that will accompany their romance. It is Carol who childishly asks for the track to be played 'Again!'. Later in the film, it is Therese who demands that Carol 'take me to bed'. Here, she verbally initiates her and Carol's first (and only full diegetic) sex scene, though she is simultaneously instructive and childlike, knowing what it is that she wants whilst asking for help to bring it into being. Any such stubborn counter-arguments thus reveal that these are complicated identifications: we are reminded by the film's title that our desire only serves to shore up the status of the desired.

In her description of what constitutes the desiring subject, Lauren Berlant articulates that she 'is well served by the formalism of desire: although desire is anarchic and restless, the objects to which desire becomes attached stabilize the subject and enable her to assume a stable-enough identity' (2012b: 76). Therese occupies a kind of openness to the experiencing of desire. She lingers in a space of receptiveness. She waits for Carol to switch on her seductive glances, to offer moments of confirmation. As Berlant goes on, this object to which one's desires attach is not a stable thing; it is not even a singular object but rather a *'cluster* of fantasmatic investments' (Ibid., emphasis added). To see the object as something that will restore you, that will help to consolidate

Figure 6.9. Frame grab from *Carol*. Carol solicits our gaze.

Figure 6.10. Frame grab from *Carol*. Therese is obscured in sympathy.

your sense of yourself, is to be out of sync. The first image of 'Carol' seen from Therese's point of view is a simulacrum: the camera pauses on a woman on the pavement with a fur coat and red scarf over blonde hair. We are lured, just as Therese is, into thinking it is, must be, Carol. But it isn't Carol, only the *idea* of her transplanted onto a stranger walking down the street. This is also a memory, unreliable as a dream; visually, for the spectator, a placeholder for Carol serves the *mise en scène* just as well. If Carol is Blanchett, Kelly and Rebecca de Winter all at once, she is always already a simulacrum of our fantasy of the woman who might satisfy our spectatorial desire. Haynes gave a copy of Roland Barthes's *A Lover's Discourse* to everyone on set to read (see White, 2015: 11), and indicated his own investment in this theoretical conceptualisation of desire, discussing the film's melancholy mood as the defining 'isolation of the desiring subject' (in Davis, 2015: 32). Much of the film's temporality is defined by the waiting that Barthes so acutely and agonis-ingly documents in that text (2002 [1977]). I understand it as the feeling of waiting for your beloved to think of you in just the same moment that you are conscious of wanting to be in receipt of their thoughts: the feeling of wanting to share a moment *in time*, if only *across space*. Even when Carol does appear, in Therese's memory – a car journey through the city with friends and a repeated musical motif brings to mind her shared journey with Carol – we see her through a hazy green filter (see Figure 6.9). Carol's image is distorted by Therese's fantasy; Therese is then distorted in sympathy by the *mise en scène*, which shrouds her behind a rainy window pane, the reflection of red traffic lights first brightening and then obscuring her face. A fantasy of the object must always also be a fantasy of the subject (see Figure 6.10).

(Ex)citing Genres

In a manifesto on the constitution of the queer text, 'Queer Texts, Bad Habits, and the Issue of a Future', de Lauretis writes that 'the unnegotiable demands of most readers, viewers, or listeners to identify and to *identify with* [. . .] are the normative requirements with which fiction is expected to comply' (2011: 244, original emphasis). We demand, de Lauretis writes, to understand 'what's happening, to know who's who in the diegesis, to find some incitement to fantasy or some versions of oneself in the mirror of the text, be it only the ego's sense of mastery over the object-text' (Ibid.). The text that refuses such unnegotiable demands is, for de Lauretis, that text which manages to exhibit its sexuality at the level of (queer) form, rather than merely at the level of (we could say lesbian) narrative. In comparison to Djuna Barnes's modernist novel *Nightwood* (2007 [1936]) and David Cronenberg's J. G. Ballard adaptation *Crash* (1996), *Carol* is surely not such a text. Its neat subscription to the period drama offers a manageable façade for difficult feelings; romance is its confirmed starting point for desire. It appears to 'comply' with fiction's 'normative requirements'. Highsmith's novel is focalised through Therese but lacks her narrative voice-over. We might feel close to her, but the novel is not written in Therese's first person, and she remains to some extent an enigma. Haynes's film carefully adapts this dynamic. Without the tools of narration, Therese lacks full mastery over her desire. The film offers us entry points for identification. However, it resists their full realisation. Even as we want to assert her command of the film's compass through an expansive gaze, it is withdrawn from her.

Carol and Therese take a road trip across the American Midwest to distract from the assorted suffocations of their New York lives. The grand house where Carol has brought up her daughter still belongs to her estranged husband Harge (Kyle Chandler); when Therese visits it early in the narrative, her departure is quickly necessitated by Harge's defiant entrance and his proclamation of ownership – not only of the house, but of Carol herself. Carol and Therese's voyage thus gives a subsidiary outlet to what has, until now, been a flirtation, at times heady with possibility and at others almost quaint with hesitation and politeness. The narrative climax juxtaposes these two motivations: seeking desire and escaping responsibility. The road trip must come to an abrupt end when Carol realises the high stakes of this game – that the reveal of her affair with Therese could mean losing her daughter. They – and we – discover only belatedly that Harge has employed a private detective (Cory Michael Smith) to follow Carol and Therese, whose first and only diegetic sex scene is later revealed to have been recorded by him. The isolation of a single sex scene (reduced from the novel's drawn out unfolding of physical intimacy) joltingly and disappointingly associates sex with misfortune. In her foreword to the novel, Val McDermid describes its generic affiliation as extending 'the drive of a thriller but the imagery of a romance' (2010: vii). Carol and Therese's first tentative flirtations are interrupted by Harge's arrival; the sex scene is immediately met by the discovery of the detective's deception; their next embrace is followed in the subsequent shot by Carol's sudden departure and the unannounced arrival of Abby (Sarah Paulson), the friend recruited to escort Therese home. Drifting romance is consistently threatened with interruption by insistent plot, and the two storylines (romance and thriller) are jarringly juxtaposed.

Carol's sexual and narrative climax is met by the kind of dismantling of privacy that characterises *Circumstance*'s scenario of lesbian desire; all moments of intimacy have the potential *to have been mediated*. *Carol* tells a story of the 1950s, mimicking the cultural dominion of the Hays Code. However, it was filmed in 2014 and released in 2015; it emerges from a United States in which, after a slow uptake of equal marriage from one state to the next, same-sex marriage was federally recognised in all fifty states under Barack Obama's presidency in June 2015 (of course, the subsequent election of President Donald Trump and Vice President Mike Pence provides a sinister appendix to this process of looking backwards). One version of the sexual liberation that – as I argued in Chapter 3 – is culturally associated with the USA is assured; *Carol* looks back to its national history from a privileged standpoint. In 'The Times of the Hours' (2013), Julianne Pidduck puts forward an analysis of what she calls the contemporary 'queer melodrama'. Haynes's *Far from Heaven* and Stephen Daldry's *The Hours* (2002), made within a year of each other in the early 2000s, deal with the past from the vantage point of a contemporary American moment: with marriage equality on the horizon, the terms of queer kinships are confronted with change by the possibility of normative recognition (see also Padva, 2014). Against this context, the films 'probe a lingering and ambivalent attachment to an enduring fantasy of the nuclear family within feminist and queer cultural production and criticism' (Pidduck, 2013: 40). The nuclear family is precisely what *Carol* resurrects and pushes against, forcing its protagonist to choose. The decision Carol finally makes not only to seek romantic love but also to risk motherhood is radical even in the twenty-first century.

The film awards Therese a camera, given to her by Carol as a gift in advance of their trip. This camera awards *us* the possibility of the diegetic lesbian gaze. However, this promise is hastily undermined by a decisive imposition. Looking becomes sinister, as voyeuristic mechanisms of desire merge with those of homophobic inspection. *Carol* thus resurrects a mid-twentieth-century past of secrecy and surveillance. It thereby takes on a strategy of engagement with the contemporary via a past not just narratively but aesthetically cited. The climactic reveal of the detective's presence and the narrative drive that stems from it reveal the aesthetic measures enforced by the melodrama to procure a heightening of emotional angst and jeopardy. In her introduction to a seminal collection of essays on the genre, Christine

Gledhill writes that the melodrama 'addresses us within the limitations of the status quo, of the ideologically permissible' (1987: 38).[4] With his feature debut *Poison* (1991), one of the definitive texts of the New Queer Cinema, Haynes sought to find out what 'the industry [could] bear' (in Rich, 2013: 17). At first sight, *Carol* seems to shift, with Haynes's auteurism, into a different form, to fit neatly into the visually pleasurable and accessible *mise en scène* of a bearable genre. However, the melodrama has itself been a strategy of subversive cinematic expression, providing the opportunity to critique dominant society and industry even while remaining within its terms. The contemporary citation of twentieth-century melodrama is itself part of a very queer genealogy embraced by directors such as François Ozon and Pedro Almodóvar. Haynes's *Far from Heaven* adapts Douglas Sirk's *All That Heaven Allows* (1955) via Rainer Werner Fassbinder's *Ali: Fear Eats the Soul* (1974), which radically reworks Sirk's tale of class and prohibition with an intergenerational romance between an elderly working woman and a younger Moroccan immigrant. All three films – Sirk's, Fassbinder's and Haynes's – proffer narratives of unacceptable desire played out in the interstitial spaces allowed within domestic settings. Together, they form layers of pastiche that radically transcend the presumed heterosexuality of the melodrama's generic trajectories (see Dyer, 1997b).

Thomas Elsaesser writes of Fassbinder's work that, 'amid the beautifully executed camera movements, the classically balanced shots, and the languid pans, another rupture is also present' (1997: 19–20). It is precisely this rupture that is signalled by these intertextual aestheticisations of domesticity's suffocation. Lisa Cholodenko also cites Fassbinder's work with aesthetic and narrative allusions to *The Bitter Tears of Petra von Kant* (1972) in her feature film *High Art* (1998), which, according to B. Ruby Rich, 'gilded the lily and therefore also sounded the death knell of NQC [New Queer Cinema]' (2000: 133; see also Wallace, 2009). Cholodenko juxtaposes here the critical theory of Barthes and the photography of Nan Goldin to reflect at once an intellectual endeavour and an uncompromising encounter with queer counterculture. Lucy (Ally Sheedy) is a photographer whose sexuality is manifested through her work. Her camera is an extension of her desiring eye; she turns her partner, friends, lover and mother into objects of an artist's gaze. For Rich, *High Art* 'push[ed] the envelope of queer consumer expectation and force[d] viewers to move beyond comfortable boundaries to confront the less visible and less savory aspects of our most intimate interactions with those we claim to love' (1999: 83). In its 'melancholy echo of an ideal world yet to be shamed into existence' – to repurpose Elsaesser's description of Fassbinder's work (1997: 19–20) – we can see the subtext of a citation of queer tragedy. No promising epilogue is available in *High Art* to redeem the queer pathologies of Fassbinder, Goldin and Barthes: the film had, in Rich's words, 'the *nerve* to go for an unhappy ending' (2000: 17, emphasis added). The film might be read as the underside of *Carol*'s hopeful lesbian register: an irreverent queer text premised on citation.

THE LABOUR OF QUEER PLEASURE

In the original article that announced the New Queer Cinema, Rich described the movement as a queer *sensation* (1992a). In *Carol*, such sensation *itself* provides pleasure, an affect 'self-validating with or without any further referent' (Tomkins, 1991: 404, cited in Sedgwick and Frank, 1995: 7). Pleasure's referent is external to *Carol*'s diegesis; its citational texture provides cinematic signs of both pleasure and restraint even as it doesn't always name them. *Carol* delivers its period's 'signs of gayness' (Dyer, 1983: 2): a lesbian couple in a record store signified by costume and stare; knowing looks shared across a room at a party. These are codes of recognisability. They are, moreover, the foundation for identification: what we see, and what we have seen, is all we know. In other words, subtext is all intertext. The figurations of *Rebecca*, a diegetic screening of *Sunset Boulevard* (Billy Wilder, 1951), the abstract longing of *A Lover's Discourse*: even beyond its status as adaptation and beyond these allusions, *Carol*'s very visual texture feels citational. The film is not so very far away from the account of 'retrospectatorship' that closes White's *Uninvited*, in which she argues that Haynes's radically queer short film *Dottie Gets Spanked* (1992) 'not only theorises the structuring role of popular culture in perverse desire, it *performs* it' (1999: 199).

We cannot but see *Carol* as a dream of what a lesbian film could be. Chronologically the final film of this book's principal case studies, it is also the most commercially successful, taking $40,272,135 at the box office worldwide.[5] It trades in cinematic heritage, box office returns, Hollywood stars and romance. It solicits, but refuses, the universal application of the love story. Its presumed lesbian sensibility is overdetermined. Eagerly anticipated throughout its long gestation, *Carol* is in the realm of the already *thought, felt, wished*. Of course I cannot write a book about twenty-first-century lesbian cinema, now, without its inclusion. And yet, what is also recognisable is a paradoxical citation of representability's opposing structures: to be made cinematically legible as a 1950s period text is simultaneously to put onto the screen the prevailing terms of *in*visibility. In other words: *Carol* makes us work for our pleasure.

Our relationship to *Carol*'s scene of desire evokes for me what Barthes, in *The Pleasure of the Text* (1975 [1973]), names as the intractability of drifting pleasure: when a text remains just beyond our reach, just as Therese's look doesn't seduce, as Carol's does, but defers our gratification. For Barthes:

The pleasure of the text is not necessarily of a triumphant, heroic, muscular type. No need to throw out one's chest. My pleasure can very well take the form of a drift. *Drifting* occurs whenever *I do not respect the whole*, and whenever, by dint of seeming driven about by language's illusions, seductions, and intimidations, like a cork on the waves, I remain motionless, pivoting on the *intractable* bliss that binds me to the text (to the world). (Ibid.: 18)

Carol seems to deliver more the texture of Barthes's driftingly pleasurable text than of Highsmith's satisfyingly plot-driven novel. If Carol's looks are instructive and solicitous, Therese's are wondering and wandering. Just as we watch Therese drift through her desire for Carol, we can only drift in our watching of the film, from the repetitive patterning of the grate that begins the film in close-up to the repetitive movement of piano and wind on the soundtrack. We are bound to the text by its irresistible display of colour and texture, but we must contend with its stubbornness. Therese's entryway to that which we desire – Carol – is halted by a refusal to yield: from always saying 'Yes to everything,' she switches, in a crucial moment, when Carol asks for a reunion, to a disappointing 'No, I don't think so.' The film sustains the 'game' that produces, for Barthes, 'a dialectics of desire, [. . .] an *unpredictability* of bliss: the bets are not placed' (Ibid.: 4, original emphasis).

We go to a text like *Carol* for bliss, for the overdetermination of the lesbian sensibility, and we are met with precisely this: *unpredictability*. At the moment in which we might feel secure in the consummation of desire we are reminded of its precariousness. If orchestration in the melodramatic genre 'allow[s] for complex aesthetic patterns' (Elsaesser, 1987: 51), the patterns here, both musical and aesthetic, flash back and forth between memory and fantasy, between the heightening of desire and its rejection, refusal or interruption. Edward Lachman's cinematography and Carter Burwell's score are met by the narrative's disjunctive chronology. Directly citing the looping beginning/ ending of *Brief Encounter* (David Lean, 1945), *Carol*'s romance – like the road trip that consummates it – doubles back, its momentum unreliable. Cycles of desire mimic instead the train set that provides the pretext for their first meeting in the department store; it orbits, never reaching the promised West Coast. *Carol* begins out of sequence, like Lean's film, which famously reveals the relationship between Laura (Celia Johnston) and Alec (Trevor Howard) to be ill-fated before it has even begun. The ending arrives at the beginning: we see the moment of goodbye before we see the first hello. This temporal allusion to *Brief Encounter*'s cyclical heartbreak includes a precise replication of the visual coding of the agony of Johnston and Howard's farewell: his hand squeezing her shoulder gently as their final moment together is thwarted by a stranger and a surer display of public intimacy is abandoned (see Figure 6.11). As in *Brief Encounter*, Carol squeezes Therese's shoulder in a tearoom as she

Figure 6.11. Frame grab from *Carol*. The beginning/an ending.

gets up to leave, their possible reunion thwarted by the interruption of an unremarkable acquaintance (Catherine Grant's video essay on the film [2015] is an ode to this comparison). Unlike in the novel, which proceeds chronologically, in Haynes's film, as in Lean's, this unbearable moment must happen twice. Pidduck describes the contemporary queer melodrama's 'strange temporal and affective modalities' (2013: 39); the genre must look backwards in order to deal with and compensate for our ambivalent relations to newly possible homonormative assurances. Here is the temporality of Elsaesser's 'melancholy echo' (1997: 19–20) – we do not yet know what would define the ideal (queer) world.

Upon its publication, *The Price of Salt* undermined the narrative precedents of its peers, making possible a lesbian happy ending – as prospect if not as guarantee. The famous final lines of Highsmith's novel read: 'Therese waited. Then as she was about to go to her, Carol saw her, seemed to stare at her incredulously a moment while Therese watched the small smile growing, before her arm lifted suddenly, her hand waved a quick, eager greeting that Therese had never seen before. Therese walked towards her.' (1991 [1952]: 307) The glance of assertive desire in this scene belongs, finally, to Therese. In the film, we see Carol's receipt of and facial response to Therese's choice; the wilful acceptance of the gaze belongs, as ever, to Carol. The final shot of the film is of Carol, poised for a seductive glance, cut off just as she delivers it and before it can be returned.

The films of the New Queer Cinema were not 'all the same and don't share a single aesthetic vocabulary, strategy or concern' but were all, as Rich wrote at the time, 'irreverent, energetic, alternately minimalist, and excessive. And above all, they [were] full of pleasure' (1992: 32). As we embark on a viewing of *Carol* the film, we are assured of a happy ending. And indeed, we are awarded it, as an epilogue. We are also, however, forced to reconcile ourselves to the notion that – like in Lean's film – the 'goodbye' sets the tone for the whole of the narrative. If desire is ever-present, it is also precarious. Cinematic textures of desire eclipse the singular eponymous figure while conclusions hover just beyond the final frame. *Carol* delivers to us not the simply legible lesbian pleasure of Highsmith's happy ending but the queer lesbian *pleasure of the text*. No need to throw out one's chest.

Conclusion: The Queerness of Lesbian Cinema

If the figuration of lesbianism is now a sustained device of popular culture, then figuring lesbianism beyond the fixing of singularity, and indeed figuring (out) the ways in which the lesbian might still modify and not only particularise, is a project that has more critical urgency than ever before. Responding to the interplay between the lesbian's singular and coupled figurations, the starting point for my first case study was Teresa de Lauretis's argument that 'it takes two women, not one, to make a lesbian' (1994: 120). *Lesbian Cinema after Queer Theory* has read this provocation as an evocation of the lesbian as the woman, doubled: an amplification of the woman's existing threat, marked by, and constituted through, the simultaneous impossibility and paradoxical inevitability of the presence of the other in desire. In short: the cinematic lesbian was visually doubled before she was narratively coupled.

The trace of this cinematic history is found in the visual doublings and figural reflections that, rather than simply invoking past pathologisations, instead resist the containment of lesbian desire in the positive image of uncensored sex or culturally endorsed outness. The lesbian charge in the films discussed over the course of these chapters generates an image whose interruption becomes part of its register. The corpus exposes the various technologies at work in the image's capture and reception. The mechanisms of rehearsal, impersonation, modelling and performance reveal paradoxical tensions. Sameness and difference, self-reflection and identification, eroticism and narcissism all reduce the ease with which we might suggest that any one 'lesbian' has been 'made visible'. Moving from the visual impossibility of lesbianism in the twentieth century, and forwards to the limits of the visually acceptable, I have argued in this book that, in the era of the visible in which the lesbian has now been recognised in law and representation, the sexuality she stands for exceeds the confines of both her singular *and* her coupled figurations. Thus, rather than shoring up her categorisation in the newly available terms of the visible, the films in this corpus, and my readings of them, have questioned and explained the lesbian's very on-screen legibility.

Lesbian representation can be charted through three distinct trends. First comes invisibility, in which, because of her dual marginalisation – sexualised and gendered as both non-heterosexual and non-male – the lesbian falls, in Annamarie Jagose's words, 'outside sexuality's visual field' (2002: 2). Patricia White (1999) and Lee Wallace (2009) have argued meanwhile that, in this context, her sexuality is evidenced on-screen through other devices. Secondly, the lesbian's sexuality is made representable but perverse: she becomes a figure of violence or tragedy. Finally, she is welcomed into the romance genre and her singular figuration makes way for the coupling that accompanies her social and political transformation from discrimination to normative legitimacy. I have used the word 'finally' here to denote the latest incarnation of representability. The word also reiterates the definitive status that this particular figuration purports to hold. However, through a focus on the interruption or subversion, rather than celebration, of the lesbian's new-found visibility, I have resisted the seductive narrative of lesbian film in which the past twenty years are seen to have delivered a representational endpoint. In *Lesbian Cinema after Queer Theory*, I have focused on films that rebel against what we might call the visibility imperative: the necessity to embrace the era of the visible and the positivity that it promises as a corollary of 'progress'.

Taking the notion of making visible to mean, as Peggy Phelan (1993: 1) has argued, the fixing of a set idea in the image, this book has both highlighted a visual response to the new availability of that fixing and questioned the presumed progress that lies therein. The issue addressed by Phelan over twenty-five years ago is even more acutely pronounced in the twenty-first century, in which visibility is more than ever about the shaping of cultural identities into forms that can be made recognisable on the screen. This visual context has had particular implications for the representation of sexuality. Even previously marginalised or censored sexualities have now found visual form in the mainstream. Moreover, this visual form legitimately includes, and even prioritises, the sexual act: can sexuality now be taken seriously without it? As such, a new kind of marginalisation occurs through the fixing of meaning in the prescriptive image.

In the specificity of this screen context, *Lesbian Cinema after Queer Theory* has responded to the renewed vitality of a question posed in the mid-1990s by Valerie Traub (1995: 115) – 'What is a lesbian?' – by focusing not on an answer that implants a social category of identity into cinema, but rather one that considers the ways in which the category of lesbianism, if it is a category, has been constructed by cinema itself. In an unparalleled context in which we can observe the extreme privileging of the visual, the easy answer to Traub's question is that a lesbian is categorised by the visual evidence of sex. In this sexualised form, visibility is neither necessarily indicative of progress, nor authoritatively definitive: sexual visibility obscures other forms of eroticism while desire fails, and refuses, to live up to its own image.

What reveals itself here is the intensified relationship between the singular figuration of the lesbian and the multiple registers of her desire and sexuality. Jackie Stacey (1994: 27) addresses these problems by choosing a psychic rather than a social category to describe cinematic processes of desire: foregrounding homoeroticism instead of lesbianism. In her response to Stacey, de Lauretis maintains reservations about what she reads as the implication that 'desire between women is not sexual' (1991: 262). Twenty-five years on, queer theory has given us a vocabulary for exploring the complex facets of lesbian sexuality invoked by this debate. The fluid possibilities of queer theory in the academy have threatened to flatten out gender difference, using this lack of difference to shield the lack of availability or interest that in fact makes the lesbian disappear altogether. This trend is echoed in the queer film festivals whose titles often obscure the overwhelming bias in programming towards gay male narratives. The New Queer Cinema reclaimed the homophobic notion of queer pathology, rejecting the ubiquity of representational positivity. To identify the queerness of lesbian cinema, in the face of the lesbian's commodification in the positive image, is to enable queer readings of the very traits through which she has historically been marginalised.

The lesbian is double the image of the woman who is, already, an imitation of her prior representations. Reading contemporary films *through* cinematic history turns the lesbian's visible figuration into a necessary pastiche, that which 'acknowledges itself as being in the realm of the already said' (Dyer, 1997b: 179). This could look like a retreat to genre or cliché, both variously perceived as damaging instruments of pathologisation. While a pastiche of melodrama acknowledges itself as being directly referential to an existing genre, contemporary replications, imitations and parodies of lesbian cinematic history expose the constitutive force of these very generic structures. However, through subtext, adaptation or affect, they not only cite but also *exceed* the 'already said'. Just as Lauren Berlant writes that genre is 'an aesthetic structure of affective expectation' through which the 'persons transacting with it will experience the pleasure of encountering what they expected', so the contemporary cinematic encounter with the lesbian promises a genre made less familiar by queer modulation (2008: 4).

The imperative becomes, instead, to consider lesbianism beyond the concrete intentionality of spectatorial identification and the over-investment in sex as evidence, both of which may not only enforce our anxieties about queer's fluctuations but also buy into the more general commodification of sex. The contemporary films explored in this book have responded to the simultaneity of queer affects of lesbian desire with the new language of identity's coherence and installation in the public representational sphere. I have examined the conceptual centrality of the body, but through affective traces that eroticise the spaces in-between as supplements to, rather than precursors of, the sexual touch that endorses the relationship between subject and object. The importance of space in the representation of desire and sexuality not only means the coding of *particular* spaces, but also the cinematic rendering of those spaces as erotic through the structuring of the *mise en scène* and its echoes. The swimming pool, for instance, is not inherently erotic, but evokes a watery motif whose repetition across space and time generates an affective charge. Like our suspense in a Hitchcockian thriller even after the main denouement, our immersion in desire's spatialisation lingers beyond the unfolding of what are presumed to be the necessary narrative details. The mood of sexual potential that characterises this queer spatialisation of lesbian desire is captured even through a recollective or anticipatory potential that moves beyond the scope of the film's own running time. To read lesbian cinema through queer theory in this way has enabled, rather than flattened out, the paradoxes inherent in the representation of sexuality, unsettling rather than bolstering its coherence in the visible image.

While lesbian representation has ostensibly emerged from the insufficiency of the marginalised figurations of the past, it is this marginality that continues to provoke and seduce. This is an era in which positive representations of the lesbian have figured her in ways that have historically been impossible (as mother; as partner; as wife; indeed, quite simply, as protagonist). Rather than accepting this apparent representational terminus as a closing down of new possibilities for theorisation, I have instead argued that to understand lesbian representation in the contemporary context is to trouble her easily narrativised legibility while observing it in other forms.

These other forms have been conceptualised as the queer affects, genres, sequences and spaces of lesbian desire. Such cinematic qualities, departing as they do from the particularisation of sexual acts or coming out declarations, have been made conceptually intelligible through the enabling terms of queer theory. Yet they also remain indebted to the feminist film theories that root this book in the history of the lesbian (non-)image. I have thus combined two sets of knowledge practices that, together, expose the complex and sometimes contradictory aesthetic registers that exceed the singular characterisation of gender or sexuality. Having begun as a project about lesbian cinema, *Lesbian Cinema after Queer Theory* has unsettled the assumptions inherent in that term while simultaneously holding on to its terminological commitments. Through a feminist reading of lesbian cinema after queer theory, I have offered a methodological challenge to the notion that the past twenty years have offered the definitive and final encapsulation of lesbianism, deeming it past or done with. Contrary to the static figurations of these discursive responses to its commodification on the contemporary screen, lesbian cinema – in its queer form – has never been more mobile and dynamic.

Notes

Preface

1. To take one example, Frances McDormand demanded in her Oscars acceptance speech in March 2018 that actors take contractual responsibility for diverse workforces via so-called 'inclusion riders' (see Belam and Levin, 2018).
2. These are the kinds of questions that I explored with a group of scholars at a workshop on 'Lesbian Studies in Queer Times' organised by Valerie Traub and Susan Lanser at the University of Michigan in spring 2016.

Introduction

1. Cult or minority-interest lesbian films are often those lesbian-directed, low-budget features that might be shown in a network of international queer film festivals but not in major film festivals, distributed in straight-to-DVD releases by speciality distributors like Peccadillo Pictures and TLA Releasing in the UK but very rarely screened in cinemas on general release (this has started to change in recent years, as Peccadillo has increasingly distributed films in theatres following its spearheading of the travelling LGBTQ+ film festival PoutFest). When it comes to the archive, there are often surprising cases where significant lesbian films have not been made available; *Maidens in Uniform* (Leontine Sagan, 1931) is an example for instance of an historically important film that is regularly discussed in scholarship on lesbian cinema but has yet to be released on DVD in the UK.
2. The directorial team for *The L Word* included, over the course of its six seasons, Rose Troche (who, aside from short films and television episodes, has directed the feature films *Go Fish*, 1994; *Bedrooms and Hallways*, 1998; *The Safety of Objects*, 2001), Angela Robinson (*D.E.B.S.*, 2004; *Herbie Fully Loaded*, 2005; *Professor Marston and the Wonder Women*, 2017), Jamie Babbit (*But I'm a Cheerleader*, 1999; *The Quiet*, 2005; *Itty Bitty Titty Committee*, 2007; *Breaking the Girls*, 2012; *Addicted to Fresno*, 2015), Lisa Cholodenko (*High Art*, 1998; *Laurel Canyon*, 2002; *Cavedweller*, 2004; *The Kids Are All Right*, 2010), and Kimberly Peirce (*Boys Don't Cry*, 1999; *Stop-Loss*, 2008; *Carrie*, 2013). Many of the show's cast members also found cameo roles in the comedy musical satire *Girltrash: All Night Long* (Alex Martinez Kondracke, 2014), written by Robinson.

3. The allocation of 'family values' beyond heterosexuality inevitably boosted the circulation of this comic drama about a lesbian couple, by a lesbian director, described by Timothy Smith of the London Film Festival as a film whose narrative 'resonate(s) with an audience in a universal way' (2011), and scathingly dismissed by David Cox as a 'cosily reassuring message [that] could have been devised to delight midwestern Tea Party moms, whatever their views on lesbianism' (2010).

4. Here, profession is pitted against family; secure domesticity that does not trouble the status quo is the ultimate goal. The feminist study of postfeminist media culture has an extensive bibliography, but key contributions include McRobbie (2009), Negra (2009), Negra and Tasker (2007), Projansky (2014, 2001), Gwynne and Muller (2013), and Winch (2013).

5. These structuring devices of anti-normativity have been thoroughly examined and contested within queer theory's broad church. See the special issue of *differences* on queerness and anti-normativity edited by Robyn Wiegman and Elizabeth Wilson (2015).

6. GLAAD (formerly the Gay and Lesbian Alliance Against Defamation) produces an annual report on 'inclusiveness' in the major studios. In 2017, of 125 major studio releases, only twenty-three 'contained LGBTQ characters'. Ten of those (43 per cent) 'included less than one minute of screen time for their LGBTQ characters' (GLAAD, 2017).

7. Those films are, in date order of nomination: *Declaration of War* (Valérie Donzelli, 2011); *My Little Princess* (Eva Ionesco, 2011); *Augustine* (Alice Winocour, 2012); *Noor* (Çağla Zencirci and Guillaume Giovanetti, 2012); *Sarah Prefers to Run* (Chloé Robichaud, 2013); *Opium* (Arielle Dombasle, 2013); *Girlhood* (Céline Sciamma, 2014); *A Girl at My Door* (July Jung, 2014); *Party Girl* (Marie Amachoukeli, et al., 2014); *Respire* (Mélanie Laurent, 2014); *Marguerite & Julien* (Valérie Donzelli, 2015); *Mustang* (Deniz Gamze Ergüven, 2015); *Oh La La Pauline!* (Émilie Brisavoine, 2015); *The Dancer* (Stéphanie Di Giusto, 2016); *Divines* (Houda Benyamina, 2016); *Raw* (Julia Ducournau, 2016); *Willy 1er* (Ludovic Boukherma, et al., 2016); *They* (Anahita Ghazvinizadeh, 2017); *Marlina the Murderer in Four Acts* (Mouly Surya, 2014); *The Prince of Nothingwood* (Sonia Kronlund, 2017); *Carmen and Lola* (Arantxa Echevarria, 2018); *Cassandro the Exotico!* (Arantxa Echevarria, 2018); *Euphoria* (Valeria Golino, 2018); *Friend* (Wanuri Kahiu, 2018). Seven of these were nominated in 2018 (of a total of sixteen nominations that year), an indication of a possible change of direction for female representation.

8. An infographic by New York Film Academy reveals the alarming statistics associated with gender bias in Hollywood in particular, where, for instance, there is a ratio of five men to one woman working 'behind the scenes' in film (Zurko, 2013). An updated version, produced in 2018 in the wake of the #timesup movement, reveals that this ratio remains identical (Peronne, 2018). The first (and still only) woman to have received an Oscar for Best Director was Kathryn Bigelow for the Iraq war film *The Hurt Locker* (2008). It is a significant paradox that while a female director can only win such mainstream recognition for what has been

argued to be a male genre, traditionally 'female' genres like the romance can only receive mainstream recognition when mediated by a male director. For a longer discussion of Bigelow's work, see White (2015: 3). See also the edition of *Cahiers du Cinéma* entitled 'Où sont les femmes?' (Where are the women?). Ironically, the image used for the cover of the edition is a faceless graphic: a movie camera with legs whose only identifying female feature is a pair of high-heeled shoes. Of particular interest is the filmmaker Céline Sciamma's contribution (2012).

9. On Google Scholar, for instance, a search for titles including the words lesbian and cinema (or film or screen) yields 61 results between 1990 and 1995, 96 between 1995 and 2000, 53 between 2000 and 2005, 45 between 2005 and 2010 and 58 results between 2010 and 2015. Since 2015, there are just 27 results. A search for the equivalent 'queer' titles yields forty-seven between 1990 and 1995, 66 between 1995 and 2000, 120 between 2000 and 2005, 194 between 2005 and 2010, 240 between 2010 and 2015, and 191 since 2015.

10. In her study of disciplinary imaginaries, *Object Lessons*, Robyn Wiegman explores the ways in which these polarised positions have shifted over the course of the disciplinarisation of feminist and queer theory, arguing that 'feminism has diverged repeatedly from itself, proliferated in contradiction across academic, social, institutional, national, and political domains, and recognized, even when repeating, its own contradictions and complicities' (2012: 112).

Chapter 1

1. A collection of essays on *Twin Peaks* (Lavery, 1995) reveals the extent of cita- tional games Lynch and co-creator Frost play with the show, including the insur- ance agent who shows up under the name of Walter Neff (Fred MacMurray's character in *Double Indemnity* [Billy Wilder, 1944]).

2. Lynch explored this effect to the extreme in his next feature, *Inland Empire* (2006), the first of his films shot entirely on a digital camera.

3. This is not just a generic necessity but a fascination of all cultural forms. Elisabeth Bronfen writes that 'because the feminine body is culturally constructed as the superlative site of alterity, culture uses art to dream the deaths of beautiful women' (1992: xi). While the body that ensues is treated as being 'other', it also indirectly represents a general fear of death so that 'what is plainly visible – the beautiful feminine corpse – also stands in for something else' (Ibid.).

4. The male double recurs too, though with different emphases: in *Fight Club* (David Fincher, 1999), the nameless protagonist (Edward Norton) discovers, by the end, that his macho co-conspirator Tyler Durden (Brad Pitt) is really an imagined version of himself. In contrast to the inevitable destruction of the woman in the films listed in the main text, *Fight Club*'s happily united heterosexual couple watches the end of the world hand in hand (in the form of the end of capitalism as the city's financial buildings explode before them). The elimination of the male double, Tyler Durden, leaves the male protagonist not alone but in the arms of the woman whose triangulation of desire has reached its necessary conclusion.

5. See the account of the backlash against the film in, for instance, Galvin (1994). B. Ruby Rich also offers a brief and playful account of the protests in the opening of her seminal essay 'The New Queer Cinema', in which she writes that '*Basic Instinct* was picketed by the self-righteous wing of the queer community (until dykes began to discover how much fun it was)' (1992: 30).

6. The film begins with the doubling of the lesbian/bisexual murder suspects – writer Katherine Tramell (Sharon Stone) and her almost indistinguishable lover Roxy (Leilani Sarelle). But with a midway twist that reveals the potential threat of erstwhile-unsuspected Beth Gardner (Jeanne Tripplehorn), the film disturbs the generic convention for the Other Woman to be an insignificance to the plot. Beth begins as an accessory to give weight to the back story of male lead Nick Curran (Michael Douglas), doubling as the investigation's resident psychologist and as Nick's ex-girlfriend. But the twist makes Beth central to the film's thrust towards the answering of the genre's structuring question (whodunnit). By the end of the film, despite a twist that leads us towards Beth as prime suspect, we are left hanging and unsure by a final shot that points the finger again at writer (and now lover) Katherine; the third suspect, Roxy, has been killed off.

7. Interrogations of *Mulholland Drive*'s narrative (non-)trajectory abound in scholarly and popular debates. The most popular reading of the film's splintered narrative proffers its fulfilment of a dreamwork logic in which Act Two is a representation of a diegetic 'reality' whilst Act One is a wish-fulfilment fantasy dreamt up by Diane (see Schaffner, 2006; Restuccia, 2009). Others argue that this wish-fulfilment logic functions in reverse (see Young, 2007). Several scholars establish Adam as the metaphorical antagonised father figure (see Thomas, 2005; McGowan, 2004). Kelly McDowell (2005) instead focuses on Camilla as the attendant mother figure in the Oedipal triangle, arguing that Diane has been unable to graduate from this juvenile phase of desire.

8. This list could be extended to include even more film-star figures who occupy marginal spaces in the film. Most distinct is Coco, the custodian of Betty's borrowed apartment, who starts as a kindly figure but becomes increasingly sinister. She is played by Hollywood studio-system stalwart Ann Miller, known for her roles in musical films such as *Easter Parade* (Charles Walters, 1948), *On the Town* (Gene Kelly and Stanley Donen, 1949) and *Kiss Me Kate* (George Sidney, 1953).

9. In *Rebecca*, a young woman (Joan Fontaine, whose character remains nameless) marries the charming Maxim de Winter (Laurence Olivier). She finds herself in competition with Rebecca, the original and deceased but somehow more legitimate Mrs de Winter, who is still the obsession of housekeeper Mrs Danvers (Judith Anderson). Rebecca occupies an absent presence in the house through Mrs Danvers's enduring loyalty and desire. She is evoked in the scene described above when Fontaine's heroine unsuccessfully (at Mrs Danvers's vindictive suggestion) tries to please her husband by dressing up for a costume ball as a family ancestor, a part already played in the past by Rebecca, who, we discover, is not the beloved late wife she is reputed to be but rather the enduring source of Maxim's disquiet and ambivalence.

10. As Stacey writes of the artist Cindy Sherman, who plays with Hitchcock's legacy in her series of photographic Hollywood 'imitations', engagement is dependent on 'our familiarity with Hitchcock's heroines' and the invitation both to identify with the image and to 'retrace our own steps' (1994: 7). For feminist spectators, this is an even more charged process of recognition, as explored by White in her analysis of Lucretia Martel's 'cinephilic' reference to Hitchcock's *Vertigo* in *The Headless Woman* (2008), in which she 'reflexively cite[s] her own film's place in the male-dominated art house and in the lineage of auteur cinema' (2015: 52).

11. These identifications are also brought onto the stage by the citational film at the heart of Adam's narrative, whose production self-consciously revisits classic Hollywood in both sound and image: costume, set and music. For more on the retro turn of the aural spectacle of this film-within-the-film, see Mazullo (2005).

12. Kim Newman (2002: 51) points out that blue has coloured all of Lynch's dream scenarios since *Blue Velvet*. The colour does takes on a texture as well as a visual sheen, apt for Jennifer Barker's synaesthetic reading of *Mulholland Drive* (2008).

13. In *All About Eve* (Joseph Mankiewicz, 1950), diva Margot Channing (Bette Davis) is asked by playwright Lloyd Richard (Hugh Marlowe) why she thinks she has the right to profess *his* words as if they were her own: women's space and voice in the realm of performance is made mandatory by regimes of performance. 'Just when exactly does an actress decide they're *her* words she's saying and *her* thoughts she's expressing?': brought into being by this male writer (like the male director of *Mulholland Drive*), it is not for herself that she says these words but for him.

14. The vampire film makes this transformational process a literal one. In a chapter dedicated to it, Weiss cites a whole corpus of lesbian vampire films, at the forefront of which is the Hammer horror *The Vampire Lovers* (Roy Ward Baker, 1970). Parodied in *Lesbian Vampire Killers* (Phil Claydon, 2009), the trope has been revived by *The Carmilla Movie* (Spencer Maybee, 2017). We might also think here of *Carrie* (Brian de Palma, 1976), a film whose narrative of adolescent sexualisation is made extreme through supernatural physical transformation. In *Jack and Diane* (Bradley Rust Gray, 2012), lesbian sexual desire is metaphorically associated with Jack's transformation into a werewolf. Less extreme physical 'transformation' often takes the now-clichéd form of the newfound identity and the new haircut as in *I Am Love* (Luca Guadagnino, 2009) and *Caramel* (Nadine Labaki, 2007).

15. De Lauretis begins her essay with an examination of the history of Greek myth and its centrality to enduring discourses within and about narrative structure. In her initial arrangement of the differentiation between narrative movement and narrative image, a hero like Perseus or Oedipus embodies narrative movement as he and his story move through the 'places and topoi' marked out by Medusa or the Sphinx, on his way to his 'destination and to accomplish meaning' (1984: 109).

16. In *Vertigo*, Scottie (James Stewart), a retired detective, is employed to follow Madeleine (Kim Novak), the wife of an old friend. Madeleine seems to be embodying the spirit of her great-grandmother, Carlotta Valdes. At the Mission

San Juan Bautista, Madeleine commits suicide and Scottie cannot save her. However, later, it is revealed that 'Madeleine' is in fact another woman, Judy, in disguise. This has been a plot to cover up the death of the 'real' Madeleine. There was no suicide at the mission but instead a visual trick; the murder occurred before the diegetic beginning of the film. Scottie meets and falls in love with the undisguised Judy, but is obsessed and forces her to continue to dress as Madeleine. Finally, Scottie and Judy revisit the mission, the site of the fake suicide of "Madeleine", where Judy falls accidentally to her death.

Chapter 2

1. In fact, Béart's character begins life as Marlène; it is in this scene that she changes her name to Nathalie at Catherine's instruction. This act of re-naming endorses a reading of the film through dynamics of power and, in many ways, class. However, for the sake of clarity (and since there is no name change in the remake), I use the name 'Nathalie' throughout.
2. *Chloe* was the first film that Egoyan directed but did not write. The screenplay was written by Erin Cressida Wilson, who also wrote *Secretary* (Steven Shainberg, 2002) and *Fur* (Steven Shainberg, 2006), both of which controversially challenge conventional depictions of desire, femininity and the erotic image (see also Wilson, 2009). For more on Anne Fontaine, see Ritterbusch (2008) and Wilson (2008).
3. *Chloe* made $11,702,642 worldwide across thirty-five countries, while *Nathalie . . .* made only $5,228,683 across fifteen countries (Box Office Mojo, 2018).
4. De Lauretis writes: 'In order to show that inversion was a real, functional deviation of the sexual instinct, rather than *merely* a difference in its direction or object' (1994: 17, original emphasis); 'if homosexuality is *merely* another path taken by the drive in its cathexis or choice of object' (Ibid.: xiii, original emphasis); 'here, the failure of narcissism also derives from the lack or loss of a lovable female body, not only in the subject but also in the mother, for she is also dispossessed and vilified as merely a body' (Ibid.: 244); 'no one spectator's reading of, or identification in, a film can be generalized as a property of the film (its fantasy) or merely an effect of *its* narration' (Ibid.: 130, original emphasis); 'heterosexuality stands for the *institution* of heterosexuality, and not mere heterosexual behavior, the event of sexual intercourse between a woman and a man, which may or may not occur' (Ibid.: 111, original emphasis); 'McLaughlin's recasting is no mere gender-reversal tale' (Ibid.: 90).
5. De Lauretis sums up *Crash*'s radical intervention into the representation of sexuality as more than sex: 'It cannot but be clear to every spectator that *Crash* is about more than sex. Some have called it sick; I am calling it queer. Again, not just because of the "nonnormative" sex scenes between bodies able and disabled, the fetish objects, the kinkiness of the sex. What makes this text queer is its heterotopic vision of sexuality as drive and of the radical irrelevance of gender, sexual identity, or anatomy to sexuality as such.' (2011: 248)

6. The conceptual notion of fake orgasm has its own history. Annamarie Jagose writes that 'as a critical figure, fake orgasm brings to visibility the presumptions that underpin claims to the transformative capacities or potentials of some sex acts, some amatory transactional relations or erotic spaces but not others. It therefore acts as a useful reminder that the critical value accorded to certain sex acts is often in the service of systems of discrimination more ideological than erotic' (2012: 178).

7. Famous examples of the film within a film include *Peeping Tom* (Michael Powell, 1960) and *The French Lieutenant's Woman* (Karel Reisz, 1981). The latter cleverly adapts the novelistic *mise en abîme* of the original text, John Fowles's novel *The French Lieutenant's Woman* (1969). The phrase *mise en abîme* emerged in critical theory via André Gide (1947: 30), who cited William Shakespeare's play *Hamlet* (1603) and Diego Velázquez's painting *Las Meninas* (1656) as two key early illustrations. The inner scene in all these examples comes to expose the major thematic of the artwork as a whole.

8. This claim that 'impersonation requires the repetition of duplicity' is founded on Judith Butler's famous discussion of repetition in 'Imitation and Gender Insubordination', in which she argues that 'it is through the repeated play of this sexuality that the "I" is insistently reconstituted as a lesbian "I"; paradoxically, it is precisely the *repetition* of that play that establishes as well the *instability* of the very category that it constitutes' (1991: 18, original emphases).

9. Stacey's interlocutor here is Sedgwick, with whom she asks: 'How are we to know whose desire it is that is [. . .] figured? By whom can it be figured?' (2008 [1990]: 157).

10. In the science fiction realm of *Gattaca*, Vincent, a genetically inferior 'in-valid', dreams of flying spacecraft; to do so, he must impersonate a 'valid', and so he initiates a genetic transaction with the wheelchair-bound but genetically superior Jerome.

11. This creates a kind of triangulation of unspoken female homoerotic desire or intense intimacy via the brother or father who holds a strong resemblance to the sister/daughter and is also a feature of *My Summer of Love* (Pawel Pawlikowski, 2004), *Love Sick* (Tudor Giugiu, 2006), *The Falling* (Carol Morley, 2015) and *Adore*.

12. Sedgwick observes that the status of women is 'deeply and inescapably inscribed in the structure even of relationships that seem to exclude women' (1985: 25), including marriage, which, for Claude Lévi-Strauss, 'is not established between a man and a woman, but between two groups of men, and the woman figures only as one of the objects in the exchange, not as one of the partners' (1969 [1949]: 115). We see this typified in key films of the post-Second World War period such as *Marnie* (Alfred Hitchcock, 1964), *Saratoga Trunk* (Sam Wood, 1945) and *Notorious* (Alfred Hitchcock, 1946) in which, as Mike Chopra-Gant notes, the male partner of the female protagonist is enabled 'to substitute for the father as a source of patriarchal authority, regulating the conduct of the female protagonist and restoring her to conformity with traditional norms of femininity' (2006: 76).

13. Cairns includes three sequential chapters entitled 'Bad Girls: Criminality', 'Mad

Girls: Pathology' and finally 'Girls on the Edge: Liminality' in her book *Sapphism on Screen: Lesbian Desire in French and Francophone Cinema* (2006).

14. Pidduck's coining of the term 'hypervisibility' characterises not only unprecedented visibility but 'a frenzy of visibility' (2011: 10).

Chapter 3

1. *Milk* tells the story of Harvey Milk, the first openly gay politician in the United States who, through his seat on the San Francisco Board of Supervisors, was responsible for instituting landmark gay rights legislation in the city. Milk was assassinated by a fellow board member in 1978. Described by Nicolas Rapold (2009: 30) as 'eerily of the moment' – *Milk* was released amid political tensions surrounding Proposition 8, which would revoke equal marriage rights – the film's storyline follows the defeat of the comparable Proposition 6. With more feature-film sequels still anticipated over ten years following its 1998–2004 run on HBO television, *Sex and the City* remains a landmark text about female friendship, relationships and sex (see Akass and McCabe, 2004). *Sex and the City* is often cited as the epitome of postfeminist media because of its group of empowered female friends who claim their rights to work, friendship, consumerism and family while maintaining their perpetual focus on heterosexual romance. For an elaboration of the show's lesbian potential, see Merck (2004).
2. This notion of adolescence as a time of being both *within and without*, as these films map spatially, is a common theoretical tendency extending from Jerome Hamilton Buckley's much-cited book on the *bildungsroman* (1974), whose introduction is entitled 'The Space Between'. The third part of Catherine Driscoll's account of teen film is entitled 'liminal teen film', a title that suggests a mode at the very heart of the genre that is indefinable, between childhood and adolescence (2011). Angus Gordon, however, argues that the 'theoretical tendency to treat adolescence as the utopian site of a free-floating "liminal" exploration of myriad nonbinding identifications and desires' is problematic because it masks 'the extent to which heterosexuality is privileged in the discursive construction of adolescence' (1999: 6).
3. We might compare this with what Galt calls the 'non-commodity time' of *Suddenly* (Diego Lerman, 2002), in which Argentina's economic context is the backdrop to and generator of a queer aesthetic outside of the neoliberal commodification of lesbian identity. Galt writes that to read *Suddenly* through a queer lens allows it to become 'visible both as a national and a transnational text' (2013: 70). For more on capitalism and gay identity, see Alderson (2016).
4. Whilst Rushbrook contends that a queer cosmopolitanism is formed through consumer capital that endorses, and allows for, the 'creation of multiple shifting identities' (2002: 188), Hilary Radner argues that a contemporary culture puts forward the 'concept of identity as a process of "becoming"' that 'has been understood as offering emancipatory possibilities to the individual who is invited not to take up a stable, untested and fixed position, but, rather, to see her "self,"

or even "selves", as subject to a multiple and on-going process of revision, reform and choices' (2011: 6). Radner exposes here a problematic distortion of the famous Beauvoirian principle that 'one is not born, but rather becomes, a woman' (1997 [1949]: 295). This is a tension at the heart of any discussion of both 'post'-feminism and postmodern or poststructuralist feminisms, whereby the unsettling of essentialist notions of gender identity on the one hand morph into maintainers of consumer industries, premised on women's 'choice', on the other. Carissa Showden has outlined these tensions in terminology between an *anti*-feminist postfeminism and a postfeminism that inherits the political enquiry of postmodernism, poststructuralism or postcolonialism (2009: 168–9).

5. Rosalind Gill writes that the postfeminist sensibility is 'characterized among other things by a marked intensification of the scrutiny of women's bodies [but disguised through a] discourse of freedom, choice and playfulness' (2008: 440–1); Diane Negra writes that postfeminist discourse 'fetishizes female power and desire while consistently placing these within firm limits' (2009: 4).

6. The romantic comedy *Appropriate Behaviour* externally references the latest iconic television show of contested femininity, *Girls. Appropriate Behaviour*'s director Desiree Akhavan received rave reviews from Lena Dunham and was invited to feature in the fourth season of *Girls*. Both directly reference *Sex and the City*, which leaves behind it a postfeminist legacy of New York femininity. This distinctly American network sets itself apart from the 'reinvigorated international cinephile circuit' discussed by White which 'renew[s] questions about singularity (the stock in trade of auteurism) and collectivity, national cinema and transnational reception in the context of feminist genealogies' (2015: 44).

7. For more on the relationship between cinematic space and the city, see Bruno (2002).

8. For more on zoning as a kind of alienation and the creation of what he calls the 'non-place' as nucleus of the 'supermodern' world, see Augé (1995).

Chapter 4

1. According to the website for the British equestrian vaulting team, vaulting is 'a form of gymnastics on the back of a moving horse [. . .] Through choreographed movements, it incorporates beauty and brilliance, power and strength, elegance and precision, all in harmony with the horse.' (Team GBR Equestrian, 2015) There is a petition for vaulting to be included in the Olympics. It is a very gendered sport in which, in the UK for instance, only women compete as part of Team GBR.

2. After *Water Lilies*, Sciamma made *Tomboy* (2011) and then *Girlhood* (2014). Together, these three films were retrospectively – and, I think, erroneously – dubbed a 'coming-of-age trilogy' by many reviewers (see for instance Lenarduzzi, 2015).

3. Platonic intimacy between friends complicates our reading of the eroticism of the non-sexual in the queer affects that I have described. In her book about

female friendship films (1998), Karen Hollinger includes a sub-genre, the 'erotic' female friendship film, within which she (contentiously) places *Desert Hearts* (Donna Deitch, 1985), *Personal Best* and *Go Fish* (Rose Troche, 1994) alongside *Fried Green Tomatoes* (Jon Avnet, 1991). The latter film famously left out the 'explicit' lesbian details of the book on which it was based but kept in much of what I would call the erotic affect that allowed it to remain a cult favourite with lesbian viewers (see Mayne, 2000: xvii).

4. For Karl Schoonover, writing about slow cinema, 'queerness often looks a lot like wasted time, wasted lives, wasted productivity. Queers luxuriate while others work. Queers seem always to have time to waste.' (2012: 73) These conceptual tensions between wasting and productivity, maturing and lingering in immaturity, are all key features of the discussion in a now-seminal *GLQ* roundtable on queer temporality chaired by Elizabeth Freeman (2007).

5. Halberstam's invocation of childhood sits uneasily alongside Lee Edelman's provocative assertion that '*queerness* names the side of those *not* "fighting for the children", the side outside the consensus by which all politics confirms the absolute value of reproductive futurism' (2004: 3, original emphasis). Along different theoretical pathways, scholars have increasingly begun to theorise a 'queer child' (see for instance Bruhm and Hurley, 2004).

6. Kathryn Bond Stockton explores the conceptual alignment of children and animals in literature, writing that 'as a recipient of the child's attentions – its often bent devotions – and a living screen for the child's self-projections – its mysterious bad-dog postures of sexual expression – the dog is a figure for the child beside itself, engaged in a growing quite aside from growing up' (2009: 90). Several films have explored this through the literal beside-ness of a speaking animal who projects the child's expression back to her: see, for instance, *Animals* (Marçal Forés, 2012).

7. Barbara Creed explains that 'Busby Berkeley directed musical numbers for virtually every important Warner Brothers film produced between 1933 and 1937' before going on to direct his own films after the success of his 'musical extravaganzas' (2009: 100).

8. Lindner writes that the similarity between the sports film and the musical lies in the interruption of 'straightforward narrative development' by 'athletic/musical performance "numbers"' (2011: 214). In Richard Dyer's words, where wordless music is concerned, 'the affective is to the fore' (2012: 6). This is partly to do with what he calls the 'suspension' of time and space in the musical number (Ibid.: 28).

9. In 'A Study of Envy and Gratitude', Klein writes: 'comparison with it [the object, in this case Cassandra] becomes impossible' and 'envy is counteracted' (1987 [1956]: 217).

10. Sedgwick writes that 'Klein's psychoanalysis, by contrast to Freud's, is based in affect and offers a compelling account of the developments and transformations of affective life' (2007: 628). Sedgwick reads Klein alongside Silvan Tomkins, for the sake of finding some queer/feminist critical distance from 'some of the

damaging assumptions that have shaped psychoanalysis in (what I think of as) its Oedipal mode: the defining centrality of dualistic gender difference; the primacy of genital morphology and desire; the determinative nature of childhood experience and the linear teleology toward a sharply distinct state of maturity; and especially the logic of zero-sum games and the excluded middle term, where passive is the opposite of active and desire is the opposite of identification, and where one person's getting more love means a priori that another is getting less.' (Ibid.: 630–1)

Chapter 5

1. The lesbian *bildungsroman* has been discussed in precisely those terms in scholarship about a variety of media, from literature to graphic fiction and video work. See, for instance, Carter (1998), Pearl (2008) and Zimmerman (1983).
2. This provided only the second occasion of a Palme d'Or win for a woman under any circumstances (Jane Campion won for *The Piano* in 1993). For more on the visibility of female filmmakers at Cannes, see White (2015).
3. The film's reputation is also marked by its actresses' belated attack on Kechiche's methods; reportedly, 'the 10-minute love scene at the centre of the film took a gruelling 10 days to shoot' (Child, 2013). This accusation, and its language, characterises much of the mainstream reporting on the film (see for instance Greenhouse, 2013).
4. Mavor writes that blue is 'a particularly paradoxical colour [. . .] blue is the purity of the Virgin Mary, *yet* blue names a movie as obscene. Or, blue is the colour of eternity, *yet* blue lips are a sign of approaching death' (2013: 10, original emphasis). See also Wolff (2013).
5. *Blue Is the Warmest Colour*'s French subtitle – *Chapitres 1 et 2* – suggests a continuation of Adèle's narrative, though Kechiche's professed desire to explore later 'chapters' is complicated by the controversies surrounding his working relationship with the actresses Seydoux and Exarchopoulos. The play *La Vie de Marianne* (Marivaux, 2007 [1731]), read by Adèle and her peers and cited in this title, was famously left unfinished.
6. The female homosocial classroom belongs to a somewhat different history. Lee Wallace, following Mikhail Bakhtin, introduces the school as one of four classic 'lesbian chronotopes' that 'advance specific stories' (2009: 134). Central to lesbian classics such as *Maidens in Uniform* (Leontine Sagan, 1931) and its remake (Geza Radvanyi, 1958), this popular chronotope endures into the twenty-first century in films such as *Lost and Delirious* (Léa Pool, 2001), *Loving Annabelle* (Katherine Brooks, 2006) and *Cracks* (Jordan Scott, 2009). This site has been parodied recently in Bruce La Bruce's (arguably) feminist sex comedy *The Misandrists* (Bruce La Bruce, 2017). Wallace's other chronotopes are the bar (see *If These Walls Could Talk 2* segment 2, Martha Coolidge, 2000); the college (see *Bloomington*, Fernanda Cardoso, 2010) and the prison, which has plentifully spawned films such as Cheryl Dunye's *Stranger Inside* (Cheryl Dunye, 2001) along-

side television series such as *Orange Is the New Black* (Jenji Kohan, 2013–) and *Wentworth* (Reg Watson and Lara Radulovich, 2013–). For more on the prison as a site of lesbian potential, see Mayne (2000).

7. *Boyhood* was filmed incrementally between 2002 and 2013 with the same cast of actors portraying the same family (see Clark, 2014).

8. For more on colour in cinema, see the *Screen* dossier on colour (Street, 2010).

9. *Buffy the Vampire Slayer* (Josh Whedon, 1997–2003), the first primetime US television show to include a long-term lesbian relationship between two central characters, depicted its first lesbian sex scene as eroticised, but fully clothed, witches' spellcraft. The show used the 'specter of witchcraft as a conduit of their romantic connection', as Sarah-Jane Stratford (2013) writes in an article provoked, as it happens, by the release of *Blue Is the Warmest Colour*. It is worth mentioning that *Buffy* allowed a whole season of Willow and Tara's relationship to pass before indulging in its much controversialised and since heralded 'explicit' (Ibid.) lesbian kiss, which remains a marker on timelines of lesbian televisual visibility.

10. Other industrial double standards have occurred in relation to *Fifty Shades of Grey*, the adaptation of the erotic novel by E. L. James (2011) that achieved widespread fame. In 2016, a 60-second advertisement (ScreenCrush, 2016) for *Carol*, featuring brief nudity, was banned by the American broadcasting company ABC (see Lewis, 2016). In contrast, as reported by Benjamin Lee (2017), 'the previous year, ads for heterosexual S&M "romance" *Fifty Shades of Grey* made their way to the small screen unscathed'.

11. For more on the role of film music in orchestrating spectator responses and affect, see Cohen (2001), Donnelly (2005) and Kassabian (2001).

12. In contrast, in an interview about Lars von Trier's *Nymphomaniac* (2013), the actress Stacy Martin says that 'anything that's penetrative sex, there's a porn double there. I had a prosthetic vagina [. . .] that's fake and you can't feel a thing. And that was very important for me because I'm not there to be a porn star – I'm there to be an actress' (in Jacobs, 2014).

13. Of the film's 179-minute running time, Adèle's masturbation scene is just under two minutes, Adèle and Thomas's sex scene just over two, Adèle and Emma's media-grabbing sex scenes seven, one and two minutes long. Of the six scenes in the film that we might call sex scenes – one between Thomas and Adèle, one 'alone', the rest between Adèle and Emma – only two begot such attention in the press. In the words of Rich (2014), the prolonged duration of the film 'may well be an intended bulwark against prurience: anyone going for salacious reasons will have to pay – with their time – for the privilege'. Rich's review of the film accompanied its debut DVD release by Criterion in the USA; much of the fervent debate surrounding the film's sex scenes preceded her apparently atypical observations. For more on the distribution and length of sex scenes in (non-pornographic) feature films see for instance Williams (2005: 45).

Chapter 6

1. Jill Soloway, whose television series *Transparent* (2014–) and *I Love Dick* (2016–17) have both been praised as radical platforms of female sexual empowerment, gave a keynote address at Toronto International Film Festival on 'the female gaze' (2016), calling on queer and/or female filmmakers to reconstitute the visual field through a powerful recalibration of production processes.
2. The original novel was published under the pseudonym Claire Morgan.
3. In contrast, twelve films have received double (or triple) nominations in the Best Actor category: Clark Gable, Charles Laughton and Franchot Tone were all nominated for *Mutiny on the Bounty* (Frank Lloyd, 1935); Bing Crosby and Barry Fitzgerald for *Going My Way* (Leo McCarey, 1944); Montgomery Clift and Burt Lancaster for *From Here to Eternity* (Fred Zinnemann, 1953); James Dean and Rock Hudson for *Giant* (George Stevens, 1956); Tony Curtis and Sidney Poitier for *The Defiant Ones* (Stanley Kramer, 1958); Maximilian Schell and Spencer Tracy for *Judgement at Nuremberg* (Stanley Kramer, 1961); Richard Burton and Peter O'Toole for *Becket* (Peter Glenville, 1964); Dustin Hoffman and Jon Voigt for *Midnight Cowboy* (John Schlesinger, 1969); Michael Caine and Laurence Olivier for *Sleuth* (Joseph Mankiewicz, 1972); Peter Finch and William Holden for *Network* (Sidney Lumet, 1976); Tom Courtney and Albert Finney for *The Dresser* (Peter Yates, 1983); and F. Murray Abraham and Tom Hulce for *Amadeus* (Milos Forman, 1984). There are of course comparable omissions for films with gay male narratives, including the single nominations in the Best Actor category for *Philadelphia* and *Brokeback Mountain*.
4. Pidduck responds to this assertion by pointing out that Gledhill 'associates melodrama with an ambiguous "we" of feminist film theory, a "we" that comfortably ascribes to the white Anglo-American feminist genealogy' (2013: 46).
5. *Carol* earned $40,272,135 in gross worldwide ticket sales. This compares to $34,705,850 for *The Kids Are All Right*, another lesbian film garnering several awards, and $29,027,914 for *Far from Heaven*, another Haynes film. In comparison to the other main case studies of this book, it by far extends beyond them in terms of ticket sales: $20,117,339 for *Mulholland Drive*; $11,702,642 for *Chloe*; $7,379,806 for *Blue Is the Warmest Colour*; $5,228,683 for *Nathalie . . .*; $549,148 for *Water Lilies* and $454,121 for *Circumstance* (*She Monkeys* did not receive general cinema distribution).

Filmography

20th Century Women, film, directed by Mike Mills. USA: 2015.
42nd Street, film, directed by Lloyd Bacon. USA: 1933.
52 Tuesdays, film, directed by Sophie Hyde. Australia: 2013.
The Accused, film, directed by Jonathan Kaplan. USA: 1988.
A Girl at My Door (Dohee-Ya), film, directed by July Jung. South Korea: 2014.
A League of Their Own, film, directed by Penny Marshall. USA: 1992.
A Single Man, film, directed by Tom Ford. USA: 2009.
Addicted to Fresno, film, directed by Jamie Babbit. USA: 2015.
Adore (Adoration), film, directed by Anne Fontaine. Australia, France: 2013.
Afternoon Delight, film, directed by Jill Soloway. USA: 2001.
Ali: Fear Eats the Soul (Angst Essen Seele Auf), film, directed by Rainer Werner Fassbinder. West Germany: 1974.
All About Eve, film, directed by Joseph Mankiewicz. USA: 1950.
All Over Me, film, directed by Alex Sichel. USA: 1997.
All That Heaven Allows, film, directed by Douglas Sirk. USA: 1955.
Almost Famous, film, directed by Cameron Crowe. USA: 2000.
Amadeus, film, directed by Milos Forman. USA, France, Czechoslovakia: 1984.
American Beauty, film, directed by Sam Mendes. USA: 1999.
American Idol, reality television series, created by Simon Fuller. USA: 2002–.
Animals, film, directed by Marçal Forés. Spain: 2012.
Anne Trister, film, directed by Léa Pool. Canada: 1986.
Appropriate Behaviour, film, directed by Desiree Akhavan. UK: 2014.
Atomic Blonde, film, directed by David Leitch. Germany, Sweden, USA: 2017.
Attenberg, film, directed by Athina Rachel Tsangari. Greece: 2010.
Augustine, film, directed by Alice Winocour. France: 2012.
Basic Instinct, film, directed by Paul Verhoeven. France, USA, UK: 1992.
Battle of the Sexes, film, directed by Jonathan Dayton and Valerie Faris. UK, USA: 2017.
Becket, film, directed by Peter Glenville. UK, USA: 1964.
Bedrooms and Hallways, film, directed by Rose Troche. UK: 1998.
The Beguiled, film, directed by Sofia Coppola. USA: 2017.
Bend It Like Beckham, film, directed by Gurinder Chadha. UK: 2002.
Bessie, television movie, directed by Dee Rees. USA: 2015.
Beyond the Hills (După Dealuri), film, directed by Cristian Mungiu. Romania: 2012.
The Big Sleep, film, directed by Howard Hawks. USA: 1946.

The Birds, film, directed by Alfred Hitchcock. USA: 1963.

The Bitter Tears of Petra von Kant (Die Bitteren Tränen der Petra von Kant), film, directed by Rainer Werner Fassbinder. West Germany: 1972.

The Black Dahlia, film, directed by Brian de Palma. USA: 2006.

Black Swan, film, directed by Darren Aronofsky. USA: 2010.

Black Widow, film, directed by Bob Rafelson. USA: 1987.

Blade Runner, film, directed by Ridley Scott. USA, Hong Kong: 1982.

The Bling Ring, film, directed by Sofia Coppola. USA, UK, France, Germany, Japan: 2013.

Bloomington, film, directed by Fernanda Cardoso. USA: 2010.

Blue Is the Warmest Colour (La Vie d'Adèle), film, directed by Abdellatif Kechiche. France: 2013.

Blue Velvet, film, directed by David Lynch. USA: 1986.

Body of Evidence, film, directed by Uli Edel. Germany, USA: 1993.

Bound, film, directed by Lana and Andy Wachowski. USA: 1996.

Boyhood, film, directed by Richard Linklater. USA: 2014.

Boys Don't Cry, film, directed by Kimberly Peirce. USA: 1999.

Break My Fall, film, directed by Kanchi Wichmann. USA: 2011.

Breaking the Girls, film, directed by Jamie Babbit. USA: 2013.

Breathe (Respire), film, directed by Mélanie Laurent. France: 2014.

Brief Encounter, film, directed by David Lean. UK: 1945.

Bring It On, film, directed by Peyton Reed. USA: 2000.

Brokeback Mountain, film, directed by Ang Lee. USA, Canada: 2005.

Buffy the Vampire Slayer, television series, created by Josh Whedon. USA: 1997–2003.

But I'm a Cheerleader, film, directed by Jamie Babbit. USA: 1999.

Butterfly Kiss, film, directed by Michael Winterbottom. UK: 1995.

Call Me by Your Name, film, directed by Luca Guadagnino. USA: 2017.

Caramel (Sekkar Banat), film, directed by Nadine Labaki. France, Lebanon: 2007.

Carmen and Lola (Carmen y Lola), film, directed by Arantxa Echevarria. Spain: 2018.

The Carmilla Movie, film, directed by Spencer Maybee. Canada: 2017.

Carol, film, directed by Todd Haynes. UK, USA, France: 2015.

Carrie, film, directed by Brian de Palma. USA: 1976.

Carrie, film, directed by Kimberly Peirce. USA: 2013.

Cavedweller, film, directed by Lisa Cholodenko. Canada, USA: 2004.

The Children's Hour, film, directed by William Wyler. USA: 1961.

Chloe, film, directed by Atom Egoyan. USA, Canada, France: 2009.

Circumstance, film, directed by Maryam Keshavarz. France, USA, Iran: 2011.

Claire of the Moon, film, directed by Nicole Conn. USA: 1992.

The Class (Entre les Murs), film, directed by Laurent Cantet. France: 2008.

Clouds of Sils Maria, film, directed by Olivier Assayas. France, Germany, Switzerland: 2014.

Code 46, film, directed by Michael Winterbottom. UK: 2003.

Colette, film, directed by Wash Westmoreland. UK, USA, Hungary: 2018.

Concussion, film, directed by Stacey Passon. USA: 2013.

The Conformist (*Il Conformista*), film, directed by Bernardo Bertolucci. Italy, France, West Germany: 1970.

Contempt (*Le Mépris*), film, directed by Jean-Luc Godard. France, Italy: 1963.

Coup de Foudre (*Entre Nous*), film, directed by Diane Kurys. France: 1982.

Couscous (*Le Graine et le Mulet*), film, directed by Abdellatif Kechiche. France: 2007.

Cracks, film, directed by Jordan Scott. UK, Ireland, Spain, France, Switzerland: 2009.

Crash, film, directed by David Cronenberg. Canada, UK: 1996.

Cruel Intentions, film, directed by Roger Kumble. USA: 1999.

Curse of the Cat People, film, directed by Gunther von Fritsch and Robert Wise. USA: 1944.

The Dancer (*La Danseuse*), film, directed by Stéphanie Di Giusto. France, Belgium, Czech Republic: 2016.

D.E.B.S., film, directed by Angela Robinson. USA: 2004.

Declaration of War (*La Guerre Est Déclarée*), film, directed by Valérie Donzelli. France: 2011.

The Defiant Ones, film, directed by Stanley Kramer. USA: 1958.

Desert Hearts, film, directed by Donna Deitch. USA: 1985.

Desperately Seeking Susan, film, directed by Susan Seidelman. USA: 1985.

The Devil Is a Woman, film, directed by Josef von Sternberg. USA: 1935.

Dishonoured, film, directed by Josef von Sternberg. USA: 1931.

Disobedience, film, directed by Sebastián Lelio. UK, Ireland, USA: 2017.

Divines, film, directed by Houda Benyamina. France, Qatar: 2016.

Dogtooth (*Kynodontas*), film, directed by Yorgos Lanthimos. Greece: 2009.

Dottie Gets Spanked, television short, directed by Todd Haynes. USA: 1992.

Double Indemnity, film, directed by Billy Wilder. USA: 1944.

The Double Life of Véronique (*La Double Vie de Véronique*), film, directed by Krzysztof Kieślowski. France, Poland, Norway: 1991.

Doubt, film, directed by John Patrick Shanley. USA: 2008.

The Dresser, film, directed by Peter Yates. UK: 1983.

Dry Cleaning (*Nettoyage à Sec*), film, directed by Anne Fontaine. France, Spain: 1997.

The Duke of Burgundy, film, directed by Peter Strickland. UK, Hungary: 2014.

Easter Parade, film, directed by Charles Walters. USA: 1948.

The Edge of Heaven (*Auf der Anderen Seite*), film, directed by Fatih Akin. Germany, Turkey, Italy: 2007.

Elle, film, directed by Paul Verhoeven. France, Germany, Belgium: 2016.

Euphoria, film, directed by Valeria Golino. Italy: 2018.

The Falling, film, directed by Carol Morley. UK: 2015.

Far from Heaven, film, directed by Todd Haynes. USA, France: 2002.

Fatal Attraction, film, directed by Adrian Lyne. USA: 1987.

Female Perversions, film, directed by Susan Streitfeld. Germany, USA: 1996.

Fifty Shades of Grey, film, directed by Sam Taylor-Johnson. USA: 2015.

Fight Club, film, directed by David Fincher. USA, Germany: 1999.

The Fighter, film, directed by David O. Russell. USA: 2010.

Fire, film, directed by Deepa Mehta. Canada, India: 1996.

The Fish Child (*El Niño Pez*), film, directed by Lucía Puenzo. Argentina: 2009.

Flat Is Beautiful, short film, directed by Sadie Benning. USA: 1998.

Footlight Parade, film, directed by Lloyd Bacon. USA: 1933.

The Four-Faced Liar, film, directed by Jacob Chase. USA: 2010.

Foxfire, film, directed by Annette Haywood-Carter. USA: 1996.

Foxfire, film, directed by Laurent Cantet. France, Canada: 2012.

The French Lieutenant's Woman, film, directed by Karel Reisz. UK: 1981.

Fried Green Tomatoes at the Whistle Stop Café, film, directed by Jon Avnet. USA: 1991.

Friend (*Rafiki*), film, directed by Wanuri Kahiu. Kenya: 2018.

From Here to Eternity, film, directed by Fred Zinnemann. USA: 1953.

Fuck Me (*Baise-Moi*), film, directed by Virginie Despentes and Coralie Trinh Thi. France: 2000.

Fun, film, directed by Rafal Zielinski. Canada: 1994.

Fur: An Imaginary Portrait of Diane Arbus, film, directed by Steven Shainberg. USA: 2006.

Games of Love and Chance (*L'Esquive*), film, directed by Abdellatif Kechiche. France: 2003.

Gasoline (*Benzina*), film, directed by Monica Lisa Stambrini. Italy: 2003.

Gattaca, film, directed by Andrew Niccol. USA: 1997.

Gentlemen Prefer Blondes, film, directed by Howard Hawks. USA: 1953.

Giant, film, directed by George Stevens. USA: 1956.

Gilda, film, directed by Charles Vidor. USA: 1946.

Ginger and Rosa, film, directed by Sally Potter. UK, Denmark, Canada, Croatia: 2012.

Girlhood (*Bande des Filles*), film, directed by Céline Sciamma. France: 2014.

Girls, television series, created by Lena Dunham. USA: 2012–17.

Girltrash: All Night Long, film, directed by Alex Martinez Kondracke. USA: 2014.

Go Fish, film, directed by Rose Troche. USA: 1994.

Going My Way, film, directed by Leo McCarey. USA: 1944.

Gold Diggers of 1933, film, directed by Mervyn LeRoy. USA: 1933.

Good Manners (*As Boas Maneiras*), film, directed by Marco Dutra and Juliana Rojas. Brazil, France: 2017.

Good Old Daze (*Le Péril Jeune*), film, directed by Cédric Klapisch. France: 1994.

Gosford Park, film, directed by Robert Altman. UK, USA, Italy: 2001.

Grand Central, film, directed by Rebecca Zlotowski. France, Austria: 2013.

The Hand That Rocks the Cradle, film, directed by Curtis Hanson. USA: 1992.

The Handmaiden (*Ah-Ga-Ssi*), film, directed by Park Chan-Wook. South Korea: 2016.

The Haunting, film, directed by Robert Wise. UK, USA: 1963.

The Headless Woman (*La Mujer sin Cabeza*), film, directed by Lucretia Martel. Argentina, France, Italy, Spain: 2008.

Heavenly Creatures, film, directed by Peter Jackson. New Zealand, Germany: 1994.

Herbie Fully Loaded, film, directed by Angela Robinson. USA: 2005.

High Art, film, directed by Lisa Cholodenko. USA: 1998.

Highly Strung (*Je Te Mangerais*), film, directed by Sophie Laloy. France: 2009.

The Hours, film, directed by Stephen Daldry. USA, UK: 2002.

The Hunger, film, directed by Tony Scott. UK: 1983.

The Hunger Games: Catching Fire, film, directed by Francis Lawrence. USA: 2013.

The Hurt Locker, film, directed by Kathryn Bigelow. USA: 2008.

I Am Love, film, directed by Luca Guadagnino. Italy: 2009.

I'm Not There, film, directed by Todd Haynes. Germany, Canada, USA: 2007.

I Can't Think Straight, film, directed by Shamim Sarif. UK: 2008.

I Love Dick, television series, created by Sarah Gubbins and Jill Soloway. USA: 2016–17.

If These Walls Could Talk 2, television movie, directed by Jane Anderson, Martha Coolidge and Anne Heche. USA: 2000.

Imagine Me and You, film, directed by Ol Parker. UK: 2005.

Imitation of Life, film, directed by Douglas Sirk. USA: 1959.

In Between (Bar Bahar), film, directed by Maysaloun Hamoud. Israel, France: 2016.

In My Skin (Dans Ma Peau), film, directed by Marina de Van. USA: 2002.

In the Cut, film, directed by Jane Campion. UK, Australia, USA: 2003.

The Incredibly True Adventure of Two Girls in Love, film, directed by Maria Maggenti. USA: 1995.

Inland Empire, film, directed by David Lynch. France, Poland, USA: 2006.

The Innocents, film, directed by Jack Clayton. UK: 1961.

The Innocents (Les Innocents), film, directed by Anne Fontaine. France, Poland: 2016.

The Intervention, film, directed by Clea DuVall. USA: 2016.

Intimacy, film, directed by Patrice Chéreau. France, UK, Germany, Spain: 2001.

Irreversible (Irréversible), film, directed by Gaspar Noé. France: 2002.

Itty Bitty Titty Committee, film, directed by Jamie Babbit. USA: 2007.

Jack and Diane, film, directed by Bradley Rust Gray. USA: 2012.

Je, Tu, Il, Elle, film, directed by Chantal Akerman. France, Belgium: 1974.

Jennifer's Body, film, directed by Karyn Kusama. USA: 2009.

The Journey to Forming a Family, promotional video, created by Colleen Benn, Marian Mansi and Julie Harter. USA: 2010.

Judgement at Nuremberg, film, directed by Stanley Kramer. USA: 1961.

Juno, film, directed by Jason Reitman. USA: 2007.

The Kids Are All Right, film, directed by Lisa Cholodenko. USA: 2010.

The Killing of Sister George, film, directed by Robert Aldrich. USA: 1966.

Kiss Me (Kyss Mig), film, directed by Alexandra-Therese Keining. Sweden: 2011.

Kiss Me Deadly, film, directed by Robert Aldrich. USA: 1955.

Kiss Me Kate, film, directed by George Sidney. USA: 1953.

Kissing Jessica Stein, film, directed by Charles Herman-Wurmfeld. USA: 2001.

Koyaanisqatsi, film, directed by Godrey Reggio. USA: 1982.

The L Word, television series, created by Ilene Chaiken. USA: 2004–9.

Lady Vengeance (Chinjeolhan Geumjassi), film, directed by Park Chan-Wook. South Korea: 2005.

Laura, film, directed by Otto Preminger. USA: 1944.

Laurel Canyon, film, directed by Lisa Cholodenko. USA: 2002.

Laurence Anyways, film, directed by Xavier Dolan. Canada, France: 2012.

Les Diaboliques, film, directed by Henri-Georges Clouzot. France: 1955.

Lesbian Vampire Killers, film, directed by Phil Claydon. UK: 2009.

Lianna, film, directed by John Sayles. USA: 1982.

The Life and Death of Colonel Blimp, film, directed by Michael Powell and Emeric Pressburger. UK: 1943.

Lizzie, film, directed by Craig William Macneill. USA: 2018.

Lost and Delirious, film, directed by Léa Pool. USA: 2001.

Lost Highway, film, directed by David Lynch. France, USA: 1997.

Lost in Translation, film, directed by Sofia Coppola. USA, Japan: 2004.

Love Crime (Crime d'Amour), film, directed by Alan Corneau. France: 2010.

Love Sick (Legături Bolnăvicioase), film, directed by Tudor Giugiu. Romania, France: 2006.

Lovesong, film, directed by So Yong Kim. USA: 2016.

Loving Annabelle, film, directed by Katherine Brooks. USA: 2006.

Madame X – an Absolute Ruler (Madame X – Eine Absolute Herrscherin), film, directed by Ulrike Ottinger. West Germany: 1978.

Mädchen in Uniform, film, directed by Geza Radvanyi. West Germany, France: 1958.

Maidens in Uniform (Mädchen in Uniform), film, directed by Leontine Sagan. Germany: 1931.

Manifesto, film, directed by Julian Rosefeldt. Germany: 2015.

Margarita with a Straw, film, directed by Shonali Bose and Nilesh Maniyar. India: 2014.

Marguerite & Julien (Marguerite et Julien), film, directed by Valérie Donzelli. France: 2015.

Marlina the Murderer in Four Acts, film, directed by Mouly Surya. Indonesia, France, Malaysia, Thailand: 2014.

Marnie, film, directed by Alfred Hitchcock. USA: 1964.

May Fools (Milou en Mai), film, directed by Louis Malle. France, Italy: 1990.

Mean Girls, film, directed by Mark Waters. USA, Canada: 2004.

The Meetings of Anna (Les Rendez-Vous d'Anna), film, directed by Chantal Akerman. France, Belgium, West Germany: 1979.

The Member of the Wedding, film, directed by Fred Zinnemann. USA: 1952.

Metropolis, film, directed by Fritz Lang. Germany: 1927.

Midnight Cowboy, film, directed by John Schlesinger. USA: 1969.

Mildred Pierce, film, directed by Michael Curtiz. USA: 1945.

Mildred Pierce, television mini-series, directed by Todd Haynes. USA: 2011.

Milk, film, directed by Gus van Sant. USA: 2008.

The Misandrists, film, directed by Bruce La Bruce. Germany: 2017.

The Miseducation of Cameron Post, film, directed by Desiree Akhavan. USA: 2018.

Misery, film, directed by Rob Reiner. USA: 1990.

Mogambo, film, directed by John Ford. USA: 1953.

Monster, film, directed by Patty Jenkins. USA, Germany: 2003.

Morocco, film, directed by Josef von Sternberg. USA: 1930.

Mosquita y Mari, film, directed by Aurora Guerrero. USA: 2012.

Mudbound, film, directed by Dee Rees. USA: 2017.

Mulholland Drive, film, directed by David Lynch. France, USA: 2001.

Mustang, film, directed by Deniz Gamze Ergüven. France, Germany, Turkey, Qatar: 2015.

Mutiny on the Bounty, film, directed by Frank Lloyd. USA: 1935.

My Days of Mercy, film, directed by Tali Shalom-Ezer. UK, USA: 2017.

My Little Princess, film, directed by Eva Ionesco. France: 2011.

My Summer of Love, film, directed by Pawel Pawlikowski. UK: 2004.

Nathalie . . ., film, directed by Anne Fontaine. France, Spain: 2003.

The Neon Demon, film, directed by Nicolas Winding Refn. Denmark, France, UK, USA: 2016.

Network, film, directed by Sidney Lumet. USA: 1976.

Nocturnal Animals, film, directed by Tom Ford. USA: 2016.

Noor, film, directed by Çağla Zencirci and Guillaume Giovanetti. France, Pakistan: 2012.

Notorious, film, directed by Alfred Hitchcock. USA: 1946.

Now, Voyager, film, directed by Irving Rapper. USA: 1942.

Nymphomaniac Vol. 1, film, directed by Lars von Trier. Denmark, Germany, France, Belgium, UK: 2013.

Oh la la Pauline! (*Pauline S'Arrache*), film, directed by Émilie Brisavoine. France: 2015.

Oldboy (*Oleduboi*), film, directed by Park Chan-Wook. South Korea: 2003.

On the Town, film, directed by Gene Kelly and Stanley Donen. USA: 1949.

Only Angels Have Wings, film, directed by Howard Hawks. USA: 1939.

Opium, film, directed by Arielle Dombasle. France: 2013.

Orange Is the New Black, television series, created by Jenji Kohan. USA: 2013–.

Pacific Heights, film, directed by John Schlesinger. USA: 1990.

Pariah, film, directed by Dee Rees. USA: 2011.

The Party (*La Boum*), film, directed by Claude Pinoteau. France: 1980.

The Party, film, directed by Sally Potter. UK: 2017.

Party Girl, film, directed by Marie Amachoukeli, Claire Burger and Samuel Theis. France: 2014.

Passion, film, directed by Brian de Palma. Germany, France: 2012.

Peeping Tom, film, directed by Michael Powell. UK: 1960.

Persona, film, directed by Ingmar Bergman. Sweden: 1966.

Personal Best, film, directed by Robert Towne. USA: 1982.

The Piano, film, directed by Jane Campion. New Zealand, Australia, France: 1993.

Poison, film, directed by Todd Haynes. USA: 1991.

Porcupine Lake, film, directed by Ingrid Veninger. Canada: 2017.

Portrait of a Young Girl at the End of the 60s in Brussels (*Portrait d'une Jeune Fille de la Fin des Années 60 à Bruxelles*), television mini-series, directed by Chantal Akerman. France: 1994.

Pretty Persuasion, film, directed by Marcos Siega. USA: 2005.

The Prince of Nothingwood (*Nothingwood*), film, directed by Sonia Kronlund. France, Germany: 2017.

The Private Lives of Pippa Lee, film, directed by Rebecca Miller. USA: 2009.

Producing Adults (Lapsia Ja Aikuisia – Kuinka Niitä Tehdään), film, directed by Aleksi Salmenperä. Finland, Sweden: 2004.

Professor Marston and the Wonder Women, film, directed by Angela Robinson. USA: 2017.

Puccini for Beginners, film, directed by Maria Maggenti. USA: 2006.

Queer Eye, reality television series, created by David Collins. USA: 2018–

The Quiet, film, directed by Jamie Babbit. USA: 2005.

Raw (Grave), film, directed by Julia Ducournau. France, Belgium, Italy: 2016.

Rear Window, film, directed by Alfred Hitchcock. USA: 1954.

Rebecca, film, directed by Alfred Hitchcock. USA: 1940.

River of No Return, film, directed by Otto Preminger. USA: 1954.

Room in Rome, film, directed by Julio Medem. Spain: 2010.

Safe, film, directed by Todd Haynes. UK, USA: 1995.

The Safety of Objects, film, directed by Rose Troche. UK, USA, Canada: 2001.

Sarah Prefers to Run (Sarah Préfère la Course), film, directed by Chloé Robichaud. Canada: 2013.

Saratoga Trunk, film, directed by Sam Wood. USA: 1945.

The Scarlet Empress, film, directed by Josef von Sternberg. USA: 1934.

Secretary, film, directed by Steven Shainberg. USA: 2002.

Sex and the City, television series, created by Darren Star. USA: 1998–2004.

Sex and the City, film, directed by Michael Patrick King. USA: 2008.

She Monkeys (Apflickorna), film, directed by Lisa Aschan. Sweden: 2011.

She Must Be Seeing Things, film, directed by Sheila McLaughlin. USA: 1987.

Shortbus, film, directed by John Cameron Mitchell. USA: 2006.

Show Me Love (Fucking Åmål), film, directed by Lukas Moodysson. Sweden: 1998.

Side Effects, film, directed by Steven Soderbergh. USA: 2013.

Signature Move, film, directed by Jennifer Reeder. USA: 2017.

Single White Female, film, directed by Barbet Schroeder. USA: 1992.

Sister My Sister, film, directed by Nancy Meckler. UK: 1994.

Sisters, film, directed by Brian de Palma. USA: 1973.

Sleuth, film, directed by Joseph Mankiewicz. UK, USA: 1972.

The Slope, online series, created by Desiree Akhavan and Ingrid Jungermann. USA: 2010–12.

Spider Lilies (Ci Qīng), film, directed by Zero Chou. Taiwan: 2008.

The Spiral Staircase, film, directed by Robert Siodmak. USA: 1946.

Stop-Loss, film, directed by Kimberly Peirce. USA: 2008.

The Straight Story, film, directed by David Lynch. France, UK, USA: 1999.

Stranger by the Lake (L'Inconnu du Lac), film, directed by Alain Guiraudie. France: 2013.

Stranger Inside, television movie, directed by Cheryl Dunye. USA: 2001.

Stud Life, film, directed by Cambell X. UK: 2012.

Suddenly (Tan de Repente), film, directed by Diego Lerman. Argentina, Netherlands: 2002.

Suddenly, Last Summer, film, directed by Joseph Mankiewicz. UK, USA: 1959.

Summertime (La Belle Saison), film, directed by Catherine Corsini. France, Belgium: 2015.

Sunset Boulevard, film, directed by Billy Wilder. USA: 1951.

Swimming Pool, film, directed by François Ozon. France, UK: 2003.

Sympathy for Mr. Vengeance (Boksuneun Naui Geot), film, directed by Park Chan-Wook. South Korea: 2002.

That Obscure Object of Desire (Cet Obscur Objet du Désir), film, directed by Luis Buñuel. France, Spain: 1977.

Thelma, film, directed by Joachim Trier. Denmark, France, Norway, Sweden: 2017.

Thelma and Louise, film, directed by Ridley Scott. USA, UK, France: 1991.

They, film, directed by Anahita Ghazvinizadeh. USA, Qatar: 2017.

Thin Ice, film, directed by Fiona Cunningham-Reid. UK: 1995.

Thirteen, film, directed by Catherine Hardwicke. USA: 2003.

Three Colours: Blue (Trois Couleurs: Bleu), film, directed by Krzysztof Kieślowski. France, Poland, Switzerland: 1993.

Three Veils, film, directed by Rolla Selbak. USA: 2011.

Times Square, film, directed by Alan Moyle. USA: 1980.

To Have and Have Not, film, directed by Howard Hawks. USA: 1944.

Tom at the Farm (Tom à la Ferme), film, directed by Xavier Dolan. France, Canada: 2013.

Tomboy, film, directed by Céline Sciamma. France: 2011.

Transparent, television series, created by Jill Soloway. USA: 2014–.

Trouble Every Day, film, directed by Claire Denis. France, Germany, Japan: 2001.

The Turning Point, film, directed by Herbert Ross. USA: 1977.

Twin Peaks, television series, created by Mark Frost and David Lynch. USA: 1990–1.

Twin Peaks: The Return, television series, created by Mark Frost and David Lynch. USA: 2017.

The Uninvited, film, directed by Lewis Allen. USA: 1944.

Unveiled (Fremde Haut), film, directed by Angelina Maccarone. Germany, Austria: 2005.

Up in the Air, film, directed by Jason Reitman. USA: 2009.

The Vampire Lovers, film, directed by Roy Ward Baker. UK, USA: 1970.

Vertigo, film, directed by Alfred Hitchcock. USA: 1958.

Vita and Virginia, film, directed by Chanya Button. UK, Ireland: 2018.

Water Lilies (Naissance des Pieuvres), film, directed by Céline Sciamma. France: 2007.

The Watermelon Woman, film, directed by Cheryl Dunye. USA: 1996.

Weekend, film, directed by Andrew Haigh. UK: 2011.

Wentworth, television series, created by Reg Watson and Lara Radulovich. Australia: 2013–.

When Night Is Falling, film, directed by Patricia Rozema. Canada: 1995.

Whip It, film, directed by Drew Barrymore. USA: 2009.

Wild at Heart, film, directed by David Lynch. USA: 1990.

Wild Things, film, directed by John McNaughton. USA: 1998.

Willy 1er, film, directed by Ludovic Boukherma, Zoran Boukherma, Marielle Gautier and Hugo Thomas. France: 2016.

The Woman in the Window, film, directed by Fritz Lang. USA: 1944.

Women Who Kill, film, directed by Ingrid Jungermann. USA: 2016.

The World Unseen, film, directed by Shamim Sarif. South Africa, UK: 2007.
Written on the Wind, film, directed by Douglas Sirk. USA: 1956.
Young and Wild (Joven y Alocada), film, directed by Marialy Rivas. Chile: 2012.

Bibliography

Aaron, Michele (2012), 'Passing Through: Queer Lesbian Film and *Fremde Haut*', *Journal of Lesbian Studies*, 16:3, 323–39.

Aaron, Michele (1999), 'Til Death Us Do Part: Cinema's Queer Couples Who Kill', in Michele Aaron (ed.), *The Body's Perilous Pleasures: Dangerous Desires and Contemporary Culture*, Edinburgh: Edinburgh University Press, pp. 67–86.

AfterEllen.com staff (2012), 'The Best Lesbian/Bi Movie Poll: Winners!', *AfterEllen*, 19 November, <http://www.afterellen.com/the-best-lesbianbi-movie-poll-winners/11/2012/4/> (accessed 4 April 2014).

Ahmed, Sara (2006), *Queer Phenomenology: Orientations, Objects, Others*, Durham, NC: Duke University Press.

Akass, Kim and Janet McCabe (2004), 'Introduction: Welcome to the Age of Un-Innocence', in Akass and McCabe (eds), *Reading Sex and the City*, London and New York: I. B. Tauris, pp. 1–16.

Alderson, David (2005), 'Queer Cosmopolitanism: Place, Politics, Citizenship and *Queer as Folk*', *New Formations*, 55, 73–88.

Alderson, David (2016), *Sex, Needs and Queer Culture: From Liberation to the Postgay*, London: Zed Books.

American Film Institute (2010), 'David Lynch on Digital Video Versus Film', *YouTube*, 10 May, <https://www.youtube.com/watch?v=pjtnOCfuPVQ> (accessed 5 February 2018).

Apter, Emily (2010), '"Women's Time" in Theory', *differences*, 21:1, 1–18.

Ashby, Justine (2005), 'Postfeminism in the British Frame', *Cinema Journal*, 44:2, 127–33.

Augé, Marc (1995), *Non-Places: Introduction to an Anthropology of Supermodernity*, translated by John Howe, London: Verso.

Bad Object Choices (ed.) (1991), *How Do I Look? Queer Film and Video*, Seattle, WA: Bay Press.

Bainbridge, Caroline (2008), *A Feminine Cinematics: Luce Irigaray, Women and Film*, Basingstoke and New York: Palgrave Macmillan.

Balsom, Erika and Ginette Vincendeau (2017), 'Crossing the Line', *Sight and Sound*, 27:4, 33.

Barker, Jennifer (2008), 'Out of Sync, Out of Sight: Synaesthesia and Film Spectacle', *Paragraph*, 31:2, 236–51.

Barnes, Djuna (2007 [1936]), *Nightwood*, London: Faber and Faber.

Barthes, Roland (2002 [1977]), *A Lover's Discourse: Fragments*, translated by Richard Howard, London: Vintage.

Barthes, Roland (1975 [1973]), *The Pleasure of the Text*, translated by Richard Miller, New York: Hill and Wang.

Barthes, Roland (1989 [1984]), *The Rustle of Language*, translated by Richard Howard, Berkeley: University of California Press.

Bechdel, Alison (1986), *Dykes to Watch Out For*, Ann Arbor: Firebrand Books.

Becker, Edith, Michelle Citron, Julia Lesage and B. Ruby Rich (1995), 'Lesbians and Film', in Corey Creekmur and Alexander Doty (eds), *Out in Culture: Gay, Lesbian, and Queer Essays on Popular Culture*, London: Cassell, pp. 25–43.

Beirne, Rebecca (2008), *Lesbians in Television and Text after the Millennium*, New York: Palgrave Macmillan.

Beirne, Rebecca (2014), 'New Queer Cinema 2.0? Lesbian-Focused Films and the Internet', *Screen*, 55:1, 129–38.

Belam, Martin and Sam Levin (2018), 'Woman Behind "Inclusion Rider" Explains Frances Mcdormand's Oscar Speech', *The Guardian*, 5 March, <https://www.the-guardian.com/film/2018/mar/05/what-is-an-inclusion-rider-frances-mcdorm and-oscars-2018> (accessed 16 March 2018).

Bendix, Trish (2013), 'Watch Now! Lesbians React to the Sex Scene in *Blue Is the Warmest Color*', *AfterEllen*, 11 November, <http://www.afterellen.com/watch-now-lesbians-react-to-the-sex-scene-in-blue-is-the-warmest-color/11/2013/> (accessed 1 January 2016).

Benshoff, Harry and Sean Griffin (2006), *Queer Images: A History of Gay and Lesbian Film in America*, Lanham, MD: Rowman & Littlefield.

Berenstein, Rhona (1996), 'Where the Girls Are: Riding the New Wave of Lesbian Feature Films', *GLQ*, 3:1, 125–37.

Berlant, Lauren (1999), 'The Compulsion to Repeat Femininity', in Joan Copjec and Michael Sorkin (eds), *Giving Ground: The Politics of Propinquity*, London: Verso, pp. 207–32.

Berlant, Lauren (2012a), *Cruel Optimism*, Durham, NC: Duke University Press.

Berlant, Lauren (2012b), *Desire / Love*, New York: Punctum Books.

Berlant, Lauren (2008), *The Female Complaint: The Unfinished Business of Sentimentality in American Culture*, Durham, NC: Duke University Press.

Berlant, Lauren (2015), 'Structures of Unfeeling: Mysterious Skin', *International Journal of Politics, Culture, and Society*, 28:3, 191–213.

Berlant, Lauren and Lee Edelman (2014), *Sex, or the Unbearable*, Durham, NC: Duke University Press.

Beugnet, Martine (2007), *Cinema and Sensation: French Film and the Art of Transgression*, Edinburgh: Edinburgh University Press.

Bianco, Marcie (2013), 'Is *Blue Is the Warmest Color* a "Lesbian Film"?', *AfterEllen*, 25 October, <http://www.afterellen.com/blue-is-the-warmest-color-comes-state-side/10/2013/> (accessed 5 December 2013).

Bordwell, David (1989), *Making Meaning: Inference and Rhetoric in the Interpretation of Cinema*, Cambridge, MA: Harvard University Press.

Box Office Mojo (2018), *'Blue Is the Warmest Color'*, Box Office Mojo, <http://www.boxofficemojo.com/movies/?id=bluewarm.htm> (accessed 3 March 2018).

Box Office Mojo (2018), *'Carol'*, Box Office Mojo, <http://www.boxofficemojo.com/movies/?id=carol.htm> (accessed 3 March 2018).

Box Office Mojo (2018), *'Chloe'*, Box Office Mojo, <http://www.boxofficemojo.com/movies/?id=chloe.htm> (accessed 3 March 2018).

Box Office Mojo (2018), *'Circumstance'*, Box Office Mojo, <http://www.boxofficemojo.com/movies/?id=circumstance.htm> (accessed 3 March 2018).

Box Office Mojo (2018), *'Far from Heaven'*, Box Office Mojo, <http://www.boxofficemojo.com/movies/?id=farfromheaven.htm> (accessed 3 March 2018).

Box Office Mojo (2018), *'The Kids Are All Right'*, Box Office Mojo, <http://www.boxofficemojo.com/movies/?id=kidsareallright.htm> (accessed 3 March 2018).

Box Office Mojo (2018), *'Mulholland Drive'*, Box Office Mojo, <http://www.boxofficemojo.com/movies/?id=mulhollanddrive.htm> (accessed 3 March 2018).

Box Office Mojo (2018), *'Nathalie'*, Box Office Mojo, <http://www.boxofficemojo.com/movies/?id=Nathalie .htm> (accessed 3 March 2018).

Box Office Mojo (2018), *'Water Lilies'*, Box Office Mojo, <http://www.boxofficemojo.com/movies/?id=waterlilies.htm> (accessed 3 March 2018).

Bradbury-Rance, Clara (2016), 'Desire, Outcast: Locating Queer Adolescence', in Fiona Handyside and Kate Taylor-Jones (eds), *International Cinema and the Girl: Local Issues, Transnational Contexts*, Basingstoke: Palgrave Macmillan, pp. 85–96.

Bradbury-Rance, Clara (2013), 'Querying Postfeminism in Lisa Cholodenko's *The Kids Are All Right*', in Joel Gwynne and Nadine Muller (eds), *Postfeminism and Contemporary Hollywood Cinema*, Basingstoke: Palgrave Macmillan, pp. 27–43.

Braidotti, Rosi (2002), 'Body-Images and the Pornography of Representation', in Kathleen Lennon and Margaret Whitford (eds), *Knowing the Difference: Feminist Perspectives in Epistemology*, London and New York: Routledge, pp. 17–30.

Bristow, Joseph (1997), *Sexuality*, New York: Routledge.

British Board of Film Classification (2013), *'Blue Is the Warmest Colour'*, British Board of Film Classification, 12 November, <http://www.bbfc.co.uk/releases/blue-warmest-colour-film> (accessed 5 April 2018).

British Board of Film Classification (2017), *'Fifty Shades of Grey'*, British Board of Film Classification, 3 February, <http://www.bbfc.co.uk/releases/fifty-shades-grey-2015> (accessed 5 April 2018).

British Film Institute (2018), 'UK Weekend Box Office Report: 22–24 November 2013', *British Film Institute: Weekend Box Office Figures*, <http://www.bfi.org.uk/education-research/film-industry-statistics-research/weekend-box-office-figures> (accessed 3 April 2018).

Bronfen, Elisabeth (1992), *Over Her Dead Body: Death, Femininity and the Aesthetic*, New York: Routledge.

Browne, Kath and Eduarda Ferreira (2016 [2015]), 'Introduction to Lesbian Geographies', in Kath Browne and Eduarda Ferreira (eds), *Lesbian Geographies: Gender, Place and Power*, Abingdon and New York: Routledge, pp. 1–28.

Bruhm, Steven and Natasha Hurley (2004), 'Curiouser: On the Queerness of Children', in Steven Bruhm and Natasha Hurley (eds), *Curiouser: On the Queerness of Children*, Minneapolis: University of Minnesota Press, pp. ix–xxxviii.

Bruno, Giuliana (2002), *Atlas of Emotion: Journeys in Art, Architecture, and Film*, New York: Verso.

Bruzzi, Stella (1997), *Undressing Cinema: Clothing and Identity in the Movies*, London and New York: Routledge.

Buckley, Jerome Hamilton (1974), *Season of Youth: The Bildungsroman from Dickens to Golding*, Cambridge, MA: Harvard University Press.

Butler, Judith (1993), 'Critically Queer', *GLQ*, 1:1, 17–32.

Butler, Judith (1999 [1990]), *Gender Trouble: Feminism and the Subversion of Identity*, 10th anniversary edn, London and New York: Routledge.

Butler, Judith (1991), 'Imitation and Gender Insubordination', in Diane Fuss (ed.), *Inside/Out: Lesbian Theories, Gay Theories*, London: Routledge, pp. 13–31.

Butler, Judith (2002), 'Is Kinship Always Already Heterosexual?', *differences*, 13:1, 14–44.

Cairns, Lucille (2006), *Sapphism on Screen: Lesbian Desire in French and Francophone Cinema*, Edinburgh: Edinburgh University Press.

Campbell, Jane (2017), 'Suffocation and Desire: *The Children's Hour* and *Carol*', in Jane Campbell and Theresa Carilli (eds), *Locating Queerness in the Media: A New Look*, Lanham, MA: Lexington Books, pp. 138–46.

Carter, Mia (1998), 'The Politics of Pleasure: Cross-Cultural Autobiographic Performance in the Video Works of Sadie Benning', *Signs*, 23:3, 745–69.

Castle, Terry (1993), *The Apparitional Lesbian: Female Homosexuality and Modern Culture*, Chichester and New York: Columbia University Press.

Chambers, Samuel (2006), 'Heteronormativity and *The L Word*: From a Politics of Representation to a Politics of Norms', in Kim Akass and Janet McCabe (eds), *Reading The L Word*, London: I. B. Tauris, pp. 81–98.

Chasin, Alexandra (2001), *Selling Out: The Gay and Lesbian Movement Goes to Market*, Basingstoke: Palgrave.

Child, Ben (2013), '*Blue Is the Warmest Colour* Actors Say Filming Lesbian Love Story Was "Horrible"', *The Guardian*, 4 September <http://www.theguardian.com/film/2013/sep/04/blue-is-the-warmest-colour-actors-director> (accessed 19 November 2013).

Chopra-Gant, Mike (2006), *Hollywood Genres and Postwar America: Masculinity, Family and Nation in Popular Movies and Film Noir*, London: I. B. Tauris.

Clark, Ashley (2014), 'The Interview: Richard Linklater', *Sight and Sound*, 24:8, 20–4.

Clark, Kenneth (1956), *The Nude: A Study of Ideal Art*, London: John Murray.

Coffman, Christine (2006), *Insane Passions: Lesbianism and Psychosis in Literature and Film*, Middletown, CT: Wesleyan University Press.

Cohen, Annabel (2001), 'Music as a Source of Emotion in Film', in Patrik Juslin and John Sloboda (eds), *Music and Emotion: Theory and Research*, Oxford: Oxford University Press, pp. 249–74.

Cohen, Robin (2001), *Global Diasporas: An Introduction*, Abingdon: Routledge.

Colling, Samantha (2017), *The Aesthetic Pleasures of Girl Teen Film*, London: Bloomsbury Academic.

Corber, Robert (2011), *Cold War Femme: Lesbianism, National Identity, and Hollywood Cinema*, Durham, NC: Duke University Press.

Cowie, Elizabeth (1997), *Representing the Woman: Cinema and Psychoanalysis*, Basingstoke: Macmillan.

Cox, David (2010), 'The Kids Are All Right. But Are They?', *The Guardian*, 1 November, <http://www.guardian.co.uk/film/filmblog/2010/nov/01/the-kids-are-all-right?INTCMP=SRCH> (accessed 7 August 2011).

Creed, Barbara (2009), *Darwin's Screens: Evolutionary Aesthetics, Time and Sexual Display in the Cinema*, Carlton, Victoria: Melbourne University Publishing.

Cvetkovich, Ann (2007), 'Public Feelings', *South Atlantic Quarterly*, 106:3, 459–68.

Dargis, Manohla (2013), 'Seeing You Seeing Me: The Trouble with *Blue Is the Warmest Colour*', *The New York Times*, 25 October, <http://www.nytimes.com/2013/10/27/movies/the-trouble-with-blue-is-the-warmest-color.html?_r=1&> (accessed 19 November 2013).

Davis, Lydia (2009), *The Collected Stories of Lydia Davis*, New York: Picador.

Davis, Nick (2015), 'The Object of Desire: Todd Haynes Discusses *Carol* and the Satisfactions of Telling Women's Stories', *Film Comment*, November/December, 31–5.

Davis, Nick (2008), 'The View from the *Shortbus*, or All Those Fucking Movies', *GLQ*, 14:4, 623–37.

Dawson, Leanne (ed.) (2017), *Queer European Cinema: Queering Cinematic Time and Space*, London and New York: Routledge.

de Beauvoir, Simone (1997 [1949]), *The Second Sex*, translated by H. M. Parshley, London: Vintage.

de Lauretis, Teresa (1984), *Alice Doesn't: Feminism, Semiotics, Cinema*, London: Macmillan.

de Lauretis, Teresa (1991), 'Film and the Visible', in Bad Object Choices (ed.), *How Do I Look?: Queer Film and Video*, Seattle, WA: Bay Press, pp. 223–63.

de Lauretis, Teresa (2010), *Freud's Drive: Psychoanalysis, Literature and Film*, Basingstoke: Palgrave Macmillan.

de Lauretis, Teresa (1994), *The Practice of Love: Lesbian Sexuality and Perverse Desire*, Bloomington and Indianapolis: Indiana University Press.

de Lauretis, Teresa (2011), 'Queer Texts, Bad Habits, and the Issue of a Future', *GLQ*, 17:2–3, 243–63.

de Lauretis, Teresa (1991), 'Queer Theory: Lesbian and Gay Sexualities, an Introduction', *differences*, 3:2, iii–xviii.

Derry, Charles (1988), *The Suspense Thriller: Films in the Shadow of Alfred Hitchcock*, Jefferson, NC and London: McFarland & Company.

Desai, Jigna (2002), 'Homo on the Range: Mobile and Global Sexualities', *Social Text*, 20:4, 65–89.

Dinshaw, Carolyn, Elizabeth Freeman, Lee Edelman, Roderick Ferguson, Carla

Freccero, J. Halberstam, Annamarie Jagose, Christopher Nealon and Tan Hoang Nguyen (2007), 'Theorizing Queer Temporalities: A Roundtable Discussion', *GLQ*, 13:2, 177–95.

Doane, Mary Ann (2003), 'The Close-Up: Scale and Detail in the Cinema', *differences*, 14:3, 89–111.

Doane, Mary Ann (1987), *The Desire to Desire: The Woman's Film of the 1940s*, Bloomington: Indiana University Press.

Doane, Mary Ann (1992), *Femmes Fatales: Feminism, Film Studies and Psychoanalysis*, London: Routledge.

Donnelly, Kevin (2005), *The Spectre of Sound: Music in Film and Television*, London: British Film Institute.

DP/30: The Oral History of Hollywood (2009), 'Talking *Chloe* with Anne Fontaine', *YouTube*, 20 February, <https://www.youtube.com/user/TheHotButton/fea tured> (accessed 16 December 2015).

Driscoll, Catherine (2011), *Teen Film: A Critical Introduction*, Oxford: Berg.

Duschinsky, Robbie and Emma Wilson (2015), 'Flat Affect, Joyful Politics and Enthralled Attachments: Engaging with the Work of Lauren Berlant', *International Journal of Politics, Culture, and Society*, 28:3, 179–90.

Dyer, Richard (2004), 'Idol Thoughts: Orgasm and Self-Reflexivity in Gay Pornography', in Pamela Church Gibson (ed.), *More Dirty Looks: Gender, Pornography and Power*, London: British Film Institute, pp. 102–9.

Dyer, Richard (2012), *In the Space of a Song: The Uses of Song in Film*, London: Routledge.

Dyer, Richard (1997b), *Pastiche*, London and New York: Routledge.

Dyer, Richard (1998 [1978]), 'Resistance through Charisma: Rita Hayworth and *Gilda*', in E. Ann Kaplan (ed.), *Women in Film Noir*, revised edn, London: British Film Institute, pp. 91–9.

Dyer, Richard (1983), 'Seen to Be Believed: Some Problems in the Representation of Gay People as Typical', *Studies in Visual Communication*, 9:2, 2–19.

Dyer, Richard (1997a), *White*, London and New York: Routledge.

Dyer, Richard and Julianne Pidduck (2003 [1990]), *Now You See It: Studies in Lesbian and Gay Film*, 2nd edn, London: Routledge.

Edelman, Lee (2004), *No Future: Queer Theory and the Death Drive*, Durham, NC: Duke University Press.

Elder, Glen, Lawrence Knopp and Heidi Nast (2006), 'Sexuality and Space', in Gary Gaile and Cort Willmott (eds), *Geography in America at the Dawn of the 21st Century*, Oxford: Oxford University Press, pp. 200–8.

Ellsworth, Elizabeth (1988), 'Illicit Pleasures: Feminist Spectators and *Personal Best*', in Leslie Roman, Linda Christian-Smith and Elizabeth Ellsworth (eds), *Becoming Feminine: The Politics of Popular Culture*, London and New York: Falmer Press, pp. 102–19.

Elsaesser, Thomas (1997), 'A Cinema of Vicious Circles', in Laurence Kardish and Juliane Lorenz (eds), *Rainer Werner Fassbinder*, New York: Museum of Modern Art, pp. 15–26.

Elsaesser, Thomas (1987), 'Tales of Sound and Fury: Observations on the

Family Melodrama', in Christine Gledhill (ed.), *Home Is Where the Heart Is: Studies in Melodrama and the Woman's Film*, London: British Film Institute, pp. 43–69.

Farmer, Brett (2000), *Spectacular Passions: Cinema, Fantasy, Gay Male Spectatorships*, Durham, NC: Duke University Press.

Farrimond, Katherine (2018), *The Contemporary Femme Fatale: Gender, Genre and American Cinema*, London and New York: Routledge.

Feldman, Zeena (2017), 'Introduction: Why Visibility Matters', in Zeena Feldman (ed.), *Art and the Politics of Visibility: Contesting the Global, Local and the In-Between*, London: I. B. Tauris, pp. 1–20.

Film Independent (2016), '*Carol* Parody – Kate McKinnon & Kumail Nanjiani, 2016 Film Independent Spirit Awards', *YouTube*, 27 February, <https://www.youtube.com/watch?v=_QljnNIBtaI> (accessed 30 March 2018).

Finlay, Sara-Jane and Natalie Fenton (2005), '"If You've Got a Vagina and an Attitude, That's a Deadly Combination": Sex and Heterosexuality in *Basic Instinct*, *Body of Evidence* and *Disclosure*', *Sexualities*, 8:1, 49–74.

Fletcher, John (1995), 'Primal Scenes and the Female Gothic: *Rebecca* and *Gaslight*', *Screen*, 36:4, 341–70.

Foucault, Michel (1998 [1984]), *The History of Sexuality*, translated by Robert Hurley, Vol. 1, *The Will to Knowledge*, London: Allen Lane.

Foucault, Michel (1986 [1967]), 'Of Other Spaces', *Diacritics*, translated by Jay Miskowiec, 16:1, 22–7.

Fowles, John (1969), *The French Lieutenant's Woman*, London: Jonathan Cape.

Freeman, Elizabeth (2010), *Time Binds: Queer Temporalities, Queer Histories*, Durham, NC: Duke University Press.

Galt, Rosalind (2013), 'Default Cinema: Queering Economic Crisis in Argentina and Beyond', *Screen*, 54:1, 62–81.

Galt, Rosalind (2011), *Pretty: Film and the Decorative Image*, New York and Chichester: Columbia University Press.

Galt, Rosalind and Karl Schoonover (2016), *Queer Cinema in the World*, Durham, NC: Duke University Press.

Galvin, Angela (1994), '*Basic Instinct*: Damning Dykes', in Diane Hamer and Belinda Budge (eds), *The Good, the Bad and the Gorgeous: Popular Culture's Romance with Lesbianism*, London and San Francisco, CA: Pandora Press, pp. 218–32.

Gant, Charles (2018), 'The Numbers: Hero Venues', *Sight and Sound*, 28:4, 9.

Garber, Linda (2009), 'The Curious Persistence of Lesbian Studies', in Noreen Giffney and Michael O'Rourke (eds), *The Ashgate Research Companion to Queer Theory*, Farnham and Burlington, VT: Ashgate, pp. 65–77.

Genz, Stéphanie (2010), 'Singled Out: Postfeminism's "New Woman" and the Dilemma of Having It All', *The Journal of Popular Culture*, 43:1, 97–119.

Gerhard, Jane (2011), '*Sex and the City*: Carrie Bradshaw's Queer Postfeminism', *Feminist Media Studies*, 5:1, 37–49.

Gide, André (1947), *The Journals of André Gide*, translated by Justin O'Brien, London: Secker & Warburg.

Gill, Rosalind (2008), 'Culture and Subjectivity in Neoliberal and Postfeminist Times', *Subjectivity*, 25:1, 432–45.

GLAAD (2017), '2017 Studio Responsibility Index', *GLAAD*, <https://www.glaad.org/sri/2017> (accessed 3 April 2018).

Gledhill, Christine (1987), 'The Melodramatic Field: An Investigation', in Christine Gledhill (ed.), *Home Is Where the Heart Is: Studies in Melodrama and the Woman's Film*, London: British Film Institute, pp. 5–39.

Goldfield, Hannah (@hannahgoldfield) (2018), 'Queer Eye is fine but I would like a companion show with butch women helping straight women who want to feel comfortable being less performatively feminine', *Twitter*, 26 February, <https://twitter.com/hannahgoldfield/status/968155076463398915?lang=en> (accessed 20 April 2018).

Gopinath, Gayatri (2005), *Impossible Desires: Queer Diasporas and South Asian Public Cultures*, Durham, NC: Duke University Press.

Gopinath, Gayatri (2002), 'Local Sites/Global Contexts: The Transnational Trajectories of Deepa Mehta's *Fire*', in Arnaldo Cruz-Malavé and Martin Manalansan (eds), *Queer Globalizations: Citizenship and the Afterlife of Colonialism*, New York: New York University Press, pp. 149–61.

Gordon, Angus (1999), 'Turning Back: Adolescence, Narrative, and Queer Theory', *GLQ*, 5:1, 1–24.

Grant, Catherine (2015), 'Therese & Carol & Alec & Laura (A Brief Encounter)', *Vimeo*, 22 December, <https://vimeo.com/149791810> (accessed 29 June 2018).

Greenhouse, Emily (2013), 'Did a Director Push Too Far?', *The New Yorker*, 24 October <http://www.newyorker.com/online/blogs/culture/2013/10/did-a-director-push-too-far.html> (accessed 3 December 2013).

Griffin, F. Hollis (2016), *Feeling Normal: Sexuality and Media Criticism in the Digital Age*, Bloomington and Indianapolis: Indiana University Press.

Griffiths, Robin (ed.) (2006), *British Queer Cinema*, London: Routledge.

The Guardian (2017), 'The 50 Top Films of 2017 in the UK: The Full List', *The Guardian*, 5 December, <https://www.theguardian.com/film/2017/dec/05/the-50-top-films-of-2017-in-the-uk?CMP=Share_iOSApp_Other> (accessed 3 March 2018).

Gupta, Kristina (2013), 'Picturing Space for Lesbian Nonsexualities: Rethinking Sex-Normative Commitments through *The Kids Are All Right*', *Journal of Lesbian Studies*, 17:1, 103–18.

Gwynne, Joel and Nadine Muller (eds) (2013), *Postfeminism and Contemporary Hollywood Cinema*, Basingstoke: Palgrave Macmillan.

Halberstam, J. (2006), *Female Masculinity*, Durham, NC and London: Duke University Press.

Halberstam, J. (2005), *In a Queer Time and Place: Transgender Bodies, Subcultural Lives*, New York: New York University Press.

Halberstam, J. (2011), *The Queer Art of Failure*, Durham, NC: Duke University Press.

Halberstam, J. (2007), 'The Transgender Gaze in *Boys Don't Cry*', in Jackie Stacey and Sarah Street (eds), *Queer Screen*, London and New York: Routledge, pp. 278–82.

Hall, Stuart (2003), *Representation: Cultural Representations and Signifying Practices*, Milton Keynes: Open University Press.

Halperin, David (1997), *Saint Foucault: Towards a Gay Hagiography*, New York: Oxford University Press.

Hammer, Barbara (1993), 'The Politics of Abstraction', in Martha Gever, Pratibha Parmar and John Greyson (eds), *Queer Looks: Perspectives on Lesbian and Gay Film and Video*, New York: Routledge, pp. 70–5.

Handyside, Fiona (2014), *Cinema at the Shore: The Beach in French Film*, Oxford: Peter Lang.

Handyside, Fiona (2017), 'Postcards and/of Prostitutes: Circulating the City in Atom Egoyan's *Chloe*', in Danielle Hipkins and Kate Taylor-Jones (eds), *Prostitution and Sex Work in Global Cinema*, Basingstoke: Palgrave Macmillan, pp. 243–64.

Handyside, Fiona (2012), 'Queer Filiations: Adaptation in the Films of François Ozon', *Sexualities*, 15:1, 53–67.

Handyside, Fiona (2017), *Sofia Coppola: A Cinema of Girlhood*, London and New York: I. B. Tauris.

Hanson, Ellis (1999), 'Introduction: Out Takes', *Out Takes: Essays on Queer Theory and Film*, Durham, NC: Duke University Press, pp. 1–19.

Harris, Laura and Elizabeth Crocker (1997), 'An Introduction to Sustaining Femme Gender', in Laura Harris and Elizabeth Crocker (eds), *Femme: Feminists, Lesbians, and Bad Girls*, New York: Routledge, pp. 1–14.

Hart, Lynda (1994), *Fatal Women: Lesbian Sexuality and the Mark of Aggression*, London: Routledge.

Henderson, Lisa (2013), *Love and Money: Queers, Class, and Cultural Production*, London and New York: New York University Press.

Henderson, Lisa (1999), 'Simple Pleasures: Lesbian Community and *Go Fish*', *Signs*, 25:1, 37–64.

Herring, Sean (2006), '*Brokeback Mountain* Dossier: Introduction', *GLQ*, 13:1, 93–4.

Hesford, Victoria (2013), *Feeling Women's Liberation*, Durham, NC: Duke University Press.

Hesford, Wendy (2011), *Spectacular Rhetorics: Human Rights Visions, Recognitions, Feminisms*, Durham, NC: Duke University Press.

Highsmith, Patricia (1991 [1952]), *Carol*, London: Penguin.

Hollinger, Karen (1998), *In the Company of Women: Contemporary Female Friendship Films*, Minneapolis: University of Minnesota Press.

Holmes, Jeremy (1993), *John Bowlby and Attachment Theory*, London and New York: Routledge.

Holmlund, Chris (2002), *Impossible Bodies: Femininity and Masculinity at the Movies*, London: Routledge.

hoogland, renée (1997), *Lesbian Configurations*, Cambridge: Polity.

Hooton, Christopher, Jack Shepherd and Jacob Stolworthy (2017), 'The 20 Best Films of 2017', *The Independent*, 19 December <https://www.independent. co.uk/arts-entertainment/films/features/best-films-of-2017-list-movies-critics-

20-rated-ranked-call-me-by-your-name-get-out-moonlight-good-a8118726.html> (accessed 3 March 2018).

Horak, Laura (2016), *Girls Will Be Boys: Cross-Dressed Women, Lesbians, and American Cinema, 1908–1934*, New Brunswick, NJ and London: Rutgers University Press.

Jacobs, Matthew (2014), '*Nymphomaniac* Stars Charlotte Gainsbourg and Stacy Martin on the "Boring" Filming of the Movie's Graphic Sex', *Huffington Post*, 20 March, <http://www.huffingtonpost.com/2014/03/20/nymphomaniac-charlotte-gainsbourg-stacy-martin_n_4995662.html> (accessed 7 April 2014).

Jaffe, Sara (2016), 'Phyllis Nagy: On Writing the Script for *Carol* and Creating a Different Kind of Love Story', *Lamda Literary*, 21 February, <http://www.lamb daliterary.org/features/02/21/phyllis-nagy-on-writing-the-script-for-carol-and-creating-a-different-kind-of-love-story/> (accessed 23 March 2018).

Jagose, Annamarie (2002), *Inconsequence: Lesbian Representation and the Logic of Sexual Sequence*, Ithaca, NY: Cornell University Press.

Jagose, Annamarie (1994), *Lesbian Utopics*, London and New York: Routledge.

Jagose, Annamarie (2012), *Orgasmology*, Durham, NC: Duke University Press.

James, E. L. (2011), *Fifty Shades of Grey*, London: Vintage.

James, Nick (2018), 'Category Error', *Sight and Sound*, 28:2, 5.

Jermyn, Deborah (1996), 'Rereading the Bitches from Hell: A Feminist Appropriation of the Female Psychopath', *Screen*, 37:3, 251–67.

Kabir, Shameem (1998), *Daughters of Desire: Lesbian Representations in Film*, London and Washington, DC: Cassell.

Kamen, Matt (2017), 'The Best Films of 2017', *Wired*, 26 December, <http://www.wired.co.uk/article/films-of-the-year-2017> (accessed 3 March 2018).

Kassabian, Anahid (2001), *Hearing Film: Tracking Identifications in Contemporary Hollywood Film Music*, London: Routledge.

Kearney, Mary Celeste (2002), 'Girlfriends and Girl Power: Female Adolescence in Contemporary U.S Cinema', in Frances Gateward and Murray Pomerance (eds), *Sugar, Spice, and Everything Nice: Cinemas of Girlhood*, Detroit, MI: Wayne State University Press, pp. 125–42.

Keeling, Kara, Jennifer DeClue, Yvonne Welbon, Jacqueline Stewart and Roya Rastegar (2015), '*Pariah* and Black Independent Cinema Today: A Roundtable Discussion', *GLQ*, 21:2, 423–39.

Kessler, Kelly (2003), '*Bound* Together: Lesbian Film That's Family Fun for Everyone', *Film Quarterly*, 56:4, 13–22.

Klein, Melanie (1987 [1956]), 'A Study of Envy and Gratitude', in Juliet Mitchell (ed.), *The Selected Melanie Klein*, 1st American edn, New York: Free Press, pp. 211–41.

Kohnen, Melanie (2016), *Queer Representation, Visibility, and Race in American Film and Television*, New York and London: Routledge.

Koivunen, Anu (2010), 'An Affective Turn? Reimagining the Subject of Feminist Theory', in Marianne Liljeström and Susanna Paasonen (eds), *Working with Affect in Feminist Readings: Disturbing Differences*, London and New York: Routledge, pp. 8–28.

Kristeva, Julia (1981 [1979]), 'Women's Time', *Signs*, translated by Alice Jardine and Harry Blake, 7:1, 13–35.

Kuhn, Annette (1988), *Cinema, Censorship and Sexuality, 1909–1925*, London: Routledge.

Kuhn, Annette (1982), *Women's Pictures: Feminism and Cinema*, London: Routledge & Kegan Paul.

Lachman, Edward (2015), 'Edward Lachman Shares His Secrets for Shooting Todd Haynes' *Carol*', *IndieWire*, 3 December, <http://www.indiewire.com/2015/12/edward-lachman-shares-his-secrets-for-shooting-todd-haynes-carol-48627/> (accessed 10 April 2018).

Laplanche, Jean and Jean-Bertrand Pontalis (1986 [1964]), 'Fantasy and the Origins of Sexuality', in Victor Burgin, James Donald and Cora Kaplan (eds), *Formations of Fantasy*, London: Methuen, pp. 5–34.

Lavery, David (ed.) (1995), *Full of Secrets: Critical Approaches to Twin Peaks*, Detroit, MI: Wayne State University Press.

Lee, Benjamin (2017), 'Call Me by the Wrong Name: How Studios Are Still Trying to Straight-Wash Gay Films', *The Guardian*, 8 November, <https://www.theguardian.com/film/2017/nov/08/straight-wash-gay-films-call-me-by-your-name> (accessed 9 April 2018).

Lenarduzzi, Thea (2015), 'Testing the Waters of Identity', *The Times Literary Supplement*, 20 May, <http://www.the-tls.co.uk/tls/public/article1558437.ece> (accessed 11 September 2015).

Leonard, Suzanne (2009), *Fatal Attraction*, Chichester and Malden, MA: Wiley-Blackwell.

Lévi-Strauss, Claude (1969 [1949]), *The Elementary Structures of Kinship*, edited by Rodney Needham, translated by James Harle Bell and John Richard von Sturmer, Boston: Beacon Press.

Lewis, Hilary (2016), 'ABC Rejects *Carol* Ad Featuring Nude Love Scene', *The Hollywood Reporter*, 29 January, <https://www.hollywoodreporter.com/news/carol-nude-sex-scene-abc-860416> (accessed 9 April 2018).

Lindner, Katharina (2011), 'Bodies in Action: Female Athleticism on the Cinema Screen', *Feminist Media Studies*, 11:3, 321–45.

Lindner, Katharina (2017a), *Film Bodies: Queer Feminist Encounters with Gender and Sexuality in Cinema*, London: I. B. Tauris.

Lindner, Katharina (2017b), 'Queer-ing Texture: Tactility, Spatiality, and Kinesthetic Empathy in *She Monkeys*', *Camera Obscura*, 32:3, 121–54.

Lindner, Katharina (2011), '"There Is a Reason Why Sporty Spice Is the Only One of Them without a Fella . . .": The "Lesbian Potential" of *Bend It Like Beckham*', *New Review of Film and Television Studies*, 9:2, 204–23.

Love, Heather (2016), 'Queer Messes', *Women's Studies Quarterly*, 44:3–4, 345–9.

Love, Heather (2004), 'Spectacular Failure: The Figure of the Lesbian in *Mulholland Drive*', *New Literary History*, 35:1, 117–32.

Marinucci, Mimi (2016 [2010]), *Feminism Is Queer: The Intimate Connection between Queer and Feminist Theory*, 2nd edn, London: Zed Books.

Marivaux, Pierre (2007 [1731]), *La Vie de Marianne*, Paris, France: Le Livre de Poche.

Maroh, Julie (2013), 'Le Bleu d'Adèle', *Les Coeurs Exacerbés*, 27 May, <http://www.juliemaroh.com/2013/05/27/le-bleu-dadele/> (accessed 4 December 2013).

Maroh, Julie (2010), *Le Bleu Est une Couleur Chaude*, Grenoble, France: Glénat.

Mavor, Carol (2013), *Blue Mythologies: Reflections on a Colour*, London: Reaktion Books.

Mayer, Sophie (2012), '*Circumstance* (Review)', *Sight and Sound*, 22:9, 97–8.

Mayer, Sophie (2016), *Political Animals: The New Feminist Cinema*, London and New York: I. B. Tauris.

Mayne, Judith (2000), *Framed: Lesbians, Feminists, and Media Culture*, Minneapolis and London: University of Minnesota Press.

Mayne, Judith (1990), *The Woman at the Keyhole: Feminism and Women's Cinema*, Bloomington: Indiana University Press.

Mazullo, Mark (2005), 'Remembering Pop: David Lynch and the Sound of the '60s', *American Music*, 23:4, 493–513.

McBride, Dwight (2006), 'Why I Hate That I Loved *Brokeback Mountain*', *GLQ*, 13:1, 95–7.

McDermid, Val (2010), 'Foreword', in Patricia Highsmith, *Carol*, London: Bloomsbury, pp. v–viii.

McDowell, Kelly (2005), 'Unleashing the Feminine Unconscious: Female Oedipal Desires and Lesbian Sadomasochism in *Mulholland Drive*', *The Journal of Popular Culture*, 38:6, 1037–49.

McGowan, Todd (2004), 'Lost on Mulholland Drive: Navigating David Lynch's Panegyric to Hollywood', *Cinema Journal*, 43:2, 67–89.

McRobbie, Angela (2009), *The Aftermath of Feminism: Gender, Culture and Social Change*, Los Angeles, CA and London: Sage.

Merck, Mandy (2000), *In Your Face: 9 Sexual Studies*, New York: New York University Press.

Merck, Mandy (2017), 'Negative Oedipus: *Carol* as Lesbian Romance and Maternal Melodrama', *SEQUENCE: Serial Studies in Media, Film and Music*, 2:3, 1–28.

Merck, Mandy (1993), *Perversions: Deviant Readings*, London: Virago.

Merck, Mandy (2004), 'Sexuality in the City', in Kim Akass and Janet McCabe (eds), *Reading Sex and the City*, London and New York: I. B. Tauris, pp. 48–64.

Miller, D.A. (2007), 'On the Universality of *Brokeback Mountain*', *Film Quarterly*, 60:3, 50–61.

Modleski, Tania (1988), *The Women Who Knew Too Much: Hitchcock and Feminist Theory*, London and New York: Methuen.

Monaghan, Whitney (2016), *Queer Girls, Temporality and Screen Media: Not 'Just a Phase'*, Basingstoke: Palgrave Macmillan.

Mulvey, Laura (2006), *Death 24x a Second*, London: Reaktion Books.

Mulvey, Laura (1975), 'Visual Pleasure and Narrative Cinema', *Screen*, 16:3, 6–18.

Muñoz, José Esteban (2009), *Cruising Utopia: The Then and There of Queer Futurity*, New York: New York University Press.

Neale, Steve (1980), *Genre*, London: British Film Institute.

Negra, Diane (2009), *What a Girl Wants?: Fantasizing the Reclamation of Self in Postfeminism*, London and New York: Routledge.

Newman, Kim (2002), '*Mulholland Drive* (Review)', *Sight and Sound*, 12:1, 51.

Nochimson, Martha (2004), 'All I Need Is the Girl: The Life and Death of Creativity in *Mulholland Drive*', in Erica Sheen and Annette Davison (eds), *The Cinema of David Lynch: American Dreams, Nightmare Visions*, London: Wallflower Press, pp. 165–81.

Nonrindr, Panivong (2012), 'The Cinematic Practice of a 'Cinéaste Ordinaire': Abdellatif Kechiche and French Political Cinema', *Contemporary French and Francophone Studies*, 16:1, 55–68.

Oler, Tammy (2013), 'The Problems with *Blue Is the Warmest Color*', *Bitch*, 12 November, <http://bitchmagazine.org/post/the-problems-with-blue-is-the-warmest-color> (accessed 7 April 2014).

Oumano, Elena (2010), *Cinema Today: A Conversation with Thirty-Nine Filmmakers from around the World*, New Brunswick, NJ: Rutgers University Press.

Oxford English Dictionary (2018), 'Organise', *Oxford English Dictionary Online*, <http://www.oed.com/view/Entry/132456?rskey=DRval0&result=2&isAdvanced=false#eid> (accessed 3 April 2018).

Padva, Gilad (2014), *Queer Nostalgia in Cinema and Pop Culture*, Basingstoke and New York: Palgrave Macmillan.

Palmer, Tim (2011), *Brutal Intimacy: Analyzing Contemporary French Cinema*, Hanover, NH and London: Wesleyan University Press.

Palmer, Tim (2018), 'Fine Arts and Ugly Arts: *Blue Is the Warmest Colour*, Abdellatif Kechiche's Corporeal State of the Nation', in Lindsay Coleman and Carol Siegel (eds), *Intercourse in Television and Film: The Presentaton of Explicit Sex Acts*, London: Lexington Books, pp. 3–24.

Pearl, Monica (2008), 'Graphic Language: Redrawing the Family (Romance) in Alison Bechdel's *Fun Home*', *Prose Studies*, 30:3, 286–304.

Pedwell, Carolyn and Anne Whitehead (2012), 'Affecting Feminism: Questions of Feeling in Feminist Theory', *Feminist Theory*, 13:2, 115–29.

Peele, Thomas (ed.) (2007), *Queer Popular Culture: Literature, Media, Film, and Television*, New York: Palgrave Macmillan.

Peronne, Jeanne Joe (2018), 'Gender Inequality in Film Infographic Updated in 2018', *New York Film Academy*, 8 March, <https://www.nyfa.edu/film-school-blog/gender-inequality-in-film-infographic-updated-in-2018/> (accessed 1 April 2018).

Perriam, Christopher (2013), *Spanish Queer Cinema*, Edinburgh: Edinburgh University Press.

Perriam, Christopher and Darren Waldron (2016), *French and Spanish Queer Film: Audiences, Communities and Cultural Exchange*, Edinburgh: Edinburgh University Press.

Phelan, Lyn (2000), 'Artificial Women and Male Subjectivity in *42nd Street* and *Bride of Frankenstein*', *Screen*, 41:2, 161–82.

Phelan, Peggy (1993), *Unmarked: The Politics of Performance*, New York: Routledge.

Pick, Anat (2004), 'New Queer Cinema and Lesbian Films', in Michele Aaron (ed.),

New Queer Cinema: A Critical Reader, Edinburgh: Edinburgh University Press, pp. 103–17.

Pidduck, Julianne (1995), 'The 1990s Hollywood Fatal Femme: (Dis)Figuring Feminism, Family, Irony, Violence', *Cineaction*, 38, 65–72.

Pidduck, Julianne (2013), 'The Times of *The Hours*: Queer Melodrama and the Dilemma of Marriage', *Camera Obscura*, 28:1, 37–67.

Pidduck, Julianne (2011), 'The Visible and the Sayable: The Moment and Conditions of Hypervisibility', in Florian Grandena and Cristina Johnston (eds), *Cinematic Queerness: Gay and Lesbian Hypervisibility in Contemporary Francophone Feature Films*, Oxford: Peter Lang, pp. 9–40.

Place, Janey (1998 [1978]), 'Women in Film Noir', in E. Ann Kaplan (ed.), *Women in Film Noir*, revised edn, London: British Film Institute, pp. 47–68.

Pramaggiore, Maria (1997), 'Fishing for Girls: Romancing Lesbians in New Queer Cinema', *College Literature*, 24:1, 59–75.

Projansky, Sarah (2014), *Spectacular Girls: Media Fascination and Celebrity Culture*, New York: New York University Press.

Projansky, Sarah (2001), *Watching Rape: Film and Television in Postfeminist Culture*, New York: New York University Press.

Pulver, Andrew (2013), 'Cannes 2013 Palme d'Or Goes to Film About Lesbian Romance', *The Guardian*, 26 May, <http://www.theguardian.com/film/2013/may/26/cannes-blue-is-the-warmest-colour> (accessed 20 March 2014).

Radner, Hilary (2011), *Neo-Feminist Cinema: Girly Films, Chick Flicks and Consumer Culture*, New York: Routledge.

Rapold, Nicolas (2009), 'Come with Us', *Sight and Sound*, 19:2, 28–30.

Rastegar, Roya (2011), '*Circumstance* and Dangerous Elicitations of Truth', *Huffington Post*, 6 September, <http://www.huffingtonpost.com/roya-rastegar/circumstance-and-dangerou_b_947489.html> (accessed 15 September 2014).

Rees-Roberts, Nick (2008), *French Queer Cinema*, Edinburgh: Edinburgh University Press.

Restuccia, Frances (2009), 'Kristeva's Intimate Revolt and the Thought Specular: Encountering the (Mulholland) Drive', in Kelly Oliver (ed.), *Psychoanalysis, Aesthetics, and Politics in the Work of Julia Kristeva*, Albany: State University of New York Press, pp. 65–78.

Rich, B. Ruby (2014), '*Blue Is the Warmest Color*: Feeling Blue', *The Criterion Collection*, 24 February, <http://www.criterion.com/current/posts/3072-blue-is-the-warmest-color-feeling-blue> (accessed 7 April 2014).

Rich, B. Ruby (1999), 'Collision, Catastrophe, Celebration: The Relationship between Gay and Lesbian Film Festivals and Their Publics', *GLQ*, 5:1, 79–84.

Rich, B. Ruby (1992), 'The New Queer Cinema', *Sight and Sound*, 2:9, 30–4.

Rich, B. Ruby (2013), *New Queer Cinema: The Director's Cut*, Durham, NC: Duke University Press.

Rich, B. Ruby (2011), 'Park City Remix', *Film Quarterly*, 64:3, 62–5.

Rich, B. Ruby (2000), 'Queer and Present Danger', *Sight and Sound*, 10:3, 17.

Rich, B. Ruby (1992), 'A Queer Sensation', *The Village Voice*, 24 March, 41–4.

Rich, B. Ruby (1998), 'What's a Good Gay Film?', *OUT*, 60, 58.

Richards, Stuart (2016), 'A New Queer Cinema Renaissance', *Queer Studies in Media and Popular Culture*, 1:2, 215–29.

Ritterbusch, Rachel (2008), 'Anne Fontaine and Contemporary Women's Cinema in France', *Rocky Mountain Review*, 62:2, 68–81.

Robey, Tim (2013), '*Blue Is the Warmest Colour* (Review)', *The Telegraph*, 21 November, <https://www.telegraph.co.uk/culture/film/filmreviews/10465082/Blue-is-the-Warmest-Colour-review.html> (accessed 1 December 2013).

Robinette, Dale (2017), 'The Best Films of 2017', *Time Out London*, 14 December, <https://www.timeout.com/london/film/the-best-films-of-2017> (accessed 1 April 2018).

Rodowick, D.N. (1991), *The Difficulty of Difference: Psychoanalysis, Sexual Difference & Film Theory*, London and New York: Routledge.

Romney, Jonathan (2013), 'Cannes 2013: Up Close and Physical', *Sight and Sound*, 24 May, <http://www.bfi.org.uk/news-opinion/sight-sound-magazine/comment/festivals/cannes-2013-close-physical> (accessed 19 November 2013).

Romney, Jonathan (2013), 'London Film Festival: *Blue Is the Warmest Colour*', *British Film Institute*, <https://whatson.bfi.org.uk/lff/Online/default.asp?BOparam::WScontent::loadArticle::permalink=blue-is-the-warmest-colour> (accessed 19 November 2013).

Roof, Judith (1991), *A Lure of Knowledge: Lesbian Sexuality and Theory*, New York: Columbia University Press.

Rose, Jacqueline (2005 [1986]), *Sexuality in the Field of Vision*, new edn, London: Verso.

Rosenblum, Sarah Terez (2013), 'Convincingly Queer: Léa Seydoux in *Blue Is the Warmest Color*', *AfterEllen*, 6 November, <http://www.afterellen.com/convincingly-queer-lea-seydoux-in-blue-is-the-warmest-color/11/2013/> (accessed 5 December 2013).

Rubin, Gayle (1993), 'Thinking Sex: Notes for a Radical Theory of the Politics of Sexuality', in Henry Abelove, Michele Barale and David Halperin (eds), *The Lesbian and Gay Studies Reader*, London: Routledge, pp. 3–44.

Rueschmann, Eva (2000), *Sisters on Screen: Siblings in Contemporary Cinema*, Philadelphia, PA: Temple University Press.

Rushbrook, Dereka (2002), 'Cities, Queer Space, and the Cosmopolitan Tourist', *GLQ*, 8:1–2, 183–206.

Ryberg, Ingrid (2013), '"Every Time We Fuck, We Win": The Public Sphere of Queer, Feminist, and Lesbian Porn as a (Safe) Space for Sexual Empowerment', in Tristan Taormino, Celine Parrenas Shimizu, Constance Penley and Mireille Miller-Young (eds), *The Feminist Porn Book: The Politics of Producing Pleasure*, New York: The Feminist Press, pp. 140–54.

Schaffner, Anna Katharina (2006), 'Fantasmatic Splittings and Destructive Desires: Lynch's *Lost Highway*, *Mulholland Drive* and *Inland Empire*', *Forum for Modern Language Studies*, 45:3, 270–91.

Schoonover, Karl (2012), 'Wastrels of Time: Slow Cinema's Laboring Body, the Political Spectator, and the Queer', *Framework*, 53:1, 65–78.

Sciamma, Céline (2012), 'Côté Françaises: Mieux Loties qu'Ailleurs, Mais Encore Largement Minoritaires, Comment les Cinéastes Françaises Envisagent-Elles la Question du Féminin?', *Cahiers du Cinema*, 681, September, 22–6.

ScreenCrush (2016), '*Carol* "Too Hot for TV" Commercial', *YouTube*, 29 January, <https://www.youtube.com/watch?v=o__iT4Xcx8Q> (accessed 9 April 2018).

Sedgwick, Eve Kosofsky (1985), *Between Men: English Literature and Male Homosocial Desire*, New York: Columbia University Press.

Sedgwick, Eve Kosofsky (2008 [1990]), *Epistemology of the Closet*, updated edn, Berkeley: University of California Press.

Sedgwick, Eve Kosofsky (2006), 'Foreword', in Kim Akass and Janet McCabe (eds), *Reading The L Word*, London: I. B. Tauris, pp. xix–xxiv.

Sedgwick, Eve Kosofsky (2007), 'Melanie Klein and the Difference Affect Makes', *South Atlantic Quarterly*, 106:3, 625–42.

Sedgwick, Eve Kosofsky (1993), *Tendencies*, Durham, NC: Duke University Press.

Shachar, Hila (2018), '"He Said We Can Choose Our Lives": Freedom, Intimacy, and Identity in *Blue Is the Warmest Colour*', *Studies in European Cinema*, 30 January, <https://www.tandfonline.com/doi/citedby/10.1080/17411548.2018.1432121?scroll=top&needAccess=true> (accessed 1 March 2018).

Showden, Carissa (2009), 'What's Political About the New Feminisms?', *Frontiers*, 30:2, 166–98.

Smith, Timothy (2011), 'London Film Festival: Lisa Cholodenko', *British Film Institute*, <http://www.bfi.org.uk/lff/node/1160> (accessed 21 August 2011).

Spooner, Catherine (2006), *Contemporary Gothic*, London: Reaktion Books.

Stacey, Jackie (2010), *The Cinematic Life of the Gene*, Durham, NC: Duke University Press.

Stacey, Jackie (2015), 'Crossing over with Tilda Swinton – the Mistress of "Flat Affect"', *International Journal of Politics, Culture, and Society*, 28:3, 243–71.

Stacey, Jackie (1987), 'Desperately Seeking Difference', *Screen*, 28:1, 48–61.

Stacey, Jackie (1995), '"If You Don't Play, You Can't Win": *Desert Hearts* and the Lesbian Romance Film', in Tamsin Wilton (ed.), *Immortal, Invisible: Lesbians and the Moving Image*, London: Routledge, pp. 67–84.

Stacey, Jackie (1994), *Star Gazing: Hollywood Cinema and Female Spectatorship*, London and New York: Routledge.

Stacey, Jackie and Sarah Street (eds) (2007), *Queer Screen: A Screen Reader*, London: Routledge.

Stewart, Kathleen (2005), 'Trauma Time: A Still Life', in Daniel Rosenberg and Susan Friend Harding (eds), *Histories of the Future*, Durham, NC: Duke University Press, pp. 324–39.

Stockton, Kathryn Bond (2009), *The Queer Child, or Growing Sideways in the Twentieth Century*, Durham, NC: Duke University Press.

Straayer, Chris (1984), '*Personal Best*: Lesbian/Feminist Audience', *Jump Cut*, 29, 40–4.

Stratford, Sarah-Jane (2013), 'Conservative Americans Are More Terrified of Sex Than Violence', *The Guardian*, 4 November, <http://www.theguardian.com/

commentisfree/2013/nov/04/blue-is-the-warmest-colour-shocking> (accessed 1 December 2013).

Street, Sarah (2010), 'The Colour Dossier Introduction: The Mutability of Colour Space', *Screen*, 51:4, 379–82.

Stryker, Susan (2007), 'Transgender Feminism: Queering the Woman Question', in Stacy Gillis, Gillian Howie and Rebecca Munford (eds), *Third Wave Feminism: A Critical Exploration*, Basingstoke: Palgrave Macmillan, pp. 59–70.

Swash, Rosie (2012), '*She Monkeys* Director Wanted Coming-of-Age Movie to Be "Like a Western"', *The Guardian*, 28 April, <http://www.theguardian.com/film/2012/apr/28/she-monkeys-lisa-aschan-interview> (accessed 19 September 2013).

Tarr, Carrie and Brigitte Rollet (2001), *Cinema and the Second Sex: Women's Filmmaking in France in the 1980s and 1990s*, New York: Continuum.

Tasker, Yvonne (1994), 'Pussy Galore: Lesbian Images and Lesbian Desire in the Popular Cinema', in Diane Hamer and Belinda Budge (eds), *The Good, the Bad and the Gorgeous: Popular Culture's Romance with Lesbianism*, London: Pandora Press, pp. 172–83.

Tasker, Yvonne and Diane Negra (eds) (2007), *Interrogating Postfeminism: Gender and the Politics of Popular Culture*, Durham, NC: Duke University Press.

Team GBR Equestrian (2015), 'Vaulting', *Team GBR Equestrian*, <http://www.equestrianteamgbr.co.uk/team.aspx?strTeam=non-olympic-disciplines-vaulting> (accessed 11 June 2015).

Theobald, Stephanie (2013), '*Blue*'s Lesbian Lovemaking Doesn't Hit the Spot. For Better Sex Head for the Lake', *The Guardian*, 17 October, <http://www.theguardian.com/film/filmblog/2013/oct/17/blue-warmest-colour-lesbian-bad-sex> (accessed 19 November 2013).

Thomas, Calvin (2005), 'It's No Longer Your Film', *Angelaki*, 11:2, 81–98.

TIFF Uncut (2016), 'Jill Soloway: The Female Gaze', *YouTube*, 11 September, <https://www.youtube.com/watch?time_continue=5&v=pnBvppooD9I> (accessed 8 March 2017).

Tomkins, Silvan S. (1991), *The Negative Affects: Anger and Fear, Vol. 3: Affect, Imagery, Consciousness*, New York: Springer.

Traub, Valerie (1995), 'The Ambiguities of 'Lesbian' Viewing Pleasure: The (Dis) Articulations of *Black Widow*', in Corey Creekmur and Alexander Doty (eds), *Out in Culture: Gay, Lesbian, and Queer Essays on Popular Culture*, London: Cassell, pp. 115–36.

Traub, Valerie (2015), *Thinking Sex with the Early Moderns*, Philadelphia: University of Pennsylvania Press.

Vidler, Anthony (1992), *The Architectural Uncanny: Essays in the Modern Unhomely*, Cambridge, MA and London: MIT Press.

Villarejo, Amy (2003), *Lesbian Rule: Cultural Criticism and the Value of Desire*, Durham, NC: Duke University Press.

Wallace, Lee (2009), *Lesbianism, Cinema, Space: The Sexual Life of Apartments*, New York: Routledge.

Waters, Sarah (2002), *Fingersmith*, London: Virago.

Weiss, Andrea (1992), *Vampires and Violets: Lesbians in the Cinema*, London: Jonathan Cape.

Weston, Kath (1995), 'Get Thee to a Big City: Sexual Imaginary and the Great Gay Migration', *GLQ*, 2:3, 253–77.

Whatling, Clare (1997), *Screen Dreams: Fantasising Lesbians in Film*, Manchester: Manchester University Press.

Wheatley, Catherine (2012), '*She Monkeys* (Review)', *Sight and Sound*, 22:6, 76.

White, Patricia (2018), 'Changing Circumstances: Global Flows of Lesbian Cinema', in Elena Gorfinkel and Tami Williams (eds), *Global Cinema Networks*, New Brunswick, NJ: Rutgers University Press, pp. 159–77.

White, Patricia (2008), 'Lesbian Minor Cinema', *Screen*, 49:4, 410–25.

White, Patricia (2015), '*Pariah*: Coming Out in the Middle', in Claire Perkins and Constantine Verevis (eds), *US Independent Film after 1989: Possible Films*, Edinburgh: Edinburgh University Press, pp. 133–43.

White, Patricia (2015), 'Sketchy Lesbians: *Carol* as History and Fantasy', *Film Quarterly*, 69:2, 8–18.

White, Patricia (1999), *Uninvited: Classical Hollywood Cinema and Lesbian Representability*, Bloomington: Indiana University Press.

White, Patricia (2015), *Women's Cinema, World Cinema: Projecting Contemporary Feminisms*, Durham, NC: Duke University Press.

Wiegman, Robyn (1994), 'Introduction: Mapping the Lesbian Postmodern', in Laura Doan (ed.), *The Lesbian Postmodern*, New York: Columbia University Press, pp. 1–20.

Wiegman, Robyn (2012), *Object Lessons*, Durham, NC: Duke University Press.

Wiegman, Robyn and Elizabeth Wilson (2015), 'Introduction: Antinormativity's Queer Conventions', *differences*, 26:1, 1–25.

Williams, James (2013), *Space and Being in Contemporary French Cinema*, Manchester: Manchester University Press.

Williams, Linda (2017), '*Blue Is the Warmest Color*: Or the After-Life of "Visual Pleasure and Narrative Cinema"', *New Review of Film and Television Studies*, 15:4, 465–70.

Williams, Linda (2014), 'Cinema's Sex Acts', *Film Quarterly*, 67:4, 9–25.

Williams, Linda (1986), '*Personal Best*: Women in Love', in Charlotte Brunsdon (ed.), *Films for Women*, London: British Film Institute, pp. 146–54.

Williams, Linda Ruth (2005), *The Erotic Thriller in Contemporary Cinema*, Bloomington and Indianapolis: Indiana University Press.

Wilson, Emma (2009), *Atom Egoyan*, Urbana: University of Illinois Press.

Wilson, Emma (2010), 'Desire and Technology: An Interview with Atom Egoyan', *Film Quarterly*, 64:1, 29–37.

Wilson, Emma (2014), '"The Sea Nymphs Tested This Miracle": *Water Lilies* and the Origin of Coral', in Christopher Brown and Pam Hirsch (eds), *The Cinema of the Swimming Pool*, Oxford and New York: Peter Lang, pp. 203–13.

Wilson, Emma (2008), 'The Senses and Substitution: A Conversation with Atom Egoyan', *Paragraph*, 31:2, 252–62.

Wilton, Tamsin (1995), 'Introduction: On Invisibility and Mortality', in Tamsin Wilton (ed.), *Immortal, Invisible: Lesbians and the Moving Image*, London: Routledge, pp. 1–19.

Winch, Alison (2013), *Girlfriends and Postfeminist Sisterhood*, Basingstoke: Palgrave Macmillan.

Wolff, Janet (2013), 'Colour (Mainly Blue)', *The Manchester Review*, April, <http://www.themanchesterreview.co.uk/?p=2587> (accessed 31 July 2014).

Wolff, Janet (1997), 'Reinstating Corporeality: Feminism and Body Politics', in Jane Desmond (ed.), *Meaning in Motion: New Cultural Studies of Dance*, Durham, NC: Duke University Press, pp. 81–99.

Young, Johnny (2007), 'Identity as Subterfuge: A Kleinian and Winnicottian Reading of David Lynch's *Mulholland Drive*', *Psychoanalytic Review*, 94:6, 903–18.

Zimmerman, Bonnie (1983), 'Exiting from Patriarchy: The Lesbian Novel of Development', in Elizabeth Abel, Marianne Hirsch and Elizabeth Langland (eds), *The Voyage In: Fictions of Female Development*, Hanover, NH and London: University Press of New England, pp. 244–57.

Žižek, Slavoj (2006), *The Parallax View*, Cambridge, MA and London: MIT Press.

Zurko, Nicholas (2013), 'Gender Inequality in Film', *New York Film Academy*, 25 November, <https://www.nyfa.edu/film-school-blog/gender-inequality-in-film/> (accessed 16 June 2015).

Index

CPSIA information can be obtained
at www.ICGtesting.com
Printed in the USA
JSHW031611191022
31868JS00004B/172